BETA EXERCISE
ベータ・エクササイズ

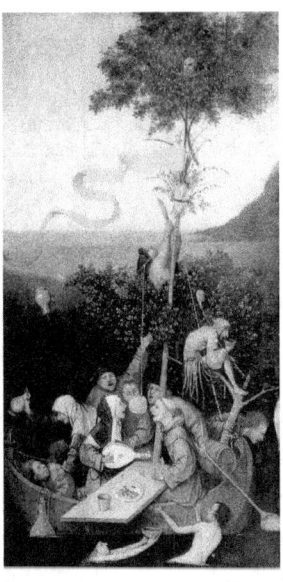

Fig. 1. Hieronymus Bosch, *Ship of Fools* (1490–1500)

First published in 2019 by punctum books, Earth, Milky Way.
https://punctumbooks.com

ISBN-13: 978-1-947447-77-6 (print)
ISBN-13: 978-1-947447-78-3 (ePDF)

LCCN: 2018953768
Library of Congress Cataloging Data is available from the Library of Congress

Book design: Vincent W.J. van Gerven Oei
Proofreading (Japanese): Keiko Tomii
Cover image: Osamu Kanemura

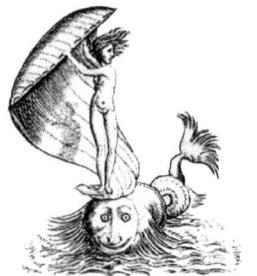

HIC SVNT MONSTRA

ベータ・エクササイズ
金村修の理論と実践

Beta Exercise
The Theory and Practice
of Osamu Kanemurg

Edited by Marco Mazzi
& Vincent W.J. van Gerven Oei
Translated by Michiyo Miyake
& Nicholas Marshall

Ⓟ

Contents

目次

Life Is a Gift

The Isetan department store in Tokyo used an advertising slogan, "Life is a Gift," for their 2015 Christmas promotion. Does this rather assertive phrase mean human life is a wonderful gift unexpectedly given by Almighty God? If gifts are connected with the grace of God, why did Isetan, an avatar of commodity society, use this word, whose real meaning runs against commercialism, in this advertisement?

If life is really a gift from Almighty God, it must be irreconcilable with a society dominated by the capitalist mode of production that produces a huge mass of commodities. A commodity requires exchange, while a gift is not supposed to be exchanged. The latter should be unilaterally given, while the former offers a network of social relationships. It reflects the entire chain of exchange that permeates society like a web. How is it possible to establish common traits between these two things?

A commodity is produced by anonymous "abstract labor." It is an accumulation of symbolic labor disconnected from concrete labor, and this concrete side of labor is always diminishing. A gift has the material trace of God inscribed, while a commodity requires no such thing. A number of commodities need to have equivalent value for exchange, which is only made possible by alienating labor from actual production.

Capitalist society detaches people from their land and means of production, and makes them nomadic and mobile. Those who have lost their land and means of production have to exchange themselves as laborers in order to survive. Once it becomes nomadic, human labor is allowed to enter the market as an exchangeable commodity. People cannot commodify their labor, nor do they need to do so, until they detach themselves from their grounded lifeworld. Only when people are alienated from their land and means of production, are they able to become a commodity. It's a process of abstraction and symbolization, and only those who have experienced it are allowed access to the market. Homogenized, abstracted humans lacking concreteness — people changing their symbolic status to transform themselves into exchangeable labor.

In capitalist society, human life bearing a special mark of divinity — in other words, the gift — is also traded as a commodity. People transform their lives, the precious gift from God, into an exchangeable unit of abstract labor in order to maintain their lives. Does Isetan's slogan, "Life is a Gift," encourage us to transform the gift into a commodity, the precious divine gift into a flat abstract concept? The commodity requires abstraction; otherwise it cannot flow freely within the market. No similarity can be found between commodity and gift; the former basically transforms concrete human labor into an abstract concept, and the latter is essentially non-symbolic, a divine favor.

For humans who cannot live without exchanging goods, the relationship involving exchange is essential for maintaining their lives. Therefore, everything has to be transformed into an exchangeable commodity. The act of exchange is so essential to human life that this process of commodification is absolutely necessary.

A gift is given voluntarily. Unlike a commodity, a gift denies the giver's ulterior motive of self-preservation. The act of gift giving is altruistic without expecting any return, which is completely different from the act of exchange. No market exists for gifts. The gift is given with no particular reason, which resembles the relationship between humans and the sun. If our life is given by grace of God, humans are basically passive, always waiting to be given to, just like we await the sunshine. The gift forms an asymmetrical relationship between giver and recipient, making the latter a passive entity. The illusion that the market hosts exchange or transaction between equal partners does not exist here from the very beginning. The recipients have no other option but to be passive.

Or does the slogan "Life is a Gift" suggest that exchanging heartfelt gifts is the most important thing in human life? A video clip displayed on a huge monitor in an Isetan store window showed people from different areas singing Letkajenkka and dancing an "extremely happy Jenkka dance." The joy of connection and its significance was the theme of this clip, and it emphasized the importance of interpersonal relationships based on gratitude, goodwill and love. This attitude is contrary to the altruistic nature of gifts; it merely reflects gift-givers' desire to be approved of by others.

The need for approval demands recognition and respect from other people; it expects affirmation from the group one belongs to. To be grateful to each other is a form of mutual recognition, which is different from the altruistic relationship found between gift-givers and recipients. Feelings that motivate gift giving, i.e., gratitude, goodwill, and love, desire approval from others and lapse into becoming instead an exchange of commodities.

The sun is not likely to shine above us out of its desire for approval, nor does it do so out of gratitude, goodwill, or love. I suspect what prompts the sun is sheer altruism without any concern about the consequences. The sun is basically indifferent toward people or things it reflects light upon. It just keeps shining and does not care at all about the consequences it may bring; it does not take heed of droughts it has caused, either. The fierce, indifferent altruism of the sun even ignores the balance of the environment. Nuclear power plants, invented to artificially create a sun, commodify the altruistic energy of the sun. The sun becomes something exchangeable. When the sun is commodified, its excessive, intense energy cannot be contained. Nuclear power plants were made on the assumption that the sun's destructive energy is controllable. It might have been an attempt to challenge the overwhelming power of the altruistic sun — in other words, the gift — and to overturn the passive, powerless condition of human beings.

Daily exchange with others is indispensable for us. Relationships with others determine our identity; likewise, interaction with others during exchange plays an essential role in our lives. Did Isetan's slogan understand the significance of exchange for us and compare it to unexpected gifts given by others? Exchange that functions as mutual help encourages us to live in reciprocal gift-giving relationships on a daily basis. But does this conceal a violent desire for approval and expectation of gratitude and love to be expressed all the time? Altruistic approval from others, approval given to others without expecting anything, exists nowhere.

Exchange is indispensable for maintaining human life. Unlike animals, human beings can only live within a network of exchange; they have to commodify everything to maintain their life. Exchange does not mean to hoard acquired wealth; that would eventually exhaust the wealth of both sides as in the potlatch of Native Americans. The concentration of wealth is a pathology of modern society; a surplus accumulates in the hands of a few, specific capitalists, and will never be used up or given to others as gifts. The act of exchange challenges this individual concentration of wealth by re-distributing the surplus, just as in case of the potlatch.

In the potlatch, the chiefs of indigenous communities compete with each other according to the amount of gifts they exchange. "When a chief cannot return the equivalent or greater goods than the gift he has received, or when he cannot give away an equivalent or greater gift to fellow members of the community, or when he cannot destroy possessions that have equivalent or higher value, he loses face in the potlatch: 'he becomes subordinate to his competitor, his power diminishes and has to tolerate being in an inferior position.' Therefore, the chiefs strive to compete with each other in gift giving. This competition became so fervent that the Canadian government banned it from 1884 to 1951."*

The cruelty of the potlatch exchange system shares something in common with the notion of gifts conceived by Isetan: people have to keep giving to others equivalent or better gifts as an expression of gratitude and love. The promotion video "Life is a Gift," which shows an image of presents wrapped up with ribbons in an endless line, overflowing into the universe, seems to demand that we keep buying things for gift giving. The slogan may imply the potlatch-like cruelty inherent in gift exchange? Or its catchy phrase probably conceals a violent desire for mutual approval, accompanying gift exchange practices in capitalist society?

Isetan's slogan fails to conceal the cruelty and violence hidden in the act of exchange. The highest level of gratitude and love is self-renunciation. As the expression "Love your neighbour as yourself" says, the renunciation of self is the ultimate expression of gratitude and love. However, where can we find self-renunciation in Isetan's notion of gifts? Gift giving is a demand for the subordination of others; it cannot fully hide the gift-givers' cruel, violent desire to control and dominate others even under the guise of Christmas gift exchange — a token of gratitude and love. We can say people are taking part in a milder form of the potlatch, which will never result in killing, nor does it destroy the hierarchy that exists in family or love relationships in bourgeois society.

A relationship involving exchange, whose initial purpose is to express gratitude and love, often conceals a struggle for supremacy. The practice of gift giving in bourgeois society hides the intention to dominate others by offering more gifts. When the recipients disapprove of this intention, "a milder form of the potlatch that does not destroy the hierarchy" is dispensed with and a violent desire to exterminate others emerges. The purpose of war is to impose one's principle upon the other, bring them

---

* Shigeru Hashimoto, *Kotowaza to kakugen no shakaigaku* [Sociology of Proverbs and Maxims], http://www5b.biglobe.ne.jp/~geru/page018.html.

to surrender and make a profit out of it, but once it becomes apparent that the enemy will not surrender, the initial purpose is easily forgotten and the agenda now becomes the extermination of the enemy. When the gift givers' strategy to initiate a bigger return fails, profit is no longer the issue and exterminating the other becomes the new goal. Isetan's slogan "Life is a Gift" conceals this kind of unconscious, violent desire.

Life Is a Gift

2015年の伊勢丹のクリスマス商品販売用のキャッチ・コピーは"Life is a Gift"だった。Life＝生命はGift＝贈物だと断定するそのコピーの意味は、人間の生命は天上の世界の絶対的な唯一神によって突然もたらされた素敵な贈物という意味なのだろうか。贈物がそのような特別な存在からの恩寵であるなら、商品社会の象徴である伊勢丹が、なぜ商品と対立する性質を持つ贈物を自分たちの宣伝に取り入れたのだろう。生命が絶対的な唯一神からの贈物であるなら、それは商品の巨大な集まりとして現れる資本主義的生産様式が支配する社会とは相容れないのではと思う。交換されることで初めて商品は、商品として成立するのであり、それに反して贈物は交換されるものではない。贈物は一方的に与えられるものだ。交換を前提として成り立つ商品は、社会的関係の網として存在する。商品には、社会の隅々にまで蜘蛛の巣のように張り巡らされた交換関係の総体が刻印されている。そのような社会的関係の総体としての商品と唯一神からの贈物のどこに共通項があるのだろう。商品は「抽象的人間労働」という匿名的な労働を注ぎ込むことで成立する。それは具体的な労働から切り離された記号的な労働の集積として現れる。商品は自らを成立させるために、労働の具体性を切り捨てるだろう。贈物に唯一神の具体性が刻印されているなら、商品にはそのような具体性は必要ない。異なる使用価値を持つ商品が交換されるためには、等価でなければ交換できない

し、具体性を切り捨て、抽象化されることで商品は交換可能な等価物として現れる。資本主義社会は、人間を土地と生産手段から切り離し、浮遊化させ、流動化させる。土地と生産手段を失った人間は、自分の生命を維持するために、自分の存在を労働力として誰かと交換しなければならなくなる。浮遊化して、初めて人間の労働は交換価値を持った商品としてマーケットに参加できるようになるだろう。実体的なものから切り離されない限り、人間は自らの労働を商品として提示できないし、提示する必要もないのだ。土地と生産手段から切り離された人間だけが交換価値を持った商品的な存在になれる。それは人間の抽象化、記号化であり、マーケットに登場できるのは、そのような抽象化、記号化された人間だけだ。実体から切り離され、均質化された抽象的な人間。マーケットにおいて交換を可能にする存在は、そのような記号的な操作が施されなければならない。特別な有徴性を刻印された生命＝贈物を資本主義下の社会では、それを商品として売買しなければならない。人間の生命が唯一神からの贈物なら、かけがえのない贈物としての生命を維持するために、贈物を「抽象的人間労働」化して交換対象に変質させる。伊勢丹の言う"Life is a Gift"は、贈物を商品に、有徴性をフラットな抽象物に変質させることを奨励することなのだろうか。商品に必要なのは抽象性であり、そうでなければ自由にマーケットの中で流通することができない。商品は具体性を持った人間の労働を、抽象化し、記号化することで成立するものであり、そのような記号的な操作を施された商品と神性という特別な有徴性を抱えた非記号的な贈物に共通する要素はどこにもないだろう。ものを交換し合うことでしか生きていけない人間にとって、交換関係こそが自らの生命を維持し続けるための重要な関係だ。そのためには、あらゆるものを交換可能なものに変質させなければいけない。交換とは人間が生きて行くうえでの必須の条件であり、商品という記号的な操作こそが人間の生命を維持するために必要な操作なのかもしれない。贈物とは無償の行為によって行われる。そこには商品とは違い、己の生存を維持するためという目的がない。それは見返りを

求めず一方的に与え続けることであり、交換を成立させる空間はどこにも存在しない。贈物にマーケットは存在しない。ただ与え続けるだけのものが贈物であり、それは太陽と人間の関係に似ている。生命が天上の世界からの恩寵なら、太陽と人間の関係のように、人間はただ与え続けられる存在であり、受動的な存在だ。受動的になる以外に何もできない非対称的な関係が贈物の関係であり、そこには交換という取引や互いが等価な存在であるというマーケットの幻想はあらかじめ廃棄されている。贈られた者に、受動以外の選択肢は存在しない。"Life is a Gift"は、それとも感謝と善意と愛情を込めた贈物を互いに交換し合うことが、人間の生活にとって一番重要なことだという意味なのだろうか。巨大なモニターを使ってディスプレされた伊勢丹のショーウィンドウの映像は、いろいろな地域の人たちが「レットキス」を歌いながら「とびきりハッピーなダンス、ジェンカ」を踊っていた。つながることの喜びと重要さを主題にした映像は、感謝と善意と愛情を共通項とした人間同士のつながりを謳歌する。それは贈物の無償性とは真逆の、他者に承認されたいという欲求を前提とした感謝と善意と愛情のような気がする。承認欲求というのが、自分が集団から価値ある存在と認められ、尊重されることを求める欲求であるなら、その欲求は自分が所属している集団の肯定が前提となる。互いが互いを感謝し合う。それはお互い認め、認め合うという相互承認であり、認めるから認めてもらうというその相互承認の関係に、贈物のような一方性は存在しない。承認の交換。承認されることをどこかで望んでいる感謝と善意と愛情は、交換可能な商品だ。太陽がそのような承認欲求を持って世界を照らしていると思えないし、太陽が感謝と善意と愛情を持って人間に日光を与えているとも思えない。それはもっと無慈悲で無関心な無償性なのではないだろうか。照らし続ける太陽は、基本的には照らしている対象に対して無関心だ。ただ照らし続けているだけで、照らしている対象がどうなろうといっこうに関心を持つことがない。照らしすぎたことで土地が干からびても意に介さない。生態系の調和すらも無視する太陽の凶暴で無関心な無償性。そのような

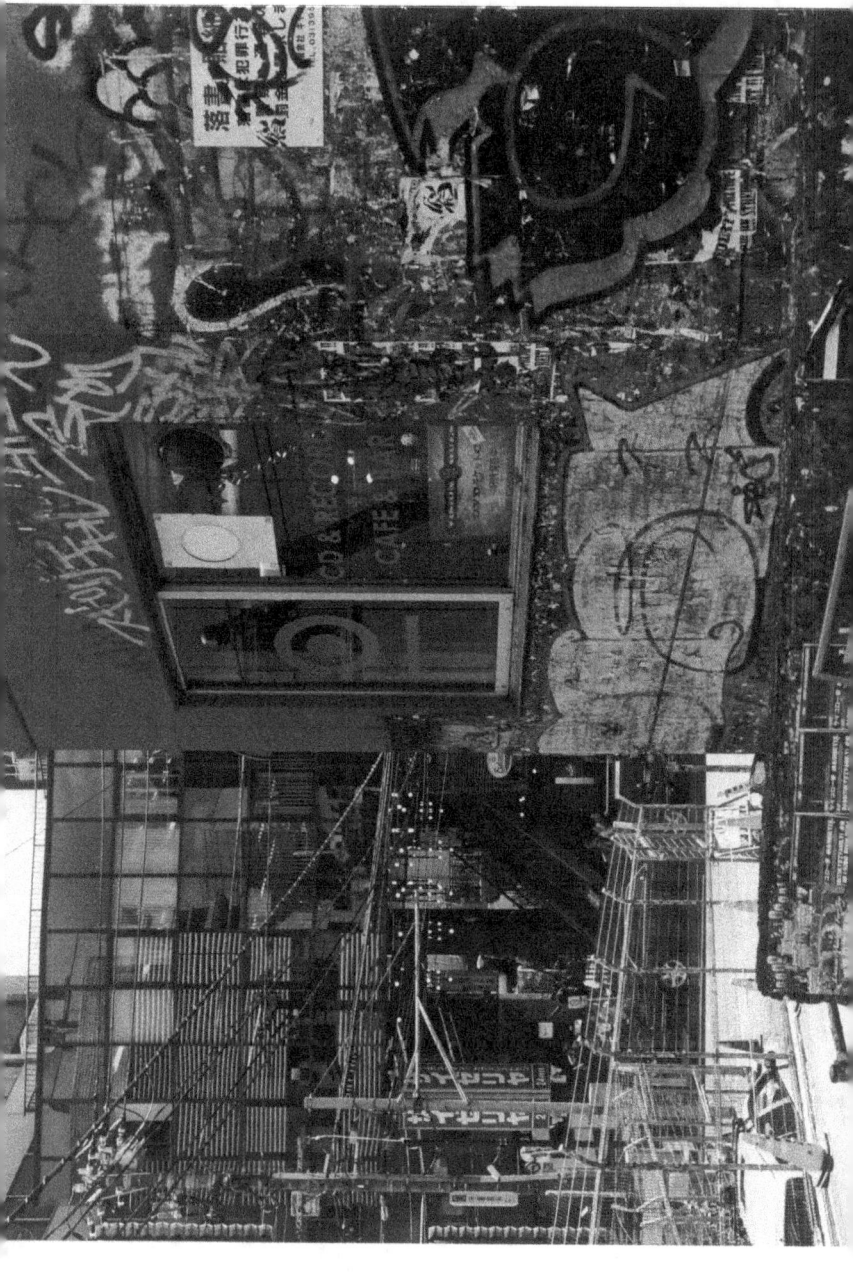

太陽を人口的に作り出そうとした原発は、太陽の無償性をエネルギーという商品に変質させる。商品として交換される原発のエネルギーは、太陽を交換可能な商品として扱う。太陽を商品体系に取り込んだとき、太陽の過剰な暴力性は必ずその体系を逸脱するだろう。原発は太陽の暴力性をコントロール可能なものと想定して扱った。それは贈物が持つ圧倒性を消去し、人間の無力な受動性を能動性に転化させようとする試みだったのかもしれない。わたしの存在が他者との日々の交換によって成り立つ。他者との関係によってしか自分のアイデンティティーが決定されないように、交換という関係を通してしか人間は生きていけない。交換という関係の束によって決定される自分の生命や生活。伊勢丹のコピーは、そんな交換を他者からの思いがけないGiftという贈物に例えたのだろうか。助け合いとしての交換。それは贈物を日々送り、送られる関係を推奨する。けれどそこには感謝と愛情を日々表せという相互承認の暴力性が隠蔽されているのではないだろうか。他者に自分が承認されなくても、自分は他者を承認する。そのような無償の承認回路はどこにもない。生命を維持するためには交換が必要になる。動物の生活と違い、交換関係の中でしか生きていけない人間の生活は、自らの生活を維持するために、あらゆるものを交換可能なものに変化させなければならない。交換とはだから人間の生命を維持するために必要な関係であり、獲得した富を貯め込むことではなく、ポトラッチのように最終的には、互いの富の消尽を交換は目指すだろう。余剰なものが消尽されることなく、特定の資本家に蓄積し、民に贈与されることがない、富の自己増殖という近代社会の病理。生命維持としての交換は、そのような富の自己増殖に対してポトラッチのような過剰に生産された富の破壊を試みる。相互に交換する贈物の量で、部族民に対する贈物の量で、競争し合うポトラッチ。「もし同等あるいはそれ以上の贈物を返せない時、また、部族民に同等あるいはそれ以上の物を贈れない時、また同等あるいはそれ以上の財産を壊せない時、その酋長はポトラッチの敗者となり、相手に『従属し、家来や召使になり、小さくなり、よ

り低い地位（従僕）に落ちる』のである。それ故、酋長たちは『負けじ』と競争するのである。その競争があまりにも過激になったので、カナダ政府によって1884年代から1951年代まで禁止された」（橋本茂「諺と格言の社会学」）。ポトラッチという破滅的な交換は、伊勢丹がイメージする感謝と愛情の発露としての贈物に似ている。同等あるいはそれ以上の贈物を相手にプレゼントし続けること。リボン掛けされたプレゼントが地球の果てまで続いていく“Life is a Gift”の映像は、プレゼントをするためにいつまでも買物し続けることを強要しているようだった。“Life is a Gift”というコピーは、贈物の交換にそのようなポトラッチ的な暴力性を加味するためだったのだろうか。それとも資本主義社会下での贈物交換の暴力性を、そのキャッチーなコピーで隠蔽することだったのだろうか。伊勢丹のコピーは、その暴力性を隠蔽することに失敗する。感謝と愛情の最高形態は自己を捨て去ることであり、自分を愛するように他人を愛せという言葉があるように、自分を捨てることが感謝と愛情の究極的な表現だ。けれど伊勢丹的な贈物のどこに自己の放棄があるのだろう。贈物を送るということは、相手の自分に対する従属を要求することであり、それがクリスマスのプレゼント交換という感謝と愛情の表現で包みながらも、どこかに支配欲や自己との同一化を迫る暴力性は隠しきれない。それは互いの破壊にまでは至らないポトラッチであり、ブルジョア社会が要求する家族関係や恋人関係という支配関係の枠組みを破壊しない程度のポトラッチなのだ。感謝と愛情を目的とした交換関係に、支配のイニシアチブを誰が握るかという階級的戦いが見え隠れする。より多くの贈物を与えることで支配力のイニシアチブを握ろうというブルジョア社会の贈物攻勢は、相手が自分の支配欲求を受け入れないとき、“支配関係の枠組みを破壊しない程度のポトラッチ”の範囲を超えて、相手の存在を殲滅する暴力性が現れる。自らの意思を相手に強要し、屈服させ、そこに利潤を得ることを目的とする戦争が、相手が屈服しないと分かれば、屈服させることで利潤を得るという当初の目的から逸脱して、相手の殲滅が目的になるように、贈物を渡すことでそれ以上の

利潤を得ることを目指した贈物攻勢が挫折したとき、今度は利潤を度外視して、相手の存在を破壊することが目的となるだろう。伊勢丹の"Life is a Gift"のコピーは、そのような破壊的な欲望を無意識下に抱えているような気がする。

Essay 01

If you want to take good photographs, you should know how to use the different functions of a camera. Using a deep focus lens and normal exposure setting, or using a printer with an impurity removal function — anyone can do it. Photographic technique is no longer something people need to make a great effort to learn. The functions on a device assure that you have a good enough technique; good computers and printers will take care of the rest.

With the invention of digital cameras, the good old days are gone. The era when acquiring skills took a fair amount of time and taking better photos meant improving technique is gone; the time when people believed photographers' talent lay in making the best use of learnt techniques and put more trust in technical skill is over. Photographers can no longer specialize in techniques that ordinary people have no access to. The quality of the picture improves when you purchase an expensive device. A photographer's identity cannot be expressed by technique any-more. The fact that anyone can take good pictures means the re-sult will be the same no matter who holds the camera. In short, it does not matter who take the pictures. Digital photography will accelerate this absence or erasure of the artist.

The distinction between good or bad photos does not mean anything when the monopoly of techniques comes to an end, photographic techniques are accessible to all, and it becomes possible for anyone to take good pictures. Good photos cannot exist without bad photos; when it is possible for anyone to take good pictures, their value ceases to exist. When there is no difference in value, you only see a boring uniformity. What is at the base of digital photography is this monotonous homogeneity. The absence of authors and homogenized pictures: it almost resembles an empty wilderness lying there.

Photography contests caused inflation in skill levels and left us with a huge amount of "good" photos. Digital photography will do the same thing: photographers' technique will have no meaning. Whether someone can take good pictures or not becomes a matter of functions or camera performance, rather than individual technique. Artists' techniques used to leave the mark of the human hand on photography and people could believe the illusion about the hegemony of our hand over the camera, the illusion that humans still hold sway through the manipulation of machinery. However, the relationship between human beings and technique, the former as agent and the latter as its means, has collapsed. Technique has become the new subject and humans are reduced to the role of servants.

The Futurists, who hailed new war technologies, such as airplanes and cannons, as the art of the twentieth century, gave technology a higher position than humans and tried to expel the latter from art. Their admiration for technology in the end affirmed the tragedy of World War I in which the latest technology eradicated human life. They declared, "War is beautiful," and attached more significance to robots with steel bodies than to the organic human body. The Futurists' faith in technology demanded that technology act as an agent independent of humans. As military technology advances, technology will take control of wars. Human beings become merely replaceable elements in the machine.

The invention of photography in the early twentieth century diminished or removed traces of the human hand from art. However, looking at the history of photography, people are still under the illusion that the trace of human agency remains. Nobody has taken serious note of the true nature of cameras, which negates the human hand in art. This fact has been covered up and photography has been falsely believed to be an art in which humans still have agency. Viewers admiring the sensibility of the artist try to discover meanings expressed by authors in their prints. The myth that photographs are marked with photographers' feelings has been nurtured.

People should know that the lyricism and beauty captured through "my feeling" or "my naked eye," which some believe to be unique and precious, is in fact replaceable by the uniform mechanical expression of digital cameras. Digital technology demonstrates that there is no difference between "my feeling" or "naked eye" and those of somebody else. Photography has become homogenized to the point where no matter who takes a picture, the result is more or less the same. Here, the "I" disappears: when everyone engages with subjects in a similar way, photographs cannot represent "my feeling." This "feeling" is merely installed in the camera as pre-set function; pictures are taken mechanically by the device, not by me or anyone else. The "I" is thus obliterated. Therefore, the expression "a unique digital photo" is an oxymoron. The digital photo is a bit like a roller levelling the ground; not only does it invalidate photographers' contradictory desires to take beautiful pictures like everyone else but also to have an individual quality that distinguishes their work from that of others. The digital device removes human individuality, but this is the result of the exposure of the hidden, true nature of photography.

Photography is an embodiment of modern technology; the secret desire of digital cameras for homogenization and de-humanization has been revealed. The digital, therefore, deprives us of the last role remaining for our individual hands. The vestiges of human "sensibility," which barely survived in film photography, will eventually be completely removed.

Is "sensibility" given to us a priori? I believe it is an invention and creation of our linguistic system; it did not exist from the beginning nor was it discovered. This "sensibility" came to be understood as common, innate human nature because the system of language and logic attached meaning to it. It became a convenient app to explain something incomprehensible, and so was circulated and shared among people. "Sensibility" as a concept emerged from the mechanical system of language and logos, which is a kind of technology; therefore, we can say "sensibility" is a product of this technology. It is inevitable that products of old technology become obsolete as new technologies emerge. The case of digital photography demonstrates that "sensibility," which once was considered to be a foundation of art or source of artistic inspiration, has become outdated.

The fact that anyone can take good pictures means that there is no distinct difference between them, and this accelerates the tendency that all photos look identical and have no individuality. There is no technical value (good or bad) or distinguishable individual quality in digital photos. This demonstrates that essential photographic value cannot be ascribed to technique or the individual talents of photographers. When we cannot seek the basis of value in artists themselves, then where can we look for it?

Photography embraces the exterior in order to maintain its own value. In music, for example, digitization has steadily progressed but most of its value still relies on the technique of instrument performers. Also in paintings, sketch techniques of artists determine the value of the canvas. In established genres of art, the techniques of artists are normally indispensable; however, in digital photography, this technical framework is not necessary. Both in music and painting, the human hand is still widely in use and people are central to the creative process; while in photography, the initiative does not lie in human hands.

Can you think of any genres of art, apart from photography, that depend on machines for their technique? In this sense, we can say that modern technology constitutes photographic technique. Technique for musicians or painters is based on handwork and resembles the secret art of alchemy more than modern technology. On the other hand, photography has dismissed this alchemic dimension from art; the world of photography has become ruled by the modern concept of technology. That is why no aura exists in photography; photography is an anonymous, depersonalized art that resembles the production of industrial goods. The difference between a tone of paint spread on canvas and that of ink printed on photographic papers is that the former is something beautiful wrought by a human hand, while the latter is an industrial thing of beauty, made of photographic paper without a trace of a human hand or aesthetics. Photography dismisses the human hand, the very aura, from art. Instead of personal beauty realized by the artist's touch, photography adopts the depersonalised beauty of ready-made industrial goods. The aura of photography arises from the beauty dwelling in industrial goods, not our hands.

The acquisition of technique in art is a kind of labor. For example, learning to play a musical instrument is as tedious as menial drudgery. Digital photography, which does not derive meaning through the repetitive process of learning unfamiliar techniques, overtly ridicules the artisitic hand. Artistic identity is usually gained through repetition of practice and study, while in digital photography this basic training is not necessary. What sort of training is necessary if anyone can easily take digital photos with the same results? The more accessible digital photography is, the more difficult it becomes to establish your individual quality as an artist. For digital photographers, it is very difficult to establish an identity as an artist through technical elaboration. Photographs lack individuality because anybody can easily produce them, and there is no need for technical training to develop individual talent.

Photography lacks the pleasure you often find, for example, in agriculture: the joy of celebrating a harvest season each year. Agricultural products harvested as a result of constant care have a kind of pleasure that art used to give us. What pleasure do digital photos give us when we can shoot them too easily and check the results immediately on the spot? Simple, accessible digital technology wipes out the joy of handwork that photographs once provided us with.

Nevertheless, since the beginning, homogeneity, not individuality, has been characteristic of photography. Who wished to see in Eugène Atget or Berenice Abbott the individual quality of the artist? What people wanted to see were the streetscapes of Paris or spectacles bristling with tall buildings in New York, not any artistic individuality. They expected verisimilitude from the photographers. It was the mission of artists to provide an equivalence or similitude to reality, not some artistic sensibility. Photography was a reproduction of reality and its value lay in the effect of verisimilitude. The value of pictures was determined by what reality they captured, not by the pictures themselves. In this regard, photography resembled a currency or language; neither of them is able to determine their value by themselves. They always require an exterior criterion to establish their value.

In order to distinguish yourself from other artists in digital photography, which nullifies difference based on individual technique, extrinsic elements such as concepts, themes, and the vision of the artist will become increasingly significant. With the invention of the digital camera, photographers are not allowed to just take photos as they used to. Without additional elements, their work is insufficient in terms of expression. As the documentary filmmaker Fumio Kamei once said, the cameraman is a blindfolded horse; just taking pictures does not create anything. Photography is, by itself, dependent and meaningless; it cannot hold any value without some exterior criteria.

Photography cannot express its value by itself; it is essentially dependent on its exterior. Photographs always needed captions because without them what was shown was obscure. Without captions, people see a picture of the American Civil War and think it just captures people lying dead by the roadside. Many photographers took pictures of urban landscapes and titled them "Cityscape"; they did this because, even when the subjects seemed obvious, photographs required words to explain what had been captured in them. Therefore, photography is essentially dependant on extrinsic, non-photographic elements to establish a basis of identity. Seeing Atget's pictures without captions, you are only aware that they show an old city. You know nothing more than what you see, an expanse of sleazy streets. The same is true about Weegee's photos; looking at them without clues, you just see well-dressed corpses and know nothing more than that. Photography captures, freezes, and fixates a reality — this was supposed to be done for the purpose of understanding it better, but when photographed, reality actually becomes even more incomprehensible. Seeing Diane Arbus's picture of a boy holding a toy grenade, can you understand her intention or the meaning of this grenade? Once it is captured in photographs, an ordinary reality becomes mysterious.

Without words, you cannot understand photographs; however, have they become somewhat comprehensible with the help of words? The camera separates subjects from reality and during this process something is lost; subjects are transformed into a likeness of what once existed. That is why their identity has to be repeatedly confirmed using captions. Subjects that require words for their identity to be affirmed — they stop being a similitude of reality.

You can say their identity is vulnerable; you need the word "table" only when the meaning of this word has been obscured. In photography, the meaning of table is always questioned. Photography questions and redefines reality.

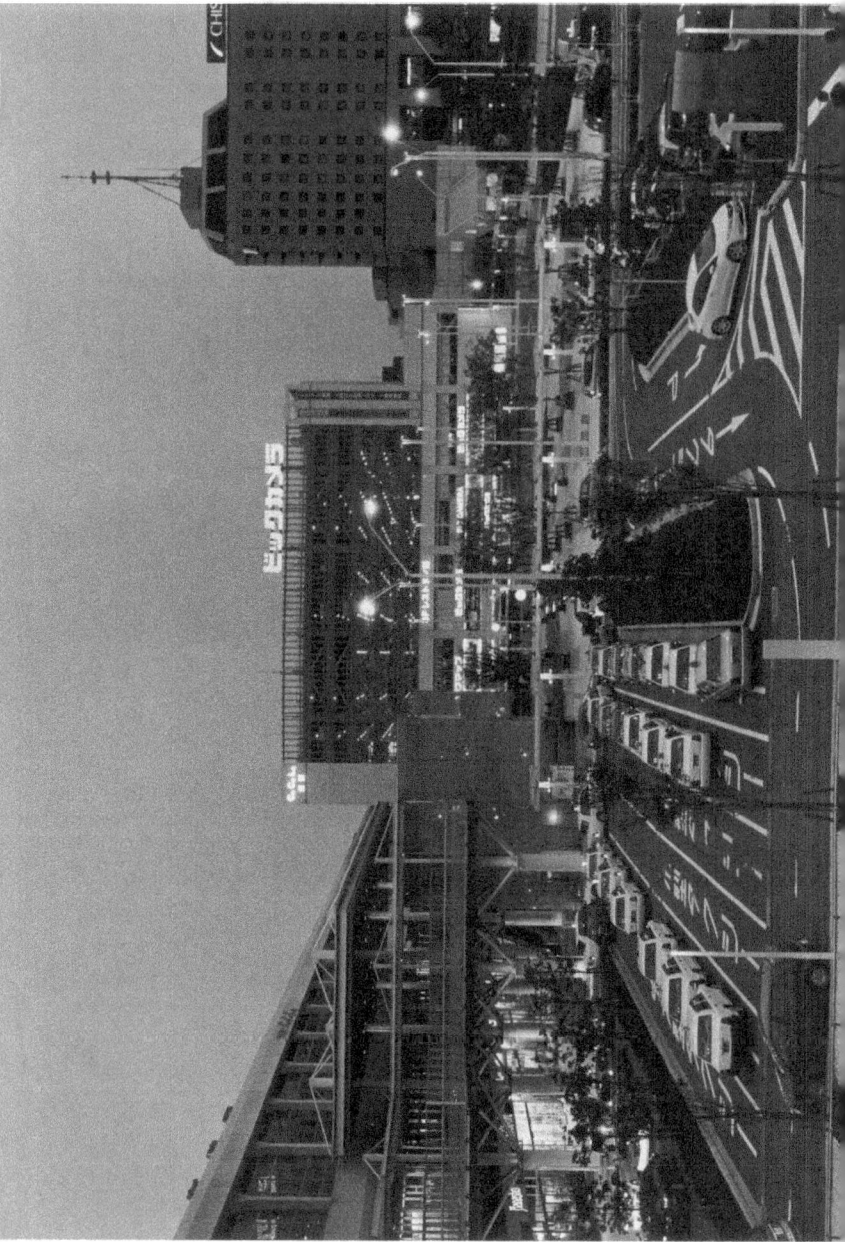

エッセイ01

　カメラの機能に任せておけば自動的にきれいな写真が撮れる。ピントはパンフォーカスになり、露出はノーマルに設定され、後はプリンターが濁りを自動的に取ってくれれば誰にでもきれいな写真が撮れる。写真において技術というのは、苦労して覚えることではなくなった。カメラに付いている機能で技術はもう十分で、後はパソコン、プリンターの性能によって画質のレベルが決定される。

　技術の習得にはそれなりの時間がかかるので、技術の向上と写真の良し悪しが同じだった時代、技術を覚えてそれを自在に駆使できることが写真家の才能なのだと、技術信仰がまだありえた時代、そんな時代がデジタルカメラの出現で終わりを迎えた。みんなが知らない技術を知っているという技術の独占が意味を持たなくなった。価格の高いカメラを買えば画面の質は向上する。写真家のアイデンティティーを技術に求めることがもう成立しなくなった。誰にでもいい写真が撮れるという事実は、誰が撮っても同じということだから、"誰が撮った"の"誰"がどこにも存在しなくなる。作者がいなくても撮れるという作者の不在、作者の抹消をデジタル写真はさらに促進するだろう。

　技術の独占状態が崩壊し、写真技術がすべての人間に開かれ、誰にでも上手い写真を撮れることが可能なったとき、上手いとか下手だとかという価値は意味をなくす。下手な写真があるから上手いという価値が成り立つ

のだから、すべての人間が上手い写真を撮れるなら、そこにはもう上手いという価値が成立する余地がない。価値は差異によって生まれるものであり、差異のない状況で生まれるものは退屈な均一性だけだ。デジタル写真は退屈な均一性をその根底に抱えている。作者の不在と均一化される写真。それはほとんど何もない荒野のようだ。

　上手さの飽和状態化としたコンテスト写真が、上手い写真の残骸でしかなくなったように、デジタルは技術を残骸化するだろう。写真が上手いということが作品の問題ではなくカメラの機能の問題でしかなくなり、技術があるかないかの問題は機械の優劣の問題でしかなくなった。技術はかつて写真の中で、唯一人間の手の痕跡を感じさせる領域であり、カメラという機械を操る人間の手という、人間がまだ機械に対して主体的に振る舞うことができるという幻想が成立していた領域だった。人間という主体に対して、技術は手段であるという関係性はすでに崩壊し始めている。技術こそが新しい主体であり、人間はその新しい主体の元で下僕のように振る舞う以外に何もできなくなるだろう。

　飛行機や大砲といった新しい戦争技術を20世紀の芸術そのものだと礼賛した未来派は、技術を人間よりも上位に置くことで、芸術から人間を追放しようとした。未来派の技術礼賛は、最先端の技術によって人間の生を根こそぎに剥奪しようとした第一次世界大戦の現実を礼賛することになるだろう。「戦争は美しい」と宣言した未来派は、有機的器官で構成される人間の肉体ではなく、鋼鉄の肉体を持つロボットを肯定する。それは人間よりもテクノロジーを肯定することであり、手段としてのテクノロジーが人間の立場を押しのけて主体の立場につくことを要求することだ。戦争技術の進歩が、戦争の主体を人間ではなく技術に明け渡す。人間はたんに交換可能な機械の部品でしかないだろう。

　二十世紀初頭における写真の登場は、芸術から人間の手の痕跡の縮減または追放を要求した。けれど写真の歴史は、手の痕跡がそこに保存されているかのような幻想をいまだに与え続けている。人間の手を追放しよう

とする写真の本性を誰も見ようとしなかった。その本性を隠し続け、人間が主体的に操れる芸術のように写真を偽装させた。作者の感性を賛美し、プリントから作者の手の痕跡を発見しようとし続ける。写真の裏側には写真家の心情があるかのような振る舞いが偽装されていた。

　この世界で交換不可能な唯一なものと思われていた"わたしの気持ち"や"わたしの肉眼"の叙情や美しさが、デジタルカメラの均一な表現によって交換可能なものであることを知るだろう。"誰かの気持ちや肉眼"と"わたしの気持ちや肉眼"の間には、どこにも差異がないことを証明する。"わたしの気持ち"や"わたしの肉眼"が選択した美しさは、誰が撮っても同じように写り、あなたじゃなくても構わない、誰が撮ってもいいというところにまで均質化されたのだ。それはもう"わたし"ではない。誰が撮っても同じものしか表すことのできない"わたしの気持ち"は、すでに"わたしの気持ち"ではない。それはすでにプリセットされた"わたしの気持ち"だ。"わたし"が撮ったものではなく、誰が撮ったものでもない、カメラがただ撮ったものでしかないだろう。"わたし"は抹消される。個性的なデジタル写真というのはだから形容矛盾なのだ。みんなと同じようにきれいな写真が撮りたいけれど、他の写真と識別できるような個性も欲しいという形容矛盾をデジタル写真は、ローラーで地を均すように均質化する。デジタルは人間の個性を抹消するための装置であり、それは写真がもともと隠し持っていた本性が曝け出された結果なのだ。

　写真は近代のテクノロジーそのものであり、近代的テクノロジーが隠し持っていた世界の均質化と非人間化をデジタルカメラが露わにし始める。デジタルはだから人間の手のその最後の領域を剥奪するだろう。フィルム写真の中で、いまだに残滓のように残っていた人間の"感性"がそこでは徹底的に排除される。

　"感性"というのは、先天的にわたし達に与えられたものなのだろうか。"感性"はそこに始めから存在していたものでも発見されたものでもなく、それは言語システムが製造し、発明したものではないだろうか。そんな

"感性"が先天的に人間に備わっているものとして共有されるようになったのは、言語システムが生みだしたロジックによって"感性"に意味が与えられたからであり、理解不可能なものを説明するときに便利なアプリとして使用される。"感性"は、便利なアプリとして、そこで初めて共有可能な存在として流通できるようになった。"感性"はロジックという言語システムによって事後的に製造される。それはシステムの動きによって事後的に操作されたものであり、言語システムというメカニカルなシステムが"感性"を製造した。言語システムというのは一つのテクノロジーであり、"感性"の存在はテクノロジーによって製造されたものでしかないのだ。"感性"はテクノロジーの一種だった。かつてのテクノロジーで製造されたものが、新しいテクノロジーの手によって駆逐されるのは当然のことであり、芸術の根拠として、芸術のインスピレーションの源として存在していた"感性"は、もはや時代に合わない枯渇した源泉でしかなくなったことをデジタル写真は証明する。

　すべての人間が上手い写真を撮れるようになったということは、そこに差異が消滅したということであり、それはどの写真もみんな同じに見えるという非個別化を促進させる。デジタル写真には上手いも下手もない。識別できる個性もない。デジタル写真によるそんな技術的価値や個別性の無効化は、写真の価値を支えるものが、写真家の技術や個性ではないことを証明する。価値の源泉が写真家に存在しないならば、写真は一体どこに価値を求めればいいのだろう。

　写真の外部から価値を支えるものを招き寄せることで、写真は自らの価値を支え続ける。デジタル化がかなり進行した音楽の場合でも、音楽の価値を支えるものは楽器演奏者の技術に頼っている領域がまだ数多くあるだろうし、絵画に関してもデッサン等の技術がその価値を支え続けている。あるジャンルを成立させるには、そのジャンルを成立させる下部構造としての人間の技術が必要とされるのに対して、デジタル写真の場合は人間の技術を必要としない。音楽や絵画ではかなりの部分で人間の手が使用され、

だからこそ人間がそこでは主体的にまだ振る舞えるのに対して、写真には人間が主体的に振る舞える領域がほとんど存在しないのだ。

　技術的領域のすべてが機械というテクノロジー任せの芸術が、写真以外にあり得るだろうか。その意味では写真における技術は、近代テクノロジーなのだ。音楽や絵画における技術が近代的な意味でのテクノロジーではなく、手の作業を重要視するという意味ではむしろ錬金術的な秘術に近いのに対して、写真は芸術からその秘術的な領域を追放する。秘術に変わってテクノロジーという近代的な概念が写真の世界を支配する。写真にはだからアウラというものを必要としない。アウラのない芸術が写真であり、それは工業製品のような無記名で没個性的な芸術として現れるだろう。キャンバスに描かれた絵の具のトーンと印画紙が表出するトーンのこの二つのトーンの差異は、前者の美しさが人間の手の痕跡を感じさせる美しさなのに対して、印画紙におけるトーンの美しさは、手の痕跡や作者の美意識の無い、印画紙という工業製品の美しさだ。芸術のアウラを成立させる人間の手を写真は否定するのだ。写真は人間の手という個別性の美しさに対して、既製の工業製品の没個別的な美しさを対置する。写真のアウラは人間の手ではなく、工業製品の美しさによって成立するだろう。

　芸術において技術というのは労働に近いものであり、例えば楽器技術の習得過程は、単純労働の過程の退屈さに近い。そのような単純労働的な要素の積み重ねによって技術を習得することに意味を見出せないデジタル写真は、あからさまに人間の手を嘲笑うだろう。練習や習作を繰り返し、それの積み重ねによって芸術家のアイデンティティーが獲得されるのに対して、デジタル写真はその基礎となる練習や習作の繰り返しと積み重ねという修行的な要素を必要としない。誰でもすぐ撮れるのであり、誰が撮っても同じである芸術に一体どんな修行が必要なのだろうか。デジタル写真の敷居の低さと写真作家として個性を成立させるための困難さは反比例する。むしろデジタル写真においては、修行によって自己のアイデンティティーを確立することが困難になるだろう。写真には個性がないのは、すぐに

撮れてしまうからであり、個性が成り立つような修行の場がそこにはそもそも存在しないからだ。

　四季の変化を通して一年の収穫を迎える農業のような喜びが写真には欠けている。丹念に手を入れた結果として収穫の時期を迎える農作物は、かつての芸術のような喜びがあるだろう。すぐに撮れてすぐにその場で何を撮ったか確認できるデジタル写真には、一体どんな喜びがあるのだろうか。誰にでもすぐ撮れる簡易なデジタル写真は、人間の手の喜びとして存在したかつての写真を追放するだろう。

　写真は出始めのときから個性ではなく、むしろ同質化が要求されていた。誰がアジェやアボットに芸術家の個性を求めていただろう。彼や彼女に求められていたのは作家的な個性ではなくパリの街並みや林立するニューヨークのビル群の光景だった。写真に要求されたことは、現実をそっくりに写すことであり、それが写真に求められたミッションだった。作者の感性ではなく、現実と同じもの、現実と寸分変わりのないものを求められていた。写真は現実の再現であり、現実と同じであることが写真の価値だった。写真の価値は写真そのものではなく、写っている現実が写真の価値を表出する。写真の価値はだから写真の中にあるのではなく、写真が再現し、指し示した現実が写真の価値を決定する。写真が貨幣や言語と共通の性格を持っているのは、どれもそれ自身では価値を表出できないことであり、価値を示すためにはつねに外部の何かを必要とするところだ。

　技術による差異化の仕組みを不可能にしたデジタル写真で他者との差異化を図るには、コンセプトやテーマ、または作家の世界観というような写真以外の分野から選択されるだろう。デジタルの出現によって、写真家は写真だけ撮っていればいいという時代は終わった。写真を撮っているだけでは、何かを表していることにならなくなった。ドキュメンタリー監督の亀井文夫がカメラマンというのは目隠しされた馬だと言ったように、撮っているだけではそこに何も生まれない。写真はそれ自体では自立できない無意味な

芸術であり、何らかの外部の存在がないかぎり、写真は価値を持つことができない。

　写真はそれ自身ではその価値を表明することができない。写真は写真だけで自立することができない芸術なのだ。写真がつねにキャプションという言葉を必要としたのも、言葉という外部がなくては、何を見せているのか分からなかったからではないだろうか。キャプションがなければ、南北戦争の写真を見てもそれは人が行き倒れになっている光景にしか見えない。都会の写真を撮って、その写真に"都会"というタイトルを多くの写真家がつけていたのも、写真は分かりきったことでさえも言葉によって再確認し続けなければ何を写しているのか分かってもらえないからだ。写した被写体を説明するキャプションの力によって成立していた写真は、当初から写真以外の分野に自らのアイデンティティーの根拠を求めていたのではないだろうか。アジェの写真をキャプションなしで見ればそれがどこか昔の都会らしいということ以外には何も分からない。汚らしい街並みが続いている以外の情報をそこから受け取ることができない。ウィージーの写真も何の情報もなく見れば高級そうな洋服を着た屍体が写っている以外に何も分からない。写真は現実を切り取り静止させ、そこに定着させた。それは現実をより理解するためになされた行為のはずなのに、写真化されたことで余計に分からなくなった。アーバスのオモチャの手榴弾を持った少年の写真を見て、それが一体何のために撮られたのか、その手榴弾が何を意味するかを理解できるだろうか。写真化することで当たり前だった現実が謎に包まれていく。

　言葉なしでは写真は理解することができない。けれど言葉を付け足したことで、写真は理解可能なものになったのだろうか。被写体を現実から切り出すことで成立する写真は、現実から被写体を切り出したことで、被写体の何かを喪失させる。写された被写体は、それは現実に存在していた被写体のよく似たものに変質させられる。だからキャプションでこれは何を

写したものなのか何度も確認するようになるのだ。言葉によってその存在を確認される被写体は、もう現実の被写体ではない。

　言葉によってそのつど確認されなければならない存在は、すでにそれは何者でもないだろう。テーブルを、これはテーブルだとつねに言葉で確認し続けなければならないのは、テーブルの意味がそこで崩壊しているからだ。テーブルを構成する意味を写真は失調させる。写真は現実を失調させる。

Interview

What do you think of the Plaubel Makina? How important is this camera in the process of composition in your photography? Were you working with other cameras before creating your famous black and white cityscapes?

The Plaubel Makina is a camera that is hard to use. The finder coverage is not 100%, therefore, there is a gap between the image you actually see and what you get after developing. I remember being puzzled by this gap when I started using it. I thought I'd taken a shot avoiding a fence in the foreground, but when I checked the film later, the fence was in the picture. Normally people crop these parts, but I found it funny that the object I intended to take out of the frame was still there. I have come to believe that this is also interesting.

The picture seemed to acquire a feeling of motion with the existence of the fence, which I had intended to take out of the frame, because I thought it would destroy the composition. If you use an aspect ratio of 6×7, you can very easily compose images as it is close to being square. Actually, anyone can compose well-balanced images using 6×7 as it is a stable size. I used to think it was difficult to create in 6×7 the motion you see in street snaps captured by 35mm cameras. I was hoping to find a way to compose less predictable images using this size, compared with the more obvious photos that anyone can take. Therefore,

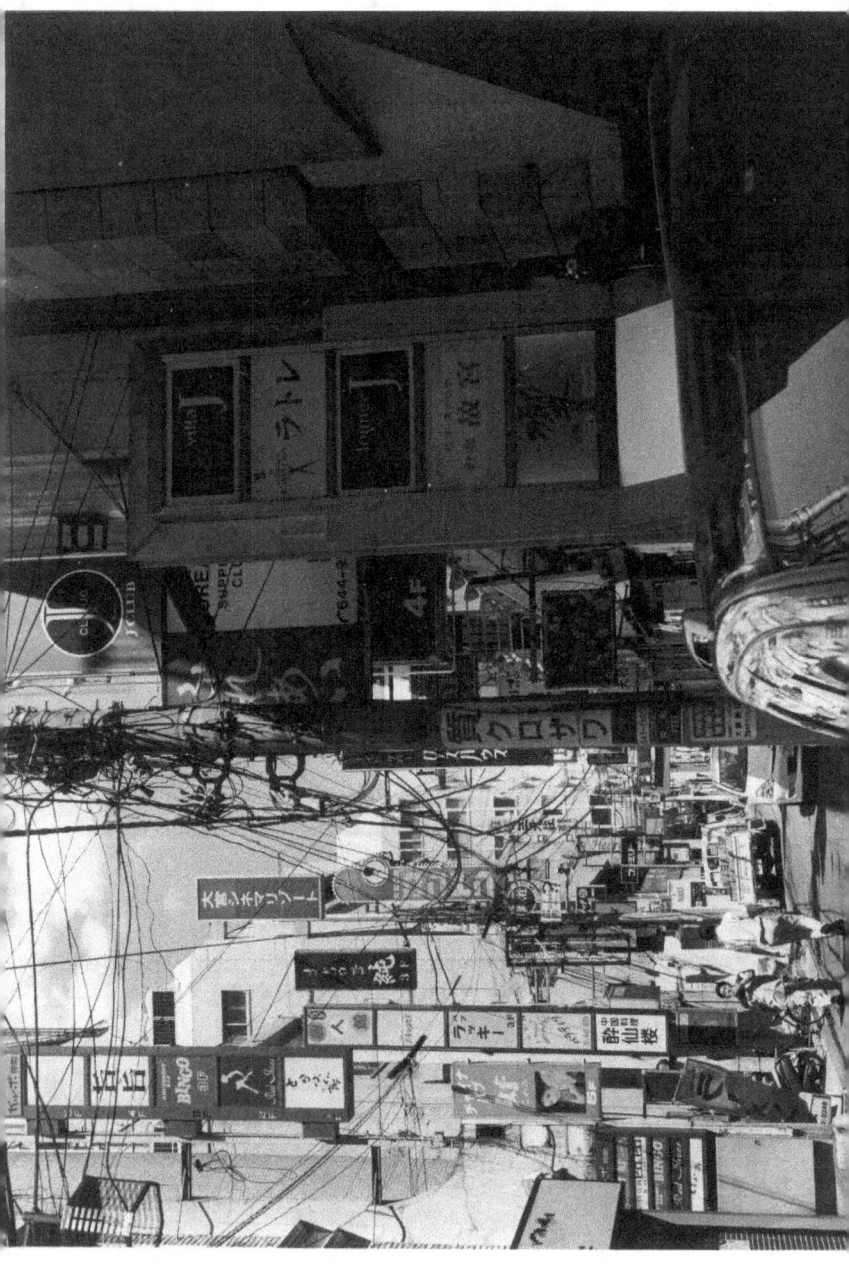

the Plaubel Makina, which creates an element of unintentional "noise," taught me the importance of unintended effects.

When I was at photography school, I liked Garry Winogrand and Lewis Baltz. At a glance, they appeared to be completely different types of photographers, but I was always thinking about how I could take pictures combining elements of both. It is difficult to intermix aspects of both artists — one uses street snaps and the other landscapes. Before the Plaubel Makina, I was using a Canon 35mm single-lens reflex camera and a Rollei 6×6. I quit the 35mm camera, because when you enlarge images, they are too grainy and details can't be seen clearly. That's how I started using a medium format Rollei 6×6, but this square 6×6 format creates symmetrical composition and so you can't avoid a kind of static impression. In contrast, the Plaubel Makina brings "noise" into the image and this adds street snap-like motion to static urban landscape photos.

Influenced by Yasujiro Ozu's framing, I was always interested in rigid composition. I chose 6×7 because it is a frame close to the size preferred by Ozu, the standard size (4×3). I admired his lean framing. My framing is also rigid in its own way, but unlike cinematography the subjects are not in motion in the photograph; therefore, too rigid framing strengthens a static impression too much. In other words, the subjects are framed too well.

Rigid framing usually increases the sophistication of the photograph. This is not exactly a criticism, but the rigidness of framing in Keiichi Tahara's photography makes me feel he is aiming at a kind of autistic beauty that consummates the photograph inside the frame. However, I was thinking of exploring a method which brings in noise while adopting rigid framing: something like cinematic framing.... To use music as an example, John Coltrane could perform all that music full of noise supported only by Elvin Jones's rigid drums in the background. It doesn't matter what is in a picture if solid framing is applied. Frame is structure. Noise is born out of a clear structure. Framing is a structure that creates indistinct noise — that's how I think.

Your pictures do include human figures. Many of your early city snapshots, your more mature works, and your recent digital works also show human traces. Also, you created a project entitled *Human Noise Amplifier*. How important and how relevant is the human body and the human figure in your work? How important is the human figure in your composition?

I'm very glad that you've brought up the human figures that appear in my photographs. Many people still think there is no trace of humans there. Possibly they don't notice them in the pictures as they're overwhelmed by electric wires, signboards, or millions of abandoned bicycles. Or their preconception of urban landscape photography might make them blind to the people in my photos.

The human figure is, in my photography, an element that is part of the larger composition. I consider people as elements in the same way as electric wires, signboards, or the abandoned bicycles that constitute the whole image. This isn't because I'm a misanthrope, it's because I don't want to provide a main character and create a central focus in the image. The things in my pictures are all equivalent — that's how I think. Human beings in photographs usually have such a powerful presence that they immediately attract people's attention. And thus, people are inclined to acquire a human-centred way of seeing photographs. I don't want people to interpret my photos in terms of hierarchical relations between the elements seen in them. I expect people to see them from a multi-layered perspective; I mean, the human being isn't the only center: signboards, electric wires, all elements that constitute cityscapes are for me important. Everything shown in pictures is significant. I don't want to express hierarchy between different components.

Human beings are also an important element in cityscapes, but it doesn't mean they are its main characters. What interests me is the moment when relationships arise between things shown in photographs. That's why I don't capture images of single objects. What relationships exist between humans, electric wires, and signboards in a single photograph? I'm interested in the connections between them inside the urban system.

When watching films — it can be any film — my interest is gradually directed toward things in the background or landscape rather than the people who play the protagonists. Therefore, what the protagonist said doesn't stay in my memory, but the scenic composition in the background does. My interest is drawn toward something that is different from the intention of film directors.

Human beings are for me equivalent to signboards and electric wires. There is nothing special to say about them. But it doesn't mean they don't mean anything. They exist in the place they should be. Without them there, the image doesn't function. This doesn't just apply to human beings, as the same is true for signboards and cars. They are inevitably there at that time. About the presence of humans in my photographs, I feel they are inevitable — they exist where they should be. While shooting, I don't pay attention to humans; in fact, quite often I am not actually aware of them at all. But when you look at the photo, you sometimes find humans in the arrangement as if I had calculated the effect to be like this.

Some photographers take pictures of cities that show no humans and the fact that none appear is somehow meaningful. But I have no interest in this kind of expression — the meaning that a desolate city suggests. I have no interest in photos that imply something. I'm interested in the possibility of the photograph that doesn't imply anything, cut off from any implication or meaning. The photograph that has nothing hidden behind and shows nothing but the things captured. The photograph that does not seek meaning; rather, is disconnected from meaning — I consider the photograph to be something cut off from the world. Reality and the photograph are parallel. These parallel lines do not meet.

The presence of humans is powerful. It is such a strong force that human existence, once casually brought into the frame, usually dominates the entire photo. Humans tend to become the focus of images. Rejecting this significance of humans from

45

images; this is how I conceive of humans in my work — treating them as inanimate objects. I am interested in people, but not in their inner minds. Furthermore, the photograph can only capture the surface. It cannot capture the human mind. Humans without mind — I am interested in people in a way similar to electric wires or signboards.

You have told me that you feel human traces in my work. Traces are inanimate substances. I want to transform human existence into traces, that is, a kind of substance.

> In your early video work, editing was included in the shooting process. I mean, you shot short segments and when you had enough the video was complete. This method makes me think you were using the video camera as a tape recorder. How important is the presence of sound in your video work and how do you deal with sound when it comes to recording video sequences?

Until around 2013, as you said, I was using the video camera as a tape recorder. Why I didn't edit: there was the technical reason that I didn't own a computer then, but I was also interested in non-editing. Non-editing is an irreversible technique. You can select photos after the shooting, but you can't do the same with non-edited video. Once you shoot, it's done. Therefore, there was a feeling of tension when shooting with video camera that is different from what you feel when taking pictures.

Aren't non-edited images similar to improvised music? Let me quote Derek Bailey's words: "The Japanese use a word for Free Improvisation — *sokkyo* — meaning 'let rise here and now.' [...] such aestheticising abolition of past and future [...]"; Like Dada, Free Improvisation is conversational, here-and-now, aggressively banal."*

---

* ベン・ワトソン著『デレク・ベイリー　インプロヴィゼーションの物語』[Ben Watson, *Derek Bailey and the Story of Free Improvisation*] 木幡和枝訳 (工作舎: 2014), 437.

Shooting without editing has no past, no future. You have to keep concentrating on the here-and-now. It doesn't matter whether or not this very shot will connect well to the next one. You can't sacrifice the present for the sake of the future. It may be banal, as Derek Bailey has said, but it makes us work in constant tension. Shooting images while thinking about how to eventually connect them, forces all shots into a pre-established arrangement. I had no interest in how the footage I shot would turn out in sequence. What whole view would emerge when shots of the here-and-now are mechanically connected together in the camera — nobody knows until the shooting ends. This ad-hoc aspect of the non-editing method interested me.

When I started using a video camera, I was interested in street sounds. I didn't care much about what I was shooting. I was just responding to sounds, and these somehow connected the images into a sequence. Walking with the video camera, it was the sounds that caught my attention first. Watching the video images later, I realized that Tokyo was flooded with all these sounds, which I had never noticed before. It was a surprise to learn that we actually live in such a noisy environment. Interestingly, you don't hear street sounds while shooting with a film camera, but the sounds were suddenly audible when I first held a video camera with a sound recording function.

A tape recorder is also an instrument into which unintended sounds will naturally intrude. Both camera and tape recorder are recording instruments, but it doesn't mean they record only what you want to see or hear. They share this similarity.

In my early video work, sounds were for me more significant than the images captured by the camera. I was kind of shooting in response to sounds. Intermittently recorded sounds reminded me of noise music such as SPK and M.B that I used to listen to when I was young. Street sounds recorded on video are constantly disrupted, and unlike music, it's not comfortable listening to them. Sometimes you hear something and you don't know where it comes from. Recorded sounds are cut off from their context and gain liberation from their source; they no longer signify anything. I suppose the recording makes the sounds become themselves, without context or signified meaning.

"Sounds, unlike words, have no meaning. Sounds are nothing more than sounds, or rather, not even sounds. They are tones that, when you think you perceive them, have already disappeared; they are a constant, arrhythmic form of life that deliver and carry away these tones in waves," musician Yuji Takahashi wrote.* I think sounds and images have a similar quality. Images, too, when you think you see or perceive them, have already flown away. With photographs you can freeze what is disappearing, whereas with sound and video images you can't. Sounds and images are disappearing every moment that you see them; they are destined to evaporate at the very moment they emerge. The photograph shows "what once existed," while the video image shows the process where "what once existed" will pass away. Unlike photographs, video images can't stop what is passing away. This property of video images, different from photographs, interests me.

When you think of the term "unconscious," how do you feel? Is the concept of unconsciousness an auditory reality or a visual reality for you?

At the end of the 1990s, I had an exhibition called *Black Parachute Ears*. "Parachute" in the title is a metaphor for the uncertainty of our sight and hearing. The reason I chose this word is because a parachute is uncertain as to where it will land. Our hearing, too, is unreliable. When you are standing on the street, you can't be confident where the sounds that reach your ears are coming from.

So unconsciousness is for me auditory as well as visual. Seeing is also an ambiguous experience to the same degree that hearing is. People think that by seeing they can fully clarify things, but I

---

* 高橋悠治 [Yuji Takahashi], スライドと音楽 [Slides and Music] (2001), http://www.suigyu.com/yuji/ja-text/2001/0105.html.

think this is wrong. Photographic images don't really clarify anything, they rather lead us into a further, uncertain world. People who have actually seen places captured in my photos always say, "I know this place, but it looks completely different from your photo." What you see in pictures is the same, of course, but this same thing doesn't look the same as reality. My photographs are supposed to show things more clearly as I always focus on every detail in the picture; but the clearer the image gets, the more it looks different. The photograph is indeed mysterious.

Unconsciousness is said to hide behind consciousness, controlling it, beyond our grasp. That is to say, it doesn't emerge above the surface of the conscious. The unconscious is there, but it's something you cannot capture. Often there are people who say, "I want to show the unconscious in my work." However, the unconscious is never able to emerge itself nor are you able to grasp it yourself. Even if you perceive something unconsciously, it must already be something different from unconsciousness. As it is impossible to see or grasp it, I suppose unconsciousness only exists in negation. It doesn't exist as a substance, therefore, it merely shows itself as null or void. Something like an absent reality....

Do you think it is possible to develop a serious political artistic practice? Your photography seems to be deeply political, according to the etymological meaning of this word, since it relates to the connection between the individual and the city. Is there a political motivation that influences and drives your aesthetic?

The *Kōjien* dictionary defines politics as "the activities aimed at influencing others in a mutual way regarding to the formation and dismantling of orders in human population." Politics means to realize society through relationships between people. Aristotle called this the "good society." According to Hannah Arendt, if the role of politics is to realize "a good society," it must influence others through language to consider what is "a good society" for everyone. If I may say so, politics connects people through language. Politics is relationships between people.

Art is also a product of relationships. Therefore, art and politics can't be considered separately. But it's not about bringing political issues into art — it's not as simple as that. To use Jean-Luc Godard's rhetoric, what is at stake is not the art of politics, but the politics of art. And when you think of the politics of art, the question of representation arises. Can the photograph, which can frame only a part of reality, represent or reproduce reality as a whole? Can it also represent artists' emotions or thought? This is a question about whether it is possible for art, not only photography but any art, to represent.

A unilateral approach to subjects, imposing my aesthetics onto them, should be avoided. As you have pointed out, what is at stake is the relationships between subjects and myself. I am taking pictures of Tokyo because this city where electric wires and signboards create chaotic sights interests me for their likeness to the paintings of Jackson Pollock; on the other hand, I also have a pessimistic feeling about living in this environment, and about being surrounded by such an environment. Living under the urban capitalist system strips subjectivity from human beings, transforming them into a mere part of its system. Humans who are deprived of their subjectivity can only express themselves in relation to the system that they are involved in. The cityscape has been constructed by this relationship to the system. Therefore, I would think that the Tokyo I take pictures of is very political. That is because it shows humans who cannot exist outside the system that they are involved in, in a similar way to signboards or electric wires.

In Japanese society, "good society" means a "good society" for those in power; ordinary people have neglected to question what is "good" or make value judgments. Nobody queries the structure of vested interests by which someone makes a profit out of constantly destroying existing streets and creating new buildings. Or rather, people seem to think the newer buildings are better.

I am not a genuine Japanese. I've got half-Korean blood in my veins. Being half-Korean in Japanese society means I belong to a minority class. Maybe that's why I have always been uncomfortable in this society. Discomfort with the social system which deprives the individuality of people and diminishes humans into nodes within the social system, creates my artistic motivation.

Do you consider the city of Tokyo to be your personal studio? What is your relation to Tokyo? What is Tokyo for you? How does the constant change of the city influence the formal changes in your own art? Is there a link between the contemporary history of Tokyo and the development of your own photography?

Andy Warhol called his studio his factory. He named it factory because he considered his art activities to be a kind of labor. I also consider my taking pictures as labor, so Tokyo for me constitutes a studio as in the sense of Warhol's factory. I don't have an inner artistic inspiration that the artists in the 19th century had, and I am not interested in waiting for the god of art to descend on me. I get up punctually and keep a routine of shooting in a predetermined locale. You have to get up early because you can't shoot when it gets dark. Labor similar to routine work is the source of photographic art. Therefore, photography is for me a form of labor.

I don't like Tokyo. But I can only take photos in a city like Tokyo. I don't know why, but somehow I've become like this: I am interested in where I live. It is not quite true recently, but I never used to shoot in foreign countries in the past. I was consciously avoiding shooting abroad. The thought behind this was that if I took photos in foreign countries, not where I live, as a mere tourist, it would be no different to taking sightseeing photographs. I probably thought it would be rude if I did that. And foreign countries do look rather nice in photographs. I feel some nervousness about cityscapes, especially in Europe. There is a somewhat authoritative design in European cityscapes — wher-

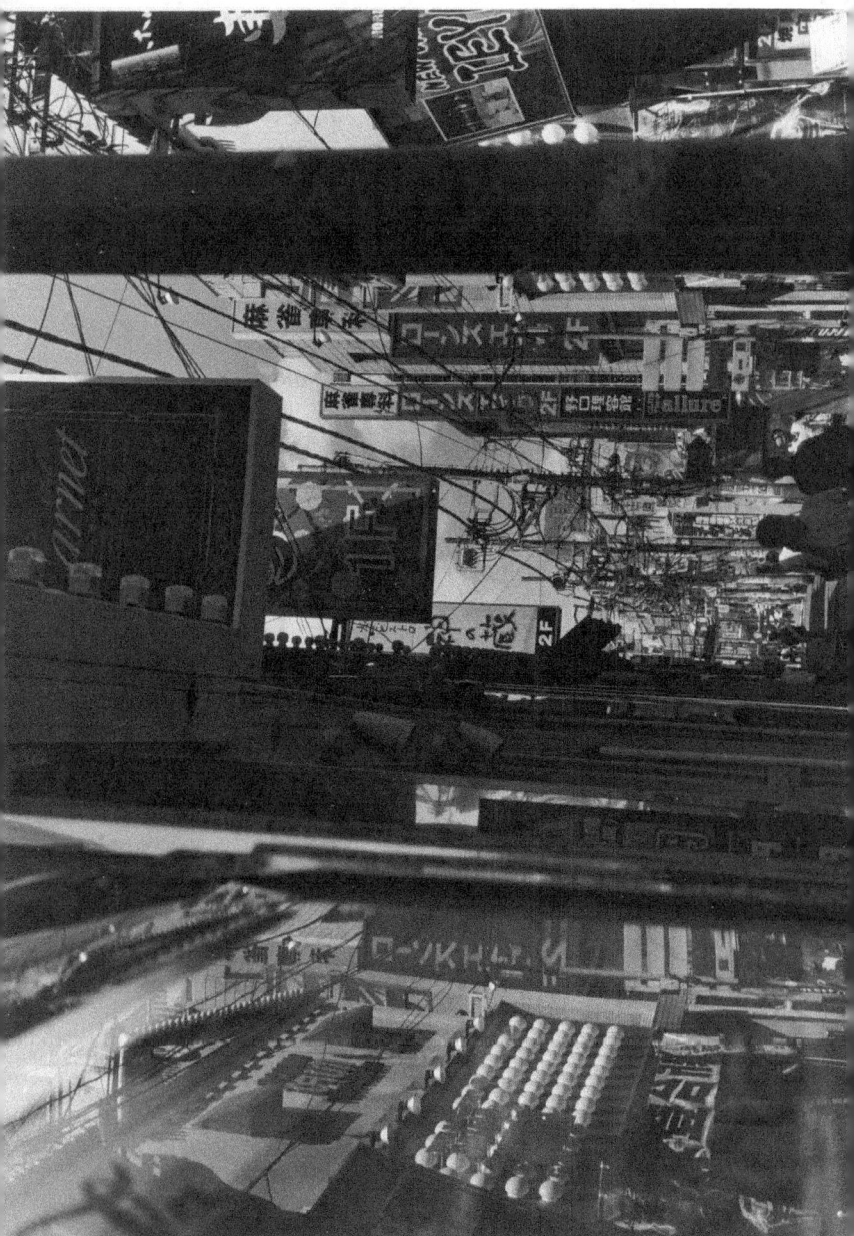

ever you go you see extensive harmonious streetscapes. Perhaps we can say they are overly controlled. Pointing a camera at this kind of scene, I feel that the landscape itself wills me to "shoot in this way." So, it is difficult for me to undermine landscapes that have been constructed by this kind of power.

Rapid changes in Tokyo have influenced my photographs, of course. I used to capture abandoned bicycles in the early days, but under increasingly tight regulation, you don't see them so much anymore. There is a plan to bury all the electric wires under the earth in preparation for the Tokyo Olympics in four years time. If that happens, you won't be able to take pictures of electric wires almost covering the sky any more. It's the fate of photographers who deal with urban landscapes that the subjects photographed should be constantly changing. Landscapes created by urban systems determine the subjects to be photographed. I can't tell what I will want to shoot. I just take photos of what is in front of me. I can't complain whether I like it or not.

If there is history in the landscape of Tokyo, it's a history created by changes in corporate power. Shibuya was a leading cultural venue in Tokyo around the 1980s and '90s; it was made possible by capital from the Seibu Corporation. In order to stimulate people's desire to consume more, the Seibu Corporation gave fashionable names to ordinary places that were actually nothing remarkable. Ordinary hills were named "Kōendori" (Park Avenue) or "Spain-zaka" (Spanish Hill) and Japanese youth at that time immediately started gathering there.

I started taking photos of Tokyo in the early '90s; what you see in those pictures is the changing history of corporate capital. For example, if you shoot in Shibuya nowadays, you can capture the transition from the Seibu Corporation to the Tokyu Corporation. Unlike Europe, the landscape in Japan is constantly changed by the power of capital. Around the '90s when I started taking photos, it was a period when regulation preventing big capital from opening supermarkets was relaxed. It was also around the same period that height restrictions for buildings were removed. High-rise apartments and large-scale commercial facilities started to emerge behind the old, nostalgic streets.

I thought it was a very imbalanced landscape. Meanwhile, construction started everywhere, and Tokyo looked like one big construction site. Prior to the 2020 Olympics, there is more construction in Tokyo than ever before. I have the feeling that we are living in a huge construction site.

However, photography can only affirm existing subjects. Even if you don't like such landscapes, you can't change them. In my opinion, the photograph starts from tentatively affirming the sight that is in front of you. Therefore, I started taking pictures of developments promoted by big capital, whose values neglect whether or not they are actually liveable for humans, although I felt uncomfortable about it.

What did it feel like to live in and photograph Tokyo in the early 2000s? What do you remember of those days?

It is impossible to be economically independent as a photographer in Japan. I don't do commercial photos, so I was taking photographs at the same time as securing a financial base by doing newspaper deliveries, etc. The situation has not changed. Delivering newspapers is a job close to the lowest rank. Thinking back, I have a feeling that I have always been looking at Japan from the lowest position. The bubble economy ended. Nevertheless, many people were still in a festive mood in the early 1990s. Meanwhile, the Tokyo subway sarin gas attack by the Aum Shinrikyo cult occurred in the mid-'90s. I felt some sympathy for their idea of trying to overthrow Japanese society.

In the early 2000s, I received many photography awards, but it didn't help me economically; life was difficult as I continued my daily job of delivering newspapers. I did this on the day following the award ceremony and it was hard to square these different realities. I appeared on two TV documentaries in those days and I remember this caused a massive response among people. When I was delivering newspapers, dozens of people said, "I saw you on TV. Please shake my hand," but nobody tried to buy my photos or photo books. I did many exhibitions in

Europe but there were very few offers in Japan. I suspect nobody was really interested in my photographs; people were merely interested in the image of artists who "commit to their vocation and continue the photographic work that they like while engaging in very low level work" — the kind of romantic image that the Japanese are fond of.

It wasn't until the early '90s that museums in Japan finally started collecting and exhibiting photographic work. A new photography museum was opened and attracted a lot of attention. Quite a number of photographers said that exhibiting photographs in museums is reactionary. Many photographers in those days were hostile toward the word "art." Around the early 2000s was a period when photography at last started receiving recognition as an art form. Everyone now admits that photography is a form of art, but I don't agree with those who either criticize it out of their inferiority complex toward painting, or those who are too optimistic so that they admit photography as an art without reservation. I say this because I've been thinking that photography is so subversive that it can destroy the system of art itself.

Do you think the work of Takuma Nakahira somehow influenced your recent color photography?

My color photographs capture the details of cities, which are slightly different from my black and white photos, but both types share a central concern with how to destabilise perspective in photography. I thought Takuma Nakahira's work had little influence on my black and white photos, but we actually do seem to have something in common in that we both look for two-dimensional expression. I particularly had this feeling when I saw Takuma Nakahira's *Circulation,* shot in 1971. It's a series of pictures he reeled off within a week on the streets of Paris, and he quickly made them into prints and exhibited them on a wall. It's very rare to see photos that have completely destabilized framing like that. They have no stable focus in the composition. For example, Lee Friedlander's photographs with solid framing and composition offer viewers cosy viewpoints to look at, but *Circulation* doesn't have this kind of stable focus. It makes you feel uneasy. Its framing doesn't make people feel comfortable, but that doesn't mean they are bad photos.

Framing interests me because I dislike it. Photographs that are nicely framed don't mean much to me. I pay attention to framings because I want to destroy them. I don't want to lock photographs in frames. I thought in *Circulation* I'd found an affirmation of my own opinion.

Probably, my color works are influenced by *Circulation* in terms of the two-dimensional element without perspective. *Circulation* is a photo book that focuses on two-dimensional expression; viewers don't find spatial elements in it. It also includes numerous copies of printed materials. Looking at this photo book, you can understand that photographs are basically two-dimensional art. Photography is a kind of trick that fabricates three-dimensional space within a two-dimensional reality. It is a fraudulent technique that makes people believe the falsity of photographs; that is, that they can reproduce reality, which is actually not true. The *Circulation* series resists this trick and strongly insists that photographs are flat, two-dimensional art. Photographs are not reproductions of reality, but construe a different reality.

In my black and white photographs, I framed objects, signboards and electric wires excessively in the foreground; this was designed *not* to create a three-dimensional perspective. I have always felt uncomfortable with photos that fabricate a three-dimensional space. I felt sympathetic toward *Circulation* for its radical will to aspire to flat expression.

You took part in an important exhibition in Italy: *Senrit-sumirai* in the Pecci Museum, Prato in 2001. This exhibition showed a whole generation of Japanese artists who were born in the 1960s to the Western public. Your work was featured together with that of other important Japanese artists of the

same generation. Is there a common background to the artists of your generation? Is that background still alive today?

People who were born in the 1960s and became active in the
early '90s, if there is a common background shared by this generation, it is the fact that "a common background doesn't exist
between them any more." Takashi Honma, Miwa Yanagi, and I
share nothing in common, I think. Until around the '80s, there
was a sort of community, but around the time when I started
taking photos, these communities were on the verge of collapse.
There were independent galleries set up by like-minded individuals who were presenting their work there, but I didn't think
this effort had much effect. Their work seemed to be restricted
within their own community, rather than using independent
galleries to launch out into possibilities outside; I thought I
would be better off making photographs by myself.

It became impossible for artists to maintain a common
background in the '90s; I suppose more or less the same thing
happened in every country. Therefore, it is now getting more
difficult to make dialogue across different genres of art. The expression "interdisciplinary" once attracted a lot of attention in
Japan, but nowadays people in different areas such as photography, painting, and film, work in isolation and their views are
narrow. One of the reasons why I have recently become keen
to produce videos is that if I withdraw into the photographers'
world, there is no future. There is no future in artists working
from an isolated perspective.

I don't think this tendency is a good thing, but it's also true
that it is difficult to interact without sharing a common background. Establishing relationships that have no shared basis is
hard; it is almost like trying to cross essentially parallel lines by
force, trying to create relationships between disconnected, dis-
crete individuals.

If there is a commonality in the artists featured in the *Senritsumirai* exhibition, it is the influence of American culture.
Honma and I are both under the strong influence of American photography. The painters in the same exhibition seem to

be strongly influenced by pop art or new painting. I remember some Italian who was involved in *Senritsumirai* pointing out that Japanese art has a strong American influence.

You might think it is naïve to evaluate American culture positively from today's point of view. But I recall not many artists who participated in the exhibition have critically reflected on this issue.

About the video work *Elvis the Positive Thinking Pelvis*: How was it born? Why did you decide to introduce editing and post-production in your video work?

I started using a video camera around 2013 and was thinking about how to exhibit my color pictures. Putting prints of color photos on the wall is not that interesting; it's just repeating the same method I use to show my black and white photos. I wanted to show them in a slightly different way, and thus *Elvis the Positive Thinking Pelvis* was made. I used a compact camera called GR and it turned out this camera can also take moving pictures. So I shot both moving and still images and I thought it would be a good opportunity to create videos again. Using 700 still and moving images, it became a 10-minute video work.

Until I made *Elvis the Positive Thinking Pelvis,* I hadn't had many opportunities to show my videos. Nobody was interested like you were, and the videos I'd created in the past were mostly ignored. Moreover, my video works are different from films; only a few opportunities were given to show them in Japan.

Because of the simple reason that I didn't have editing tools, the video works I made in the past were all non-edited. When I started using a digital camera, I found out that a friend of mine was making a living by editing videos. I thought in that case I could direct him and edit, so why not give it a try. And thus *Elvis the Positive Thinking Pelvis* was made.

Non-edited videos are interesting because they show artists' physical movements and thoughts during shootings as they are. There is a tension because you can't edit afterward. This tension still makes you feel excited when you look at them later. When you take images expecting to edit them later, this tension disappears, but you can connect different shots in unexpected ways. In non-edited videos, you can only connect images of what caught your eye because of physical constraints during shooting. But by using post-production techniques, you are released from this physical constraint and can freely connect various shots. I suppose all my videos give the impression that the shots are not well connected, but the unexpected or disconnected elements caused by editing is emphasized more.

Did your experience making videos influence your recent choice of creating digital color photographs?

Not sure. It's hard to say. I can't yet tell objectively, but I guess the experience of making videos has influenced my color photographs. Because of the education I received during four years at photography school — I was told to take photos standing still and was told that blurred pictures are not photographs — I had an instinctive hesitation in taking photos, especially black and white ones, while moving around. But I found it fairly easy to move around shooting with video or digital cameras as they didn't seem very much like cameras, in the old sense.

I create digital color photos differently from black and white ones. If something has influenced my color photos, it must be the experience of creating video work as you said.

About writing: How important is writing in your work?

For me there is no distinction between writing and taking photographs; I find both important. Looking at and taking pictures: both acts are equivalent. Likewise, writing and taking photographs are equivalent. For me, both writing and shooting, or even looking at pictures are all intuitive activities, and they are also exercises in thinking. Both activities are intuitive but analytical. The movements of body and mind during shooting, thinking about how to frame objects or how far you should approach them, etc., seem very similar to the writer's movements of body and mind, choosing words, connecting sentences, and weaving texts. Photographers and writers experience similar patterns of movements in their bodies and minds.

Generally, photographs and language are understood to signify and reproduce things. They can't exist by themselves, they always need to signify something. That is to say, they can only express themselves depending on something else and don't have autonomy in terms of their expression. However, is that really so? What Takuma Nakahira tried to say is related to this. He repeatedly claimed that photographs need not serve or complement the meanings of linguistic texts and made a strong claim about releasing photographs from meaning, with which I deeply sympathize. If photographs exist only to support what is written in language, I wouldn't have taken pictures and instead would have written something in words.

Writing was an important activity for Nakahira, I suspect. There is a clear distinction between his words and photographs, but they both organically interact in a dialectical relationship. His words criticize photographs and vice versa. He didn't write in order to complement the weakness of his photographs or to express meanings that he couldn't convey through his photographs. He used words to criticize the "expression of photographic art" itself, and moreover, criticized his own photographs within which he put his philosophy into practice. His effort was individual but seems similar to accepted art movements such as Dada and Surrealism. He tried to critically review his thoughts and activities in words and proceed to the next phase.

For Nakahira, words were a tool that he needed to move on to the next phase as a photographer, but in my case, I'm not a critic.... Well, I can probably say I'm more interested in what is created out of repetition. I have been writing similar things and also taking similar photographs. Repeating similar things — I kind of like this type of process. I was writing when I started photographs. Nowadays I write long texts even without being asked; I enjoy the act of writing itself. Perhaps it's better to write or take pictures without any purpose.

Photographs have a material base of film or printing paper. They appear not only as an image but accompany this material. And writings also appear in a material form, that is, words written on paper. I consider both photographs and words to have a material existence that accompanies images. They create another independent reality that resists representation in the very act of representing things. This other reality is something cut off from the original object.

Do you write with a computer or freehand? Is there any difference between writing freehand and with a computer?

I write with my computer. It's because my hand can't catch up with the speed of my thoughts. Plus the computer allows you to edit afterward. My thinking is not so logical, so my sentences tend to develop irrationally; my writing doesn't make sense without editing and replacing some sentences afterward.

What is the meaning of narration for you? Do your pictures form a narrative to some degree?

Narration involves a forward flow of time. Stories can only proceed forward as they basically have their own intrinsic structure.* I don't think my photographs and videos have this kind of time flow which typifies banal narratives.

My black and white pictures show similar subjects. I display four of these similar photographs arranged in vertical columns on the walls of a venue. When you are in the venue and are surrounded by similar photographs, you have the impression that

---

* Translator's note: the speaker refers to the four-part organization of Japanese narratives, *kishotenketsu*: introduction, development, turn, conclusion.

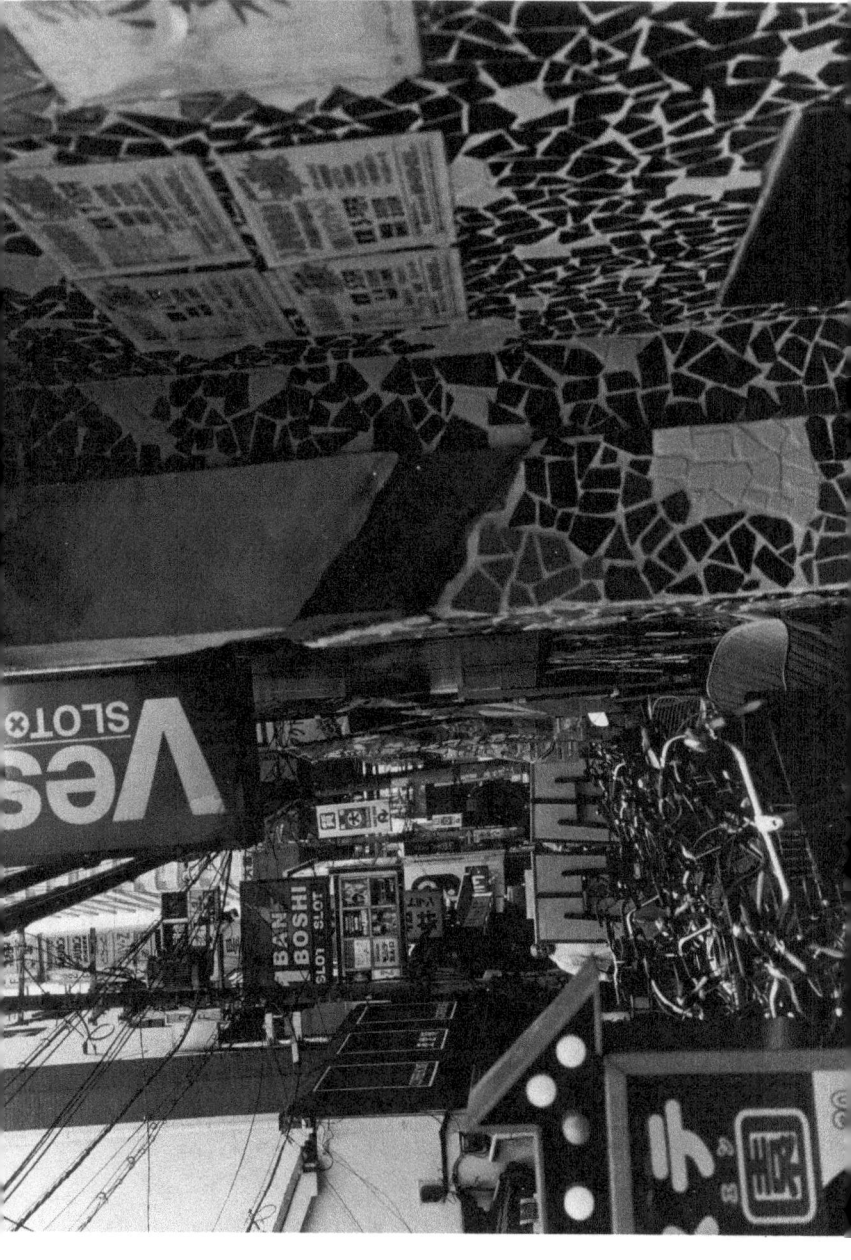

time is not moving forward or backward. Narration always requires progress in time. Are there narrations in my photographs that transcend temporal progress?

The edited video *Life Is a Gift* (2015) is an attempt to depart from the banal narrative structure of *kishotenketsu*. On the other hand, the non-edited video about Takuma Nakahira (*Takuma Nakahira, April 23, 2011*) doesn't deviate from the actual flow of time that much, but it's not completely consistent with it either. This video, which starts with a morning scene at Nakahira's home and ends at Shin-Yokohama Station, is a documentary of an ordinary day in the photographer's life; but it doesn't say much about his human nature. In terms of showing the latter, films made by other artists do it better. The main focus of my video is a scene surrounding the photographer. To be sure, I am taking images of Nakahira, but his inner qualities are not shown. The video won't tell you what's on his mind. Nakahira is the central figure, but it doesn't mean he is the protagonist. He is also one of the details of the scenes that surround him.

I am interested in the details of moving images. Blockbuster movies often omit these in order to develop the story effectively, but I consider films to be accumulations of details. Details and stories never happily coexist. There are quite a lot of films that capture the confrontational relationship between story and detail and don't reach any agreement. For example, the films by Jonas Mekas are created almost only in terms of detail. Not to mention the daily minor events shown in his films, the particular textures that appear when you blow up 16mm films for screenings — even these grainy particles that are the detail of film, are also beautiful. I think Mekas doesn't care about stories at all; I get the impression that narrative elements are kept to a minimum in his work.

What is *Z-Trash Diary* and how do you compose images with a digital camera?

"Z-Trash" is an expression meaning American third-rate pornographic movies, much lower quality than B-movies. I would say it means that there is nothing lousier or trashier. The invention of digital cameras enabled anyone to take beautiful pictures. Therefore, these days I feel the more beautiful the pictures are, the more boring they are. People used to work very hard to create beautiful photos, but because of the invention of digital cameras photographers' efforts in the past came to nothing. We've come to understand that nothing is trashier than things that are beautiful. Digital cameras have accelerated the transformation of beauty into junk or trash.

Photographs are in oversupply; they are everywhere. We live in an era when everyone takes pictures using their smartphones so that you can easily create masterpieces. Everyone takes photos like that once a day — "masterpiece" here means the imitation of masterpieces created in the past, though. But I don't think there is any possibility here for new forms of photography; plus, I am getting tired of hearing that people expect something new in photography.

I'm weary of looking at beautiful pictures or masterpieces and I don't think we will have any more masterpieces. It's more productive to think of photography as an art that throws doubt on the concept of "masterpiece." Unlike paintings, photographs have little individuality. In other words, photography is an art that deliberately makes individuality invisible. It has an anonymous quality. For example, if you collect pictures on the subject of vehicles, the pictures taken by Robert Frank and other famous photographers would look rather alike. Photography thus lacks individuality. Is it then possible that photographic art, having no individuality, can create masterpieces? Sarah Greenough reviewed Walker Evans's *Many Are Called,* a collection of photographs of people on subways and wrote: "Many Are Called and Many Are Chosen" changing the phrase "Many are Called but Few are Chosen" from the Bible. If masterpieces are born only by being chosen, Greenough's words, Many are Chosen, would probably suggest that all the photos taken were masterpieces. If all the photos are chosen and all of them are masterpieces, real masterpieces don't exist.

Nowadays, when photographs are in oversupply, we have a situation of inflation. Street snaps are good examples: the more they look like a masterpiece, the more they look like masterpieces from the past. They become a kind of craftwork. The better they look, the more they transform themselves into banal photos you've seen somewhere before. Masterpieces are nothing more than just "trash."

Unlike film photography, digital cameras don't transform banal reality into a first-rate work of art through camera skills or darkroom techniques. Digital cameras lack the element of alchemy that photography used to have. They don't transform trash into gold but they present trash as trash. Mass-produced trash-masterpiece photos are boring because people mistake trash for gold. There is no difference between trash and gold. Gold has a history of being treated as something beautiful, while trash has no such history. Trash has nothing valuable but isn't there some possibility in this nothingness?

> Do you think photography is in a state of crisis today? What is the major danger for photography today? Are people still capable of reading images?

In Japan, people have kept on saying, "Films will die soon." Although this comment has been repeated for almost thirty years, there is not the slightest indication of its death. This idea that "something will die soon" reminds me of Samuel Beckett's *Malone Dies*. Malone is supposed to die at any minute, but his death is slow coming. Instead, he lingers on in the final minutes of his life before death. Films are also lingering on just like him. The life of films doesn't end completely. They live the time just before their death without having a future or anything. It's living in suspended time that doesn't belong to life or death.

Radical filmmakers all shared the recognition that "films will die soon." Their concerns as to whether or not they could transcend Godard or François Truffaut, or whether or not there were possibilities of creating new films still remained for them. Although these concerns were a mere repetition of what Godard or Truffaut themselves had felt toward Alfred Hitchcock and American films, this kind of awareness of cessation is important. I think photography has experienced a similar crisis to this.

In the 1970s, Daidō Moriyama published a photo book *Shashin yo Sayonara* (Goodbye to Photography). I see it now as a photo book full of romantic feelings that are typical of the artist. But Moriyama, who loved photographs more than anyone else, probably had a sense of crisis to the extent that he had to say goodbye to photography.

Photography first appeared as a medium that anyone could handle, but is there any future left for it? Artists used to be in a chosen, privileged position and nobody could imitate the art they created. Cameras that could be easily handled by anyone destroyed this privilege of artists. With the invention of the digital camera, I kind of think that this tendency of good photographs, accessible to everyone, has reached a crucial phase. Anyone can create a masterpiece. When everyone can make a masterpiece, you can't call it a masterpiece any more. Outstanding photographs don't exist anywhere — the concept of masterpiece has died. All photographs are mere repetitions of masterpieces created in the past and people always see images in reference to masterpieces created before. There is no such thing as completely new images. That is because it is impossible for humans to understand something completely unknown. Unless people can relate these images to what they have seen in the past, they don't understand them. They can only understand images that refer back to existing works. That is to say, new images are repeated images. People don't see new images; they only project the images they have seen in the past. Images can only exist as the past. They lack the here-and-now.

Questions by Marco Mazzi (May 1, 2017)
Answers by Osamu Kanemura (June 12, 2017)

インタビュー

プラウベル・マキナについてどのように考えていますか？ あなたの写
真の製作過程において、このカメラはどのような重要性をもちますか？
有名であり、かつ重要な作品である、都市風景を撮影したモノクロ写
真を製作する前に、ほかのカメラをつかって撮影していましたか？

プラウベル・マキナは使いづらいカメラです。ファインダーの視野率が100
パーセントではないので、現場で実際に見ているときと、現像してからのイ
メージにずれがあります。使い始めた頃は、そんなずれに困惑した記憶が
あります。手前の柵を外して撮ったつもりが、現像してフィルムを確認した
ら、その柵が画面に入っていたりしていました。普通だったらトリミングした
りして修正するのですが、自分が外そうと思っていたものが写っているのが
不思議で、それもまた面白いのではと思うようになりました。
　ファインダーを覗いているときには、画面構成を壊す邪魔な要素だから
外そうと思ったものが写っていることで、画面に動きが出てきたような気が
しました。6×7の画面の縦横の比率は、安易な気持ちで撮っていると簡単
にまとまります。正方形に近いので構図が作りやすい。誰が撮っても6×7
だとバランスよくうまくまとまってしまいます。6×7というサイズは安定してい
るサイズです。35mmカメラのストリートスナップのような動きを6×7で出すの

は難しいと思っていました。誰が撮っても安定した画面を作れるそのサイズ
で、不安定な画面構成ができないものかと考えていたので、そのような意
図していなかったノイズ的な要素が入ってしまうプラウベル・マキナは、わた
しにノイズの重要さを教えてくれたカメラだと思います。

　写真学校時代のわたしは、ゲイリー・ウィノグランドとルイス・ボルツが好
きでした。一見するとまるで違うタイプの写真家なのですが、両方の要素
を取り入れた写真を撮れないかといつも考えていました。ストリートスナッ
プとランドスケープですから、両者の要素を混ぜ入れた写真を撮るのは難
しい。プラウベル・マキナを使う前は、キャノンの35㎜一眼レフカメラとロー
ライの6×6を使っていました。35㎜は写真を大きく伸ばすと、粒子が目立
ち、細部がよく見えないのでやめました。それで中判のローライの6×6を
使ったのですが、6×6のスクエアなフォーマットだと構図がシンメトリーにな
るので、どうしても静的な雰囲気から逃れられない。けれどプラウベル・マ
キナを使ったことで、ノイズ的な要素が画面に入り込み、そのことで静的な
都市のランドスケープの写真に、ストリートスナップ的な動きの要素がプラ
スされた感じがしました。

　わたしは小津安二郎のフレーミングに影響を受けていたので、厳密な
構図構成にはいつも興味がありました。6×7を選んだのも、小津安二郎
が常用していたサイズ、スタンダードサイズ（4:3）に近いフレームだから
です。小津の無駄のないフレーミングは憧れでもありました。自分の写真
のフレーミングもそれなりに厳密なところがあると思うのですが、写真の場
合、映画と違って被写体が動いているわけではないので、フレーミングが
厳密すぎると、静的な印象が強くなりすぎる気がします。フレームの中に収
まりすぎるというのでしょうか。

　厳密なフレーミングというのは、写真を洗練させる方向にいきがちで
す。これは批判というわけではないのですが、田原桂一の写真のフレー
ミングの厳密さは、写真をフレームの内部で完結させていくような自閉的な
美を目指しているように感じさせます。けれどフレーミングを厳密にやりなが

ら、ノイズを呼び込む方法があるのではないかと考えていました。映画的なフレーミングというか……。音楽で例えれば、エルヴィン・ジョーンズの緻密なドラムがバックを支えているから、コルトレーンはあんなにノイズまみれな演奏ができた。フレームさえしっかりしていれば、なにが写っていても構わないと思うのです。フレームというのは一つの構造です。構造が明確であるからこそノイズが生まれる。フレーミングというのは、不明瞭なノイズを生み出す構造だと考えました。

　　あなたの写真には人間の姿が含まれています。初期の都市スナップ写真の多く、より円熟した作品にも人間の姿がありますし、最近のデジタル作品にも人間や人間の痕跡があります。それから、「Human Noise Amplifier」というタイトルを冠したプロジェクトもあります。あなたの作品において、人間の身体や人間の姿はどのような重要性をもっていますか？ 人間の姿はフレーミングにおいてどのように重要ですか？

わたしの写真の中に写っている人間について言及していただいてとても嬉しいです。今でもそうなのですが、わたしの写真には人がまるで写っていないと思っている人が多いのです。彼らは電線や看板、放置自転車の群れに圧倒されて、写っている人間にまで目が届かないのかもしれないし、都市の風景写真だという先入観が、わたしの写真に写っている人間を見ないようにさせてしまうのかもしれません。
　わたしの写真にとって人間とは画面を構成する一つの部分です。わたしは人間は電線や看板や放置自転車と同じ画面の中の要素として考えています。それは人間が嫌いという私的な理由からではなく、画面の中に主役という中心をつくりたくなかったからです。画面に写っているものは、すべて等価であるとわたしは思っています。人間は強力な存在なので、画面に

人が写っていると、すぐにその人間が目に付きます。そうすればどうしても人間を中心に写真を見ようという気にさせられます。写っているものの階層的な関係の中で、わたしの写真を解釈されたくないのです。もっと重層的に見てもらいたいというか、中心は人間だけではなく、看板や電線も、あらゆる都市を構成する要素が自分にとっては重要なのです。当然ですが、重要でないものなどありません。写っているすべてのものが重要ですから、そこに階層をつけたくない。

　人間もまた都市を構成する重要な要素ですが、決して都市の主人公というわけではありません。わたしにとって興味があるのは、写っているもの同士が関係を持ち始めた瞬間です。だから単体としてのものは撮りません。人間と電線と看板が一枚の写真の中でどんな関係を持つのか。都市というシステムの中でそれらはどんな関係を結んでいるのかに興味があります。

　どんな映画でもいいのですが、わたしは映画を見ていると、だんだん主人公の人間よりも背景のモノや風景に興味を持つようになります。だから主人公が何を喋ったのかは覚えていないけれど、その背後の風景は覚えていたりします。監督の意図とは懸け離れたところに興味が行きます。

　人間はわたしにとって看板や電線と同じ存在です。特別に語られるものではない。だからといって人間はどうでもいいということでもないのです。いるべきところにいる。そこに人間がいなければ画面は成り立たない。それは人間だけではなく看板や自動車も同じです。必然的にその時そこにいるのです。わたしの写真の中に写っている人の存在には、いるべきところにいたという必然性を感じます。撮影のときに、人間に注目してはいないし、実際まったく気づかずにいることもあるのですが、写った写真を見るとまるで計算したかのような配置で人間が写っていることがあります。

　人間が一人も写っていない都市写真を撮る写真家がいますが、一人も写っていないというのは、なんだか意味深ですが、わたしはそのような表現には興味がありません。無人の都市が暗示する意味に興味がないので

す。何かを暗示する写真には興味がない。暗示という意味の連鎖ではなく、何も暗示させないもの。写っている裏側には何もない——それそのものしか写っていない写真。意味に繋がっていく写真ではなく、意味から切断された写真——写真は、世界と切断されたものだとわたしは思います。現実と写真は平行線のような気がします。平行線は交わることがない。

　人間の存在は強烈です。人間はその存在自体の意味が強いので、不用意に画面に入れると、写った人間の存在に写真全体が引っ張られていきます。どうしても人間が画面の中心になりやすい。人間が持つその強烈な意味を画面から追放することが、わたしの写真における人間に対する意識だと思います。人間をものにまで還元する。わたしは人間には興味がありますが、人間の内面には興味がないし、まして写真は表面しか写すことができない。人間の内面までは写せません。内面を欠いた人間。電線や看板と等価になった人間に興味があります。

　わたしの作品に人間の痕跡を感じられると指摘されましたが、痕跡というのは物質だと思います。人間を撮るのではなく、わたしは人間の存在を痕跡という物質に転化させたいのです。

　初期のビデオ作品では、撮影しながら編集するという手法がとられています。つまり、短いショットを撮り、多数の短い一連のショットを撮り終わったとき、編集も終わっている。その方法は、ビデオカメラをテープレコーダーとして使っているようにみえます。あなたのビデオ作品において、音の存在はどのような重要性をもちますか？　一連の場面をビデオで記録する際、音とのどのような関わりを意識しますか？

2013年ぐらいまでは、まさにテープレコーダーのようにビデオカメラを扱っていました。編集をしないのは、パソコンを持っていなかったというテクニカルな条件もあったのですが、無編集という技法に興味があったからで

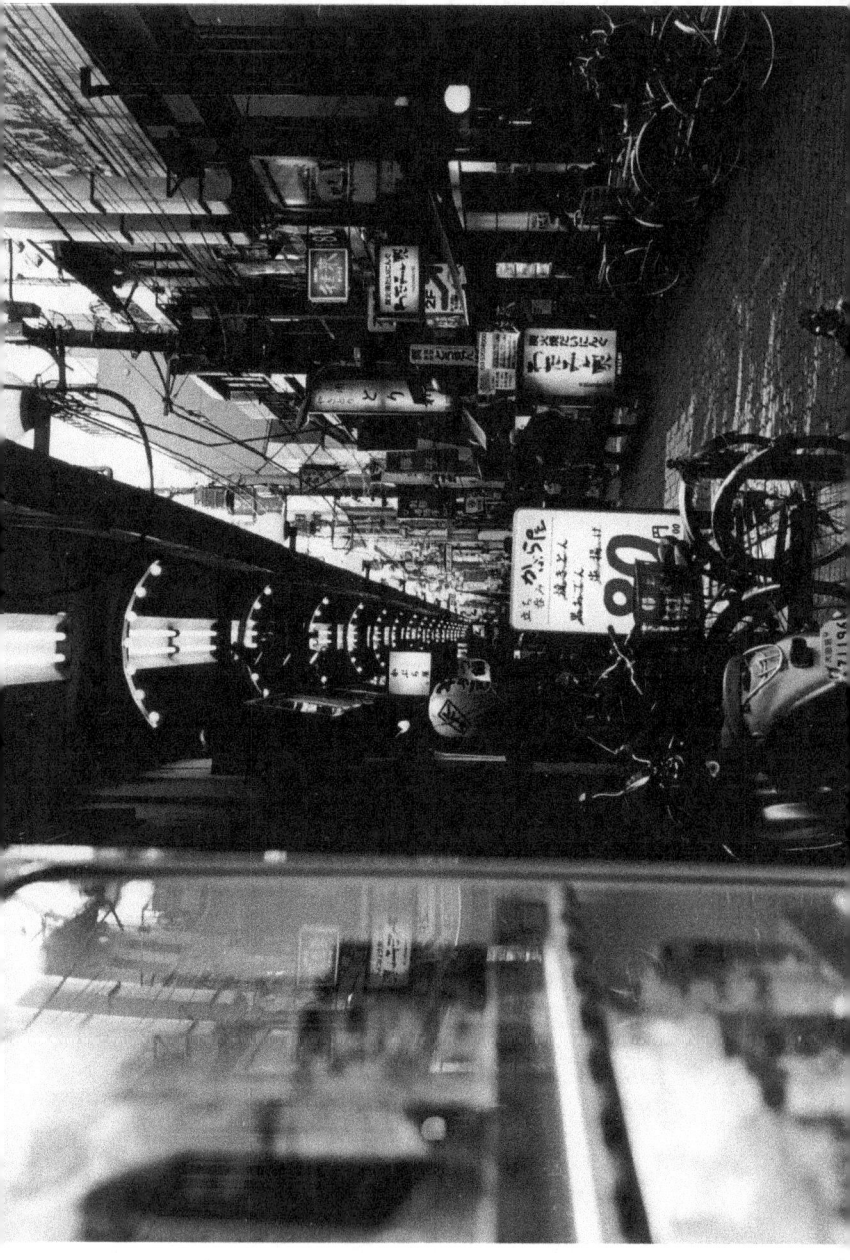

す。無編集は、取り返しがきかない技法です。写真の場合は撮ったあとでセレクトができますが、無編集のビデオ撮影ではそれができない。撮ってしまったらそれっきりです。だからビデオカメラでの撮影は、写真とは違う緊張感を強いられました。

映像における無編集というのは、音楽でいえばインプロヴィゼーションのようなものではないでしょうか。デレク・ベーリーの言葉を引いてみましょう。「「インプロヴィゼーション」の日本語「即興」は、今、ここで、興す」という字義だそうだ。過去と未来をこうした美学で帳消しにする」、「フリー・インプロヴィゼーションはダダに似て会話的であり、「今、ここ」といった実存的なものであり、また攻撃的なくらいつまらない」(『デレク・ベイリーインプロヴィゼーションの物語』/ベン・ワトソン)。

無編集の撮影は、後も先も無い撮り方です。今ここに集中し続けなければいけません。今このショットが次のショットにうまくつながるかどうかというのは、どうでもいい問題です。未来のために今を犠牲することなんてできません。それはデレク・ベイリーのいうように退屈なことなのかもしれませんが、緊張を強いられる作業です。つながりを考えて撮ることは、結局すべてのショットを予定調和的な全体に奉仕させることになります。わたしは撮り終えた映像が、どんな風に全体を構成するのかということに興味がありませんでした。今ここのショットが、カメラの中で機械的につながったとき、それがどんな全体像を見せるのか、撮影が終わるまで分からない。無編集のそんないきあたりばったりの方法に興味がありました。

ビデオカメラを使い始めの頃は、街の音に興味がありました。写っている対象はなんでもよかったところがあります。音に反応して、音が映像を結果的につなげていたという感じです。ビデオカメラを持って街を歩くようになって最初に気になったのは、街の音でした。それまではあまり気にしていなかったのですが、ビデオカメラで撮った画面を見ていたら、こんなに東京の街は音が溢れているのだと感じました。わたし達はこんなうるさい環境で生きていたのかという驚きがありました。不思議なもので、フィルムカメ

ラを持って撮影しているときは街の音は聞こえてこないのですが、音も録音できるビデオカメラを持ったら突然音が聞こえてきたのです。

　テープレコーダーもまた自分が志向していない音が勝手に入ってしまう機械です。カメラとテープレコーダーは共に記録する装置ですが、記録するといっても、自分が見たい、聞きたいものだけが記録されるわけではない。そんな共通性もあります。

　初期のビデオ作品は、写っている画面よりも音の方が自分としては重要でした。音に反応して撮っているところがありますから。細切れに録音された音は、わたしが若い頃聴いていたSPKやM.Bなどのノイズ音楽を思い出させました。途切れ途切れに録音されているので、ビデオカメラが記録した街の音は、音楽のように心地良い音ではありません。なんの音なのか、その由来が分からない音もあります。ビデオカメラに録音されたことで、現実から切り出された音は、何かの音という、その何かから自由になったのです。録音されたことで、音は起源から切り離され、音そのものになったのではないでしょうか。

　「音には、ことばのように、意味はない。音は音でしかない、というより、音でさえない。それは、とらえたと思ったときにはもう消滅している音色であり、それらを波のように運んできてまた運び去る、一定のリズムのない息づきである」、と書いたのは音楽家の高橋悠治でした（「スライドと音楽」/www.suigyu.com）。音と映像は似ていると思います。映像も見た、とらえたと思ったとき、それはすでに流れ去っています。写真は流れ去って行くものをせき止めることができますが、音や映像にはそれができない。見ていく瞬間ごとに音や画像が消滅していく。音も映像も表れた瞬間に消滅していくものです。写真は"かつてあった"ものを写しますが、ビデオ映像は"かつてあった"ものが過ぎ去っていく様子までを画面の中に映します。過ぎ去っていくものを、写真のように止めることができない。そんな写真には無いビデオ映像の機能に興味があります。

　無意識という言葉を考えるとき、どのように感じますか？　あなたにとっ
　て、無意識という概念は聴覚的なリアリティですか、それとも視覚的
　なリアリティですか？

90年代の終わりに、「BlackParachuteEars」というタイトルの展覧会をしまし
た。タイトルのParachuteは、人々の視覚や聴覚のあやふやさについての
メタファーです。なぜこの言葉を使ったのかというと、Parachuteはどこに
落ちるのか分からない、着地点のあやふやなものだからです。聴覚も曖昧
なものだと思います。街に立っていると、耳に聞えている音がどこで鳴って
いるのか、はっきりと判断できない。

　わたしにとって無意識というのは聴覚的であり、視覚的なものです。そし
て見るというのは、聞くことと同じくらいあやふやな体験です。見ることでも
のを完全に確認できるというのは間違いだと思います。写真はだから撮る
ことで何かを明確にするのはなく、さらに不明瞭な世界にわたし達を連れ
ていくのではないでしょうか。わたしが写真で撮った場所を現実に見たこ
とがある人は必ず言います。「この場所知っているけど、写真と全然違う」
と。写っているものは当然同じなのですが、同じなのに、同じように見えな
い。わたしの写真は隅々までピントを合わせることにしていますから、より
明確に写っているはずなのですが、明確になればなるほど違うものに見え
てくる。写真は本当に不思議なものだと思います。

　無意識というのは、意識の背後にあり、意識をコントロールし、自分で
は把握できない意識のことだと言われています。自分でも把握できないもの
ということは、意識の表面に表れることがないということです。無意識はあ
るのかもしれないけれど、把握することができないものだと思います。よく
「無意識的なものを作品に表わしたい」という人がいますが、無意識は決
して表れることができないし、自分で把握できないものなのだから、無意
識的なものを感じたとしても、それはすでに無意識ではないのではと思い
ます。見ることも、把握することもできないのだから、無意識は無いという

形でしか存在しないのではないでしょうか。それは実体として存在しないのですから、ゼロ、空虚という形でしか表れてこないものだと思います。不在のリアリティーでしょうか…

真摯に「政治的」な芸術の実践を模索することは可能だと思いますか？ あなたの写真は非常に「政治的」——この語の語源の意味するところにおいて——であるようにみえます。個人と都市の関係性にまつわるものだからです。あなたの美学に影響を与え、その原動力となるような政治的なモチベーションはありますか？

広辞苑によると政治とは、「人間集団における秩序の形成と解体をめぐって、人が他者に対して、また他者と共に行う営み」と定義されています。政治というのは、人々の関係を通じて社会を実現することだと思います。アリストテレスはそのような社会を「善い社会」と言いました。ハンナ・アーレントによれば、政治が「善い社会」の実現であるなら、みんなにとって「善い社会」とは何かを言語を通じて、他者に働きかけることが政治です。いってみれば政治は、言語によって関係付けられることです。政治とは人々の間の関係のことだと思います。

　芸術もまた関係の産物だとわたしは思っていますから、芸術を政治と切り離して考えることはできません。けれど単純に政治的な題材を芸術に持ち込めばいいという問題でもない。ゴダール的にいえば、問題となるのは、政治の芸術ではなく、芸術の政治だと思うのです。そして芸術の政治を考えるとき、再現の問題が浮上します。現実のある部分しか切り取れない写真が、全体を表象、再現できるのか。対象の再現だけではなく、作者の感情や思考の再現は可能なのか。それは写真に限らず、芸術に再現することは可能かという問いかけでもあります。

　わたしは被写体を自分の美意識に合わせて撮るというような、一方向的に被写体に向かうことは避けたいと思っています。マルコさんの指摘のように、被写体と自分の関係が問題だと思っています。わたしが東京を撮り続けているのは、電線や看板が乱立しているこの街が、まるでジャクソン・ポロックの絵のようで面白いからという気持ちもありますが、その一方で、このような環境下でわたし達は暮らしているのだ、このような環境に囲まれているのだという暗澹たる気持ちもあります。都会という資本主義のシステム下で生きることは、人間から主体を追放して、人間をシステムの結節点に変質させます。主体性を奪われた人間は、システムの関係の中でしか自分を表わすことができない。都市の風景は、システムの関係によって作られたものです。わたしが撮る東京は、だからとても政治的だと思います。そこにはシステムの関係の中でしか存在できない人間や、看板と電線と等価的に価値付けられた人間が写っているからです。

　日本社会では、「善い社会」というのは権力者にとっての「善い社会」であり、何が「善い」のかという価値判断を民衆が問うことは、おざなりにされてきました。古い街並みを壊し続け、つねに新しい建築物をつくることで、誰かが儲かるような利権構造に対して、誰も疑問を持っていません。むしろ新しければ、新しいほど良いと思っているところがあります。

　わたしは純粋の日本人ではありません。半分朝鮮人の血が流れています。朝鮮人とのハーフであるということは、日本の社会ではマイノリティーの階級です。だからでしょうか、日本の社会に対していつも違和感を感じるのは。そのような主体性を剥奪し、人間をシステムの結節点化させている日本の社会システムへの違和感がわたしの芸術上のモチベーションになっているのではないかと思います。

　東京という都市は、あなた自身の「スタジオ」であると思いますか？東京との関わりについて教えてください。あなたにとって東京とは何で

　すか？　東京という都市の絶え間ない変化は、あなた自身の芸術にお
　ける形式上の変化に、どのような影響を与えますか？　現代の東京の
　歴史と、あなた自身の写真の推移とのあいだに、何らかの関連性は
　ありますか？

ウォーホールは自分のアトリエをファクトリーと称していました。自分の芸
術活動を労働と捉えていたから、ファクトリーと名付けたのでしょう。わた
しも写真を撮ることは、労働だと思っているので、わたしにとっての東京は
ウォーホールの言うところのファクトリーとしてのスタジオだと思います。19
世紀の芸術家のように、芸術的インスピレーションは自分の内面にはあり
ませんし、芸術の神が自分の内面に降りてくるのを待つことにも興味があり
ません。定時に起きて、決めたコースを撮り続ける。暗くなると撮れなくな
るので、早起きしなければなりません。ルーティンワークのような労働が写
真芸術の源泉だと思うのです。だからわたしにとって写真は限りなく労働に
近い。

　わたしは東京を好きではありません。けれど東京のような都会でないと
写真が撮れない。なぜ撮れないのか分からないのですが、そういう体質に
なってしまったようです。

　わたしは自分の住んで居るところに興味があります。最近ではそうでも
ないのですが、昔は外国で撮ったりはしなかった。意識的に外国で撮るこ
とを避けていました。住んで居る場所ではなく、たんある旅行者でしかな
い自分がそこで写真を撮ってもそれは、観光写真と変わらないという思い
があったのです。観光気分で写真を撮るなんて、被写体に対して失礼だ
という意識があったのでしょう。それに外国を撮ると、なんだかきれいに撮
れてしまう。都市の景観に対して、特にヨーロッパは、神経質な気がしま
す。どこに行っても調和のとれた景観の街並みが続くヨーロッパが都市風
景に、何か権力的な意思を感じるのです。管理された風景と言い換えても
いいのかもしれません。カメラを向けると、「こういう風に撮れ」という景観

そのものが持つ意思を感じるし、ある意味権力によって作りあげられた風景を崩して撮るのは、わたしにとって実際に難しいのです。

東京のめまぐるしい変化は、当然わたしの写真に影響を与えます。初期の頃、よく写していた放置自転車は、規制が厳しくなったので、もうありません。4年後の東京オリンピックに向けて、電線をすべて地中に埋めるという計画もあります。そうなったら、あの空を覆い尽くすかのような電線を撮ることもできなくなります。撮る対象がつねに変わらざるを得ないのは、都会を撮る写真家の宿命です。都会というシステムがつくった風景が、写真家の撮る対象を決定するのです。わたしには、これを撮りたいという希望を語ることができません。目の前にあるものを撮る。それが好きでも嫌いでも文句を言えない。

東京の風景に歴史があるとしたら、それは資本の変化による歴史です。80年代から90年代の頃の東京の文化を牽引していた場所は渋谷でした。けれどそれは西武という大資本による牽引でした。さらなる購買欲を喚起させるために、西武資本はどこにでもある凡庸な場所に、流行の香りのするネーミングを施してみました。たんなる坂道を「公園通り」とか「スペイン坂」と名付けると、当時の日本の若者は途端にそこに集まるようになりました。

わたしは90年代初頭から東京を撮り始めましたが、そこに写っているものは資本の変わりゆく歴史です。例えば最近の渋谷で撮影すると、西武資本から東急資本へシフトチェンジされていく姿を撮ることができます。ヨーロッパと違って日本の風景は、資本の力によってつねに変えられていきます。わたしが写真を撮り始めた90年代ぐらいの頃は、大資本によるスーパーマーケット出店の規制が緩和された頃でした。建築の高さ制限が取り払われたのがその頃だと思います。古くて情感を感じさせる街並みの背後に、高層マンションや大型商業施設が立ち並び始めました。それはすごくアンバランスな風景だと思っていました。そのうちあちこちで工事が始まり、東京はまるで工事現場のような感じになりました。2020年のオリンピッ

クを前に、以前にもまして東京はあちらこちらで工事をしています。巨大な工事現場の中でわたし達は暮らしているような気がします。

　けれども、写真は被写体に対して肯定することしかできません。いくらこんな風景は嫌だといっても、変えられないのです。とりあえず目前の光景を肯定するところから写真は始まると思うので、わたしは、人間がそこに住みやすいか否かなど度外視した、大資本の価値観による開発の姿に違和感を感じながらも、とりあえずそのような風景を写真に撮り始めました。

　　2000年代の初めに、東京に暮らしながら写真を撮るとはどのような感じでしたか？ 当時のことで覚えていることは何ですか？

写真家として経済的に自立して生活することは日本では不可能です。わたしはコマーシャル写真の仕事はしていないので、新聞の配送などをしながら経済的基盤を確保して、写真を撮っていました。それは今でも続いています。新聞の配送というのは、最下層に近い仕事です。いま思えば、わたしはつねに最下層の立場から日本を見ていたのだという気がします。バブルが終わったとはいえ、1990年代の初めは浮かれている人が多かった。そのうち90年代半ばにオウム真理教による地下鉄サリン事件が起きました。日本の社会をひっくり返せというオウム教団の気分は多少同調できるところもありました。

　2000年代初頭にわたしは写真の賞もたくさん貰いましたが、そのことで経済的に楽になるわけではなく、日常的には新聞の配送の仕事が続いて、毎日が大変でした。賞の授賞式の次の日は、新聞の配送をして、なんだかとてもちぐはぐした感じでした。

　そのころテレビのドキュメンタリー番組に二回ほど出演したことがあります。そのときの反響は凄かったのを覚えています。新聞の配送をしていたら、「昨日テレビを見ました、握手して下さい」と何十人もの人に言われま

したが、誰もわたしの写真や写真集を買おうとはしなかったことを覚えています。ヨーロッパでの展示は多かったのですが、国内ではほとんどオファーがなかった。国内ではわたしの写真は実は興味など持たれていなかったのでしょう。「下層の仕事に従事しながら自分の好きな写真を撮り続けるという、信念を曲げないで自分の道を歩く」という日本人好みの芸術家のイメージに興味を持たれただけなのです。

90年代の初頭になってから、やっと日本の美術館は写真を収集したり、展示したりするようになりました。写真専門の美術館ができたといって騒がれてもいました。写真家の中には、美術館で写真を展示するなんて反動だと言う人も結構いましたね。芸術という言葉に敵対心を持っている人が、当時の写真家には多かったのです。2000年初頭の頃は、写真が芸術としてやっと認められ始めたという黎明期でした。今では写真は芸術だとみんな言っていますが、わたしは写真というのは、芸術の制度を破壊するぐらい危険なものだと思っていたので、絵画に対するコンプレックスから芸術を批判してみたり、写真は芸術だと能天気に両手を挙げて喜んでみたりしている姿を見ると、今でもどうかと思います。

中平卓馬の作品は、何らかのかたちで、あなたの最近のカラー写真に影響を与えたと思いますか?

わたしのカラー写真は都市の細部を撮っていて、モノクロ写真とは少し違いますが、両方とも写真の遠近法をどう壊していくかという共通した考えが中心にあります。モノクロ写真に関しては、中平卓馬の影響は少ないかなと思っていましたが、平面性を志向しているという意味では、中平卓馬の考えと共通しているところがあったようです。そのことを特に感じたのは、中平卓馬が1971年のパリで撮影した『サーキュレーション』です。1週間にわたって、やみくもに撮影し、その日の内にプリントを焼いて展示した

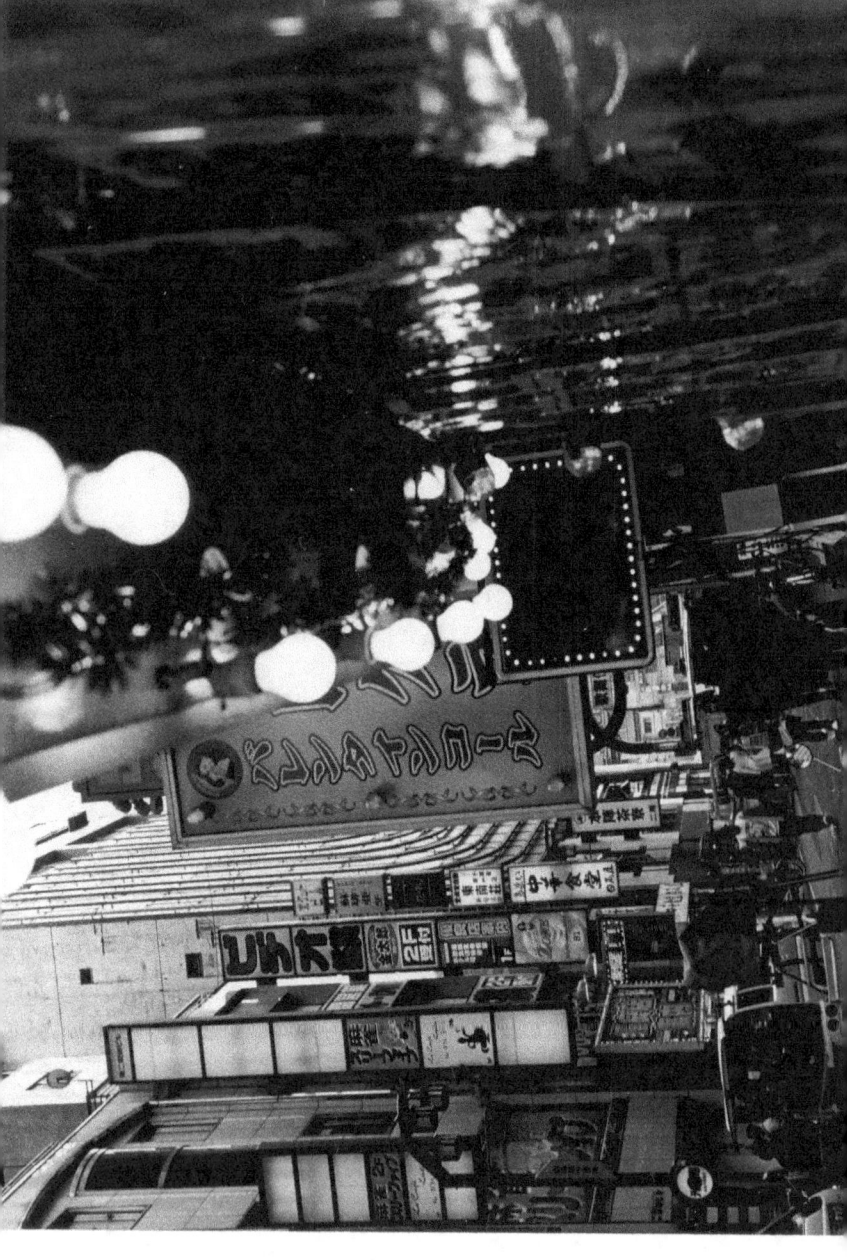

シリーズですが、あんなにフレーミングが壊れている写真も珍しいと思いました。どの写真にもキメがないというのでしょうか、フリードランダーのような写真は、フレーミングと構図がきっちり決まっていて安心して見ていられるのですが、『サーキュレーション』の写真にはそのようなキメがない。見ていてなんだか不安になる。心地の良いフレーミングではないのです。それなら下手な写真かというとそうではない。

わたしがフレーミングに興味があるのは、フレーミングが嫌いだからです。フレームの中に上手く収まっている写真なんてどうでもいい写真だと思っています。フレーミングにこだわるのは、フレーミングを壊したいからです。写真をフレームの中だけに回収させたくないのです。そんなわたしの考えが、『サーキュレーション』に実現されている気がしました。

サーキュレーションの遠近法を感じさせない平面性に、わたしのカラー写真は影響を受けているかもしれません。『サーキュレーション』は空間性を感じさせません。ひたすら平面が続く写真集です。印刷物の複写も多い。写真というのは基本的に二次元の芸術なのだということがこの写真集を見ていると分かります。二次元の世界に三次元的な空間を仮構する写真は一種の手品です。それは現実を再現できるという写真の嘘を、本当だと思わせる詐欺的な手口です。『サーキュレーション』はそのような手品に対して、写真は平面であり、二次元の芸術だという強い主張を感じさせます。写真は現実の再現ではなく、もう一つの現実なのではないでしょうか。

わたしのモノクロ写真で、手前にものや看板や電線を過剰に入れるのは、三次元的な遠近法を成り立たせないための方法でした。三次元的な空間を仮構する写真には、いつも違和感を感じていました。『サーキュレーション』の過激な平面志向に、わたしはシンパシーを感じました。

2001年にイタリア・プラートのペッチ美術館で開催された重要な展覧会「Senritsumirai」に参加なさいました。この展覧会は、60年代生ま

れの日本のアーティストたちの存在を西洋の人たちに伝えるものでした。あなたの作品は、同世代のほかの重要なアーティストたちの作品と一緒にとり上げられました。あなたと同世代のアーティストのあいだに共通のバックグラウンドはありますか？　その共通のバックグラウンドとは、今でも有効なものですか？

60年代生まれの、90年代初めに活動を本格化させた世代に共通するバックグランドがあるとしたら、それは、「共通のバックグランドはお互いの間にはもう成立しない」ということだと思います。わたしとホンマタカシさんや、やなぎみわさんに共通するものはなにも無い気がします。80年代ぐらいまでは、共通のバックグラウンドを持った人たちの共同体みたいなものがありましたが、わたしが写真を始めた頃は、そのような共同体がもう崩壊寸前でした。志を同じにする人達が自主ギャラリーをつくって、そこで発表したりしていましたが、わたしはそれがあまり有効に思えなかった。自主ギャラリーを拠点にして外に打って出ていくという感じではなく、自分たちのコミュニティーの内に自閉していく傾向が強かったように思えて、それなら一人で写真を続けていった方がいいと思っていました。

　どこの国もそうだと思いますが、1990年代に入ると、徐々に共通のバックグランドを持つことができなくなる。だからジャンルを横断したコミュニケーションも難しい時代になったような気がします。日本ではかつてジャンルの横断という言葉が流行っていましたが、今では写真は写真、絵画は絵画、映像は映像というようにジャンルの蛸壺化が進んでいます。わたしが最近になって映像を意識して発表し始めた理由の一つに、写真だけの世界に閉じこもっていては未来が無いという気持ちがありました。蛸壺化に未来はありません。

　蛸壺化していく状況をわたしはいいとは思いませんが、共通のバックグランドが無いところで、コミュニケートするのもまた難しいというのも事実です。共通するバックグランドが無いところでコミュニケーションを成立させる

ことは、孤立したまま、つながらないまま、切断されたまま関係するという、本来なら交わらない平行線を無理にでも交わらせるような力仕事だと思います。

「Senritsumirai」の出品作家に共通性というのがもしあるなら、アメリカ文化の影響ということでしょうか。わたしもホンマさんもアメリカ写真の強い影響下にいる気がします。出品していたペインティングの人達にも、ポップアートやニューペインティングの影響を強く受けているような気がしました。「Senritsumirai」の関係者のイタリア人にも日本の芸術はアメリカの影響が強いと指摘されたのを耳にしたことを覚えています。

アメリカの文化を無邪気に肯定するというのは、今の時代ではあまりにも能天気に思われるでしょう。でも、アメリカ文化の影響に対して、批判的に自己検証をしている出品者はそんなに多くはいなかったような気がします。

ビデオ作品「Elvis the Positive Thinking Pelvis」(2014)について。このビデオ作品はどのようにして生まれたのですか? ビデオ作品に編集作業とポスト・プロダクションを導入しようと思ったのはなぜですか?

2013年ごろにデジタルカメラを使うようになって、カラー写真をどういう風に発表しようかと考えていて、普通にカラー写真をプリントして壁に飾るだけでは、モノクロ写真の発表形態と同じなのであまり面白くない。少し違う形で発表しようと思い、「Elvis the Positive Thinking Pelvis」の形になりました。GRというコンパクト・カメラで撮ったのですが、そのカメラは動画も撮れることが判明しました。それで動画と静止画を撮り、いい機会だからまた映像をつくってみようかという気分になりました。静止画700点と動画本で、10分の映像作品となりました。

それと「Elvis the Positive Thinking Pelvis」をつくるまで、わたしは映像をあまり発表していませんでした。マルコさんのようにわたしの映像に興味

をもってくれた人はいなくて、わたしの過去の映像はほとんど無視されていました。それに、映画とは違うし、発表場所が日本ではほとんどなかったのです。

　編集環境が無かったという単純な理由もあって、以前のビデオ作品はすべて無編集でした。デジタルカメラで撮影を始めた頃に、わたしの友人が映像の編集を生業にしていることが判明し、それならその人に指示すれば編集ができるので、やってみようと思って作ったのが「Elvis the Positive Thinking Pelvis」です。

　無編集の映像は、撮影時の身体の動きやその時の思考がそのまま出ていて面白いです。あとで編集ができないという緊張感もあります。そんな緊張感が、今見ても生々しさを感じさせます。編集を前提にして撮ると、そのような緊張感は無くなりますが、ショット同士を唐突な感じでつなげることができます。無編集だとどうしても撮影時の身体の規制がありますから、身の回りの目に付いたものしかつなげられませんが、ポスト・プロダクションをする場合はその時の身体の制約から自由になれて、いろいろなショットをつなげることができます。わたしの映像はどれもあまりつながっていない印象を与えると思いますが、編集することで唐突さやつながらなさが、無編集とは違った感じでさらに出るのではないかと思っています。

　　ビデオ作品での経験は、最近のデジタル・カラー写真を撮影するという選択に影響を与えましたか？

どうでしょう？　わかりません。自分ではそのことはまだ客観視できていませんが、動きながら撮っていたビデオの経験が、カラー写真に影響を与えているのではと思います。

　写真は立ち止まって撮る、ブレている写真は写真じゃないという教育を写真学校で四年間受けていたので、モノクロ写真に関しては、動きながら撮

るということは生理的にできませんでしたが、ビデオカメラやデジタルカメ
ラは、あまりカメラという感じがしないので、動きながら割合気軽に撮れま
した。

　デジタル・カラー写真は、モノクロ写真を撮るようには撮影していませ
ん。カラー写真に影響を与えたものがあるとすれば、やはりビデオ作品で
の経験なのでしょう。

　　書くこと。あなたの作品において、書くことはどの程度、重要ですか？

書くことと写真を撮ることに、わたしは区別をつけていません。写真を見る
ことと撮ることが同じ撮影行為なように、書くことと撮ることもまた同じ撮影
行為だと思います。

　中平卓馬の写真と文章は、彼の中で同じ位置にあったと思います。それ
は写真が弱いから文章がその弱点を補強しているとか、写真では言い足り
ないことを文章で表現しているとかではなく、中平卓馬にとって写真は言葉
であり、言葉は写真だったと思うのです。彼にとって写真と言葉は同じ表
現であり、表現とは何かという表現批判として写真や言葉を使っていたと思
うのです。

　写真と言葉はよく似ていると思います。両方とも対象を指し示し、指示し
た対象の再現だと思われ、それ自体では独立できない。再現する対象を
持つことで初めてその存在を表すことができます。それは対象に寄生する
形でしか自らを表出できない。

　写真や言葉が対象の再現であるなら、それらは透明な存在でなければ
いけません。写真や言葉が己の存在を少しでも示そうとしたら、それは
再現機能として失敗です。再現する対象がクリアに見えなくなるからです。
対象を再現する透明な媒体だと思われているのですから。その透明で見え
ない媒体である写真や言葉の存在を、中平卓馬は暴きだそうとしたのでは

ないでしょうか。写っているイメージを支える写真は、フィルムや印画紙という物質的な基盤を持っています。写真はイメージだけではなく、物質と共に表れ、言葉は文字という紙の上に書かれた物質として表れます。写真や言葉を透明な媒体ではなく、イメージと共に表れる物質的なもう一つの存在。それは対象を再現しながらも、再現に抗うそれ自体で独立した存在です。再現機能としての写真や言葉に対する疑問です。

　文章を組み立てることは、写真のセレクトに似ていると思うのです。それは映像の編集にも似ています。単語をただ羅列するだけだったら、それは意味をなさない。言葉は文章という流れの中で初めて意味を持つと思うのです。単語という単体だけで文章が成立しないように、写真もまた一枚で成立することはできますが、作者の世界観を一枚の写真で表明することができません。その一枚の写真が他の写真とどういう流れの中で関係しているのかが重要です。

　書くことは対象を明確にします。書くことは広大な現実を言葉で切り取ります。現実のすべてを書ききることはできませんが、写真のように断片化することができます。現実のある一部分を切り取る言葉の作業は、広大すぎて理解できない未知の現実を、既知のものに変換していく作業です。けれど未知のすべてを既知化することは不可能です。既知の部分が増えれば増えるほど、未知の世界が広がっていく。撮影と言葉はよく似ています。撮影もまた、撮れば撮るほど、現実が分からなくなります。書くことと撮影は、未知の世界をさらに広めていく作業のように思えます。

　コンピューターを使って書きますか？ それとも手書きですか？ コンピューターを使って書くことと、手で書くことの違いはありますか？

コンピューターを使って書いています。手書きだと考えている速度に、手の速度が追いつかないからです。それにコンピューターだと、あとで文章の

編集ができます。わたしは論理的にものを考えていないので、文章の流れが滅茶苦茶なのですが、あとで文章を入れ替えたりして編集することでまともに読める文章になります。

あなたにとって「物語ること」とは何を意味しますか？ あなたの写真は、いくらかは物語的なのでしょうか？

「物語ること」とは、時間が前に向かって流れていくことだと思います。物語は基本的に起承転結の構造を持っていますから、前に向かって進むしかない。わたしの写真でも映像でも、そのような物語的な時間の流れはあまり感じないのではないかと思います。

　モノクロ写真では、わたしは同じような対象を撮っています。同じような写真を会場の壁面に四段掛けで貼ります。同じような写真に囲まれた会場でわたしの写真を見ていると、時間が前にも後ろにも進んでいないような気がします。物語は時間の進行を必ず要求します。時間の進み具合を感じさせないわたしの写真に物語が存在するでしょうか。

　編集を施したビデオ作品『Life is a Gift』(2015)は、起承転結というシステムからいかに離れるかという映像です。一方、無編集の中平卓馬の映像(Takuma Nakahira, April 23, 2011)は、現実の時間の流れからはそれほど逸脱していませんが、忠実に流れを再現しているわけでもない。中平宅の朝から始まって新横浜の駅で終わるこの映像は、ある日の中平卓馬の1日をドキュメントしたわけですが、中平卓馬の人間性を表しているわけではない。中平卓馬の人間性の部分なら、他の人の映像の方が十分に表しています。わたしの映像は中平卓馬を取り巻く風景を撮っている映像だと思うのです。確かに中平卓馬を撮っていますが、中平卓馬の内面は写っていません。彼が何を考えているのかは、あの映像では分からない。中平卓

馬を中心に写していますが、中平卓馬が映像の主人公というわけではありません。中平卓馬もまた彼を取り巻く風景の細部でしかない。

　わたしは映像の細部に興味があります。物語を効率良く進行させるために、メジャー映画はものの細部を端折ったりしますが、わたしは細部の集積が映像だと考えています。細部と物語が手を取り合って幸せな結合を迎える日はないと思います。物語とものの細部が対立して、折り合いのつかなくなる映画は、けっこうあると思うのです。例えばジョナス・メカスの映像はほとんどものの細部だけで成り立っている映像だと思います。写っている日常の細々したものもそうですが、上映のためにブロウアップしたときに表れる16mmフィルム特有の粒子、フィルムの細部としての粒子ですら美しいのです。メカスにとって物語は、どうでもいいものなのではないでしょうか。彼の映像は、物語的要素が最小限に抑えられている感じがします。

　「Z-TrashDiary」とは何ですか？ デジタルカメラをつかって、どのようにイメージをつくりますか？

「Z-Trash」は、B級映画よりもっと下、アメリカの三流ポルノムーヴィーのことを称した言い方です。これ以上最低でくだらないものはないという意味のようです。デジタルカメラの出現は、誰にでもきれいな写真を撮ることを可能にしました。だから最近ではきれいな写真ほど、つまらなく感じます。かつてはきれいな写真を撮るためにみんな切磋琢磨していたのに、デジタルカメラの出現で、そのようなこれまでの写真家の努力は水泡に帰しました。きれいなものほど、くだらないものはないということが分かったのです。美のジャンク化、トラッシュ化をデジタルカメラは促進しました。

　写真は、いまでは飽和状態です。どこにでも写真が溢れています。誰もがスマホで写真を撮る時代。スマホで傑作が撮れる時代です。一日一回は誰もが傑作を撮っているのではないでしょうか——この場合の傑作

は、過去の傑作を模倣しているという意味ですが。けれど新しい写真が出てくるとは思えないし、写真に新しいものを求める声こそ聞き飽きた感じがします。

きれいな写真や傑作写真はもう見飽きましたし、写真にこれ以上傑作が出てくるとは思えない。「傑作」という概念に対して疑いを提示している芸術が写真だと考えた方がよいと思います。写真は絵画と違って個性があまりない、というか、個性を意識的に殺した芸術だと思うのです。誰が撮ったのか分からないところがあります。例えば車というテーマだけで写真を集めたら、ロバート・フランクの写真も他の有名な写真家の写真も同じにように見えてしまうことでしょう。それくらい写真は個性がないのです。個性の欠けた写真芸術に傑作なんてあり得るでしょうか。ウォーカー・エヴァンスが地下鉄の車内の人々を撮影した『Many Are Called』をサラ・グリーノウは、聖書にある「Many are Called but Few are Chosen」ではなく、「Many Are Called and Many Are Chosen/多くの者が召されて、しかも多くの者が選ばれる」と評しました。選ばれることが傑作を成立させる前提なら、たくさんの人が選ばれるというその言葉は、撮られたものすべてが傑作であるという考えに近いのではないでしょうか。そしてすべてのものが選ばれ、すべてのものが傑作なら、そこに傑作は存在しません。

写真が飽和状態になった今の時代は、傑作のインフレーション状態を起こしていると思うのです。ストリートスナップがいい例ですが、スナップ写真は傑作に近づけば、近づくほど昔の傑作の写真とあまり変わらなくなる。工芸品のようになってくるのです。よくなればなるほど昔なにかで見たような凡庸な写真に変質する。傑作というのは、いまやたんなるトラッシュです。

デジタルカメラは、フィルム写真のようにカメラテクニックや暗室テクニックを使って、凡庸な現実を一級の芸術品に変質させるものではありません。デジタルカメラは、かつての写真のような錬金術を持ち合わせていないのです。ゴミを黄金に変えるのではなく、ゴミをゴミとして提出することで

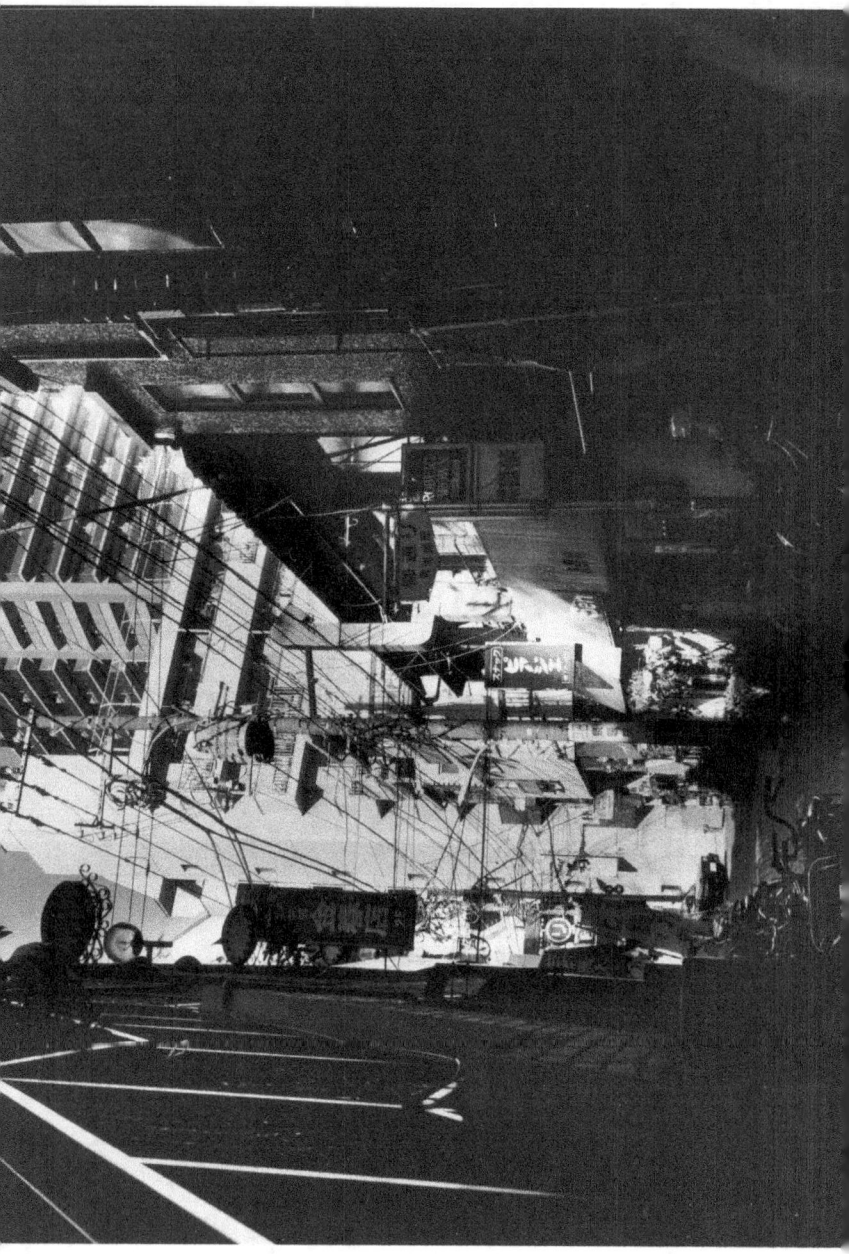

す。巷のトラッシュ化された傑作写真がつまらないのは、ゴミを黄金だと勘違いしているからです。ゴミと黄金に差はありません。黄金には、黄金が美しかったという歴史がありましたが、ゴミにはそのような歴史が存在しません。ゴミに何にも無いのですが、その何も無さにこそ、可能性があるのではないでしょうか。

　　　現在、写真は危機に瀕していると思いますか？　今日、写真にとって主な危険とは何ですか？　人びとは今なおイメージを読み取ることができるのでしょうか？

日本では、かつて"映画はもうすぐ死ぬ"と言われ続けていました。もう30年ぐらい言われ続けていましたが、いっこうに映画は死ぬ気配さえ見せません。"もうすぐ死ぬ"という認識は、ベケットの『マロウンは死ぬ』を思い出させます。マロウンは死ぬ、死ぬと言いながらなかなか死なない。むしろもうすぐ死ぬという終わる直前の時間を、いつまでも生きている。映画もそんなマロウンのような生き方をしているような気がします。完全に終わるのではない。終わる直前の未来も何もない時間。それは生の側でも、死の側でもない宙吊りの時間を生きることだと思います。
　先鋭的な映画人の中では"映画はもうすぐ死ぬ"という認識が支配的でした。ゴダールやトリュフォーを超えることができるのか、映画の可能性は彼らがすべてやり切ってしまったのではないかという認識は、当のゴダールやトリュフォーがヒッチコックやアメリカ映画に感じていたことの反復でしたが、そのような終わりの意識は重要だと思います。写真の危機もまたこれと似ていると思います。70年代には森山大道が「写真よさようなら」という写真集を出しました。いま見ると森山大道特有のロマンチックな感覚に満ち溢れている写真集だと思いますが、誰よりも写真を愛する森山大道が写真に

さようならを言わなければならないほどの危機感を抱いていたことがあったのでしょう。

　写真は誰でも撮れるメディアとして登場しましたが、誰でも撮れるものに未来があるでしょうか。誰にも真似できない、選ばれた存在が芸術家であり、芸術作品でした。写真はそのような芸術家の特権意識を、誰でも撮れるというカメラで破壊したのです。誰にでもそれなりに撮れる写真は、デジタルカメラの登場で、ある局面に達したような気がします。誰もが傑作を撮れるようになりました。誰にでも撮れる傑作は、それはもう傑作ではない。素晴らしく飛び抜けた写真はもうどこにもありません。傑作という概念が死んだのです。すべての写真は過去の傑作の反復でしかない。そしてイメージはつねに過去の傑作を参照にして見られることになります。まったく新しいイメージというのは存在しません。なぜなら人間にはまったく未知のものを理解することができないからです。過去の何かのどこかに結びつけなければ分からないのです。過去の作品と参照可能なものしか理解できないのです。それはだから反復されたイメージです。過去の同じイメージに回収されることで、イメージを初めて見ることができる。人は新しいイメージを見るのではなく、過去のイメージをそこに投影して見ているだけです。イメージは過去の中でしか存在できない。イメージには今ここがありません。

質問＝マルコ・マッツィ2017年5月1日

答＝金村修2017年6月12日

Dead Stick Landing

Kiyoshi Kurosawa wrote in his book *Eizou no Karisuma* (*Charisma of Film*): "No detail exists in Jean-Luc Godard's film *Nouvelle Vague*. Only system and entity exist."* Kurosawa considers the film to be a kind of mechanical system; he is not interested in admirable stories or beautiful shots. The film made as a machine: this approach is often found not only in Godard's *Nouvelle Vague,* but also in genre movies. Westerns, gangster movies, samurai dramas, yakuza movies, horror films, and V-Cinema (Japanese direct-to-video films): these so-called genre movies repeat patterns that have previously been laid down. These formulas that genre movies are based on are often looked down on as clichés, but they can be the essence of film.

According to Karlheinz Stockhausen, the only elements of music are start and stop. For him, music is probably nothing more than a mechanical system that is operated by switching it on and off. Stockhausen's idea can be easily applied to funk musicians. Once their performance starts, the groove endlessly continues until the end is announced; the music starts and finishes as if a switch is turned on and off. How it is performed reminds me of the mechanism of a conveyor belt. Funk is a machine that works with tempo and rhythm. It functions as a

---

*   黒沢清著 [Kiyoshi Kurosawa] 『映像のカリスマ【増補改訂版】』[Charisma of Film] (エクスナレッジ, 2006), 301.

framework, which is similar to what Kurosawa meant by machinic films.

Narrative or beautiful shots are not the only elements that determine the quality of film. Likewise, music is also affected by other elements besides melody or phrase. Both film and music begin when a switch is turned on, and finish when it is turned off. The important thing is the switch: once it is turned on, it starts a mechanism in which shots and sounds automatically flow as if on a conveyor belt. Beautiful shots or melodies are not inevitable components; what is indispensable is the mechanism that supervises these elements and controls the whole.

Music is formed when this mechanical system functions well and movements occur, not when musicians put together fragments of phrase. How smoothly this mechanism functions determines the quality of music, not the individual talent of the musician. Things like phrases or techniques associated with particular musicians do not affect it, either. The mechanism and its consistency as a whole have priority over these details.

Having well-crafted shots does not necessarily mean that you can make a good film. *Mottomo Kikenna Yūgi* (*The Most Dangerous Game*) has a scene in which Yūsaku Matsuda chases a villain's car with heroic persistence. This seems very unlikely in reality, but looks natural in the film. The reason it looks natural is that the film is loyal to the key element of a genre movie: as long as the protagonist played by Yūsaku Matsuda is good in the picture, even seemingly impossible events are accepted as natural. The beauty of Matsuda, pistol in hand, dashing into a three-storied building where villains are hiding is made possible by long tracking shots by the camera as well as the cameraman's technique. The movement of the camera creates a tension in the picture: once the recording button is switched on, the camera unerringly follows Matsuda's actions. The movement of the camera itself is the beauty and wonder.

The function of the camera is the key element in filmmaking: actors with individual characters, lines written by scenario writers and filmmakers' aesthetics — the camera combines all these elements. Actors move when the start is announced; scenario writers pay more attention to how to develop a series of images than having interesting stories, and directors announce when to start and stop. The camera plays the essential role in combining these different functions.

Once a tempo and key are set, musicians can start their performance. Depending on the genre chosen, appropriate phrases stored at a subconscious level surface and thus the musician's fingers move smoothly. Quintessential phrases for rock, jazz, etc. are retrieved and their fingers move without thinking. It looks like the choice of genre shapes the performance; musicians are not playing on their own terms. The genre functions as a mechanism that determines how people can play. Musicians in fact have no initiative in playing; they are affected by their choice of genre and its mechanical structure.

What musicians need is machine-like accuracy to keep tempo and rhythm consistent, not their own individuality. The mechanism does not demand personality: it rather disturbs rhythm and must be obliterated in order to retain the flow of music. Humans become a part of this musical machine. They must be willing to do so in order to function correctly.

The clichéd performances of V-Cinema actors show another example: they function as parts of the V-Cinema machine, which does not require any individuality. In Kurosawa's V-Cinema *Suit Yourself or Shoot Yourself,* the images of Shō Aikawa and Kōyō Maeda running are mostly shown in a distant shot, and close-ups of their faces are rarely used. You can see them running or going wild in the far distance but the details of their actual behaviour are not clearly visible. You cannot find the actors' individual personality here; the film proceeds as cliché-ridden expressions common in V-Cinema are shown one after the other. *Suit Yourself or Shoot Yourself* is a typical example of an interesting film made with only a series of images of actors running and going on a rampage. It is like the gaze of an infant who can stare at the passage of trains forever. A critic once wrote that a moving train in a film is the only thing necessary to make him feel excited. Do moving pictures infantilize our gaze?

Feel the rhythmic pulse in music, if you want to create a rhyth-mic effect. By feeling a steady beat, for example, in a fourth-, eighth-, or sixteenth-note rhythm, a rhythmic effect is achieved. This is a subdivision of sound: a similar phenomenon is seen in film movies in which twenty-four frames are recorded per second. This is probably because it is considered the best method to show movement. Sound and film both create movement by pulsing or subdividing materials, and thus succeed in making an effect that is slightly different from movement in reality.

Each of the twenty-four frames recorded per second are stat-ic; however, each of these images does not stand on its own as a photograph. These twenty-four frames cannot exist outside the series that creates the flow of a moving picture. An individual film scene, when seen by itself, looks unrelated to the whole film; likewise, the subdivided frames on a strip of film can only exist within the continuity of the whole. The essential element in films and music is not twenty-four frames or individual sounds but the mechanism that operates their sequentiality. A series of still images does not immediately create a moving picture; when it acquires continuous movement, a motion picture is made. In films and music, frames or sounds are secondary elements to the continuous movement created by the mechanism as a whole.

Music consists of both audible and inaudible sounds. For example, sounds inaudible to the human ear, a pause between beats, a subtle interval between rhythm guitar and bass line, or between bass drum, snare drum, and hi-hat — these things are indispensable for music. There is always a gap between musi-cal notes arranged into a continuous temporal flow. Doesn't this gap create the beat in music? Repetitive patterns made by sound and gaps bring continuous movement in music. Gaps between audible sounds are crucial to giving rhythmic effect to musical notes that look static when seen on the score sheet.

Do moving pictures, where shots seem to continue one after the other, have such gaps? Films record twenty-four frames per second and subtle, invisible lines appear between each frame. Our naked eye is not able to detect them, so it looks like con-tinuous movement. The movement of people, when recorded at a rate of twenty-four frames per second, is not exactly natural; we perceive it as natural because of the limitations of our vision.

The movement of these twenty-four frames looks natural in film because the film does not reproduce reality. In films that actually do reproduce reality, objects captured by camera are divided into twenty-four frames per second, and thus images of objects and invisible lines between each film frame appear one after the other. This cinematic movement occurs through a completely different process from actual movements that take place in reality. A subtle difference exists between motion in reality and that of films, and I guess the latter creates an alternative reality.

I doubt whether the motion captured by our naked eyes is genuinely real. Can our naked eyes capture objects as they are? Our eyes need extra time to recognize objects and convey information about them through pupils, corneas, and brains. I assume a slight delay occurs in this process. Probably humans are not allowed to witness reality in its true form? Pupils and corneas delay our recognition; therefore, a moving picture made of a twenty-four framed filmstrip or our naked eyes cannot capture reality as it is. Delay and gaps always exist there.

The moving picture does not show things that exist outside the frame. However, such invisible dimensions must also be a part of reality, and the moving picture always consists of this kind of invisible reality that lies outside the scope of the camera. The conflict between what is visible and invisible: the latter accentuates the former. The moving picture not only shows what the camera has captured but also what existed beyond its framing. There is no interior without an exterior; likewise, the moving picture naturally involves the invisible that exists outside the scope of the camera. The camera cannot frame everything; this mechanical condition implies what lies beyond its scope. This unseen reality may be the driving force of the moving picture? What Stockhausen said about music is probably true about the moving picture, too: start and stop are the only functions it needs. You press the same button to start and finish recording, and you need nothing else. The moving picture made as a mechanical system — you can see its mechanical framework.

Once the moving picture, even a cliché-ridden V-Cinema, starts, viewers follow its story and get a little excited as the ending approaches. Once it starts, whether they like it or not, viewers are inevitably drawn into the world depicted. The moving images are perhaps the only indispensable element of moving pictures. You find V-Cinema boring but you cannot take your eyes off the images on the screen. What then is the role of the story? Why do people get excited at the clichéd content of V-Cinema? Why do they get so thrilled at Ken Takakura and Ryō Ikebe's last raid scene that has become a routine in the *Shōwa Zankyō-den* series? The more their expressions are routine and mechanical, the more interesting the moving picture becomes. Watching their cheesy expressions, people stop thinking. Once they become like that, they feel an infantile excitement by just looking at things moving. Thinking may be the enemy of the moving picture. Those who feel sheer joy at watching moving images, stand opposed to the act of thinking.

The words "Dead Stick Landing" mean losing all power of the engines and propellers of an airplane. When the engine stops, the airplane cannot continue its flight. Mechanical continuity is lost and the plane becomes uncontrollable in the air. It stops flying and descends slowly onto the ground. If lucky, it can make a forced landing on some flat ground. Its destiny depends on luck as nobody can determine where to land under these circumstances. Probably it can land somewhere safe, or it may sink in the vast ocean without a witness. However, this will not be the end: the plane does not materially cease to exist. The aircraft forced to land on the ground or in the sea slowly corrodes, which gives it an extended form of life.

The failure of an engine or stalling of a propeller, therefore, does not immediately bring the cessation of life. The airplane remains there, corrodes, and will be slowly transformed into junk, but that does not mean that the plane ceases to exist. The process of disintegration allows the plane to live in an extended form. Its materiality lingers on after the engine stops, or even when the emergency landing ends in failure and the plane crashes. When human beings are dead, they are buried under the soil and return to the natural life cycle: things thus exist in eternal duration. If the corrosion and transformation into junk also constitutes a natural process within this eternal duration, the plane that is ruined or sunk in the sea also gains eternal life. The aeroplane, once it achieves this state, does not cease to exist even after becoming a complete wreck.

The aircraft is washed away by the waves and reaches some shore. To scavengers, the debris does not have any particular meaning: merely meaningless junk that is washed up there. The forced landing is kind of like mail directed to an unknown address. *Dead Stick Landing* is a video made for an audience whose identity is unspecified, unknown. The address is unknown and you will never know where it arrives. It, therefore, resembles a plane that has been forced to land.

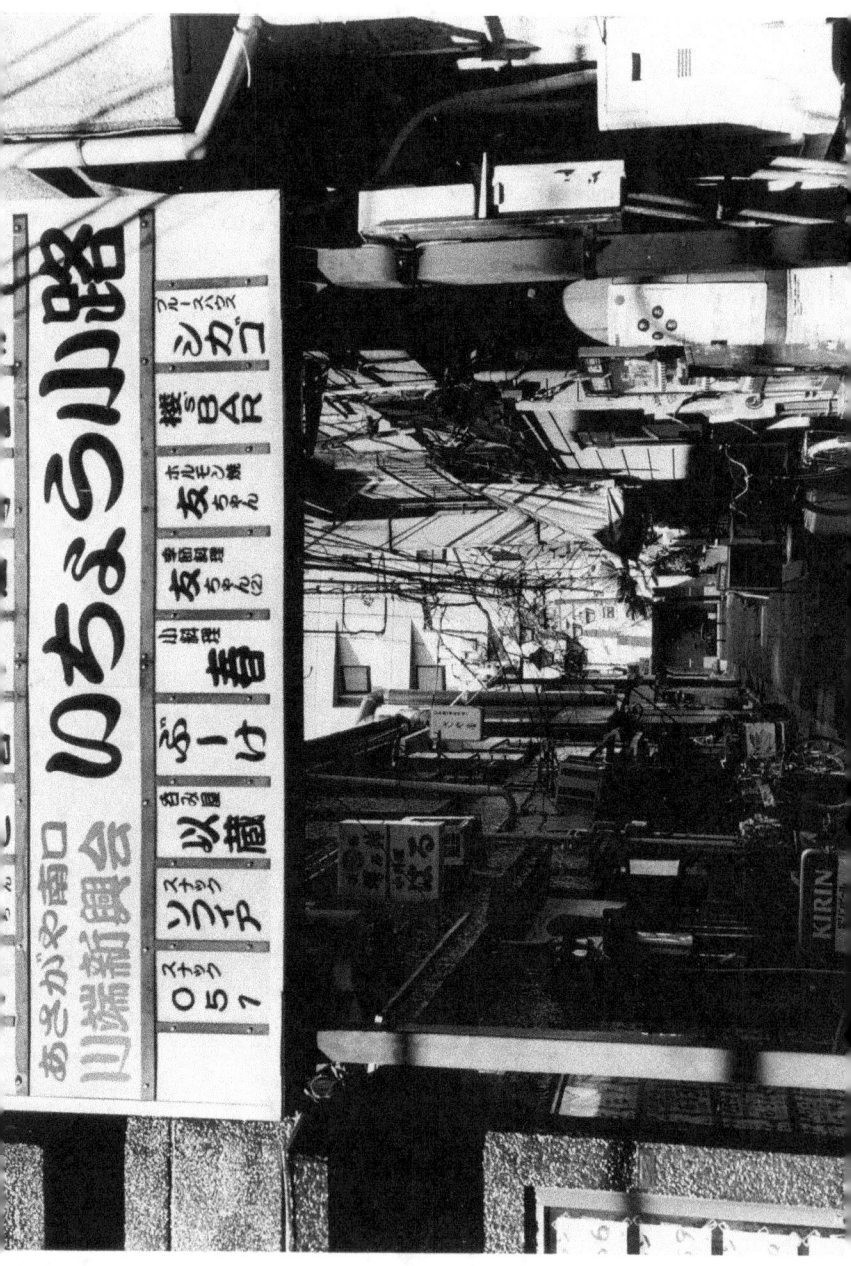

Dead Stick Landing

黒沢清は映画評論集『映像のカリスマ』で、「『ヌーヴェルヴァーグ』に細部はない。あるのはシステムと全体だけだ」と書いている。「何をどう撮ったか」というストーリーやショットの美しさを賛美することではなく、黒沢清は映画をシステムとして考えているように思える。システムとしての映画。それはゴダールの『ヌーヴェルヴァーグ』だけではなく、ジャンル映画といわれるものに顕著に見られる。西部劇やギャング映画、時代劇に、ヤクザ映画、ホラー、Vシネマ。それらのジャンル映画と呼ばれるものは、あるシステムを確立し、そのシステムが繰り返されることで成立している。お約束事で成り立っていると馬鹿にした感じで語られるジャンル映画のシステムこそが、むしろ映画の本質なのではないだろうか。シュトックハウゼンは、音楽にはスタートとストップしかないと言った。スタートとストップしかないというシュトックハウゼンにとって、音楽はスイッチのオンとオフで動く機械のシステムでしかないのだろう。シュトックハウゼンの音楽観は、ブラック・ミュージシャンの演奏するファンクに近いのではないかと思う。スタートしたら終わりの合図が出るまでグルーヴし続ける彼らの音楽は、スイッチのオンで始まりオフで終わる音楽であり、それはまるでベルトコンベアー・システムのように演奏される。テンポやリズムという進行と律動のシステムだけで成り立つファンク。それは骨組みだけで成立する音楽であって、黒沢清のいうようなシステムの映画に似ている。映画がストーリーやショットの美しさだけで

成り立つのではないように、メロディーやフレーズが音楽を決定するのではない。スイッチがオンにされることで映画や音楽は始まり、オフにすることでそれが終わる。重要なのはオンとオフのスイッチであり、スイッチをオンにすると自動的にショットや音がベルトコンベアーのように流れていくためのシステムの構築ではないだろうか。美しいショットやメロディーが必要なのではない。それらを動かし、全体を統御するシステムが必要なのだ。フレーズの断片をミュージシャンがつなぎ合わせることで音楽が成立するのではなく、システムが動き、その動きが音楽を成り立たせるのではないだろうか。ミュージシャンという個人が音楽を決定するのではなく、システムの流れが音楽を決定する。あのミュージシャンのフレーズやテクニックがどうのという細部が音楽を決定するわけではない。全体の持続とシステムが、細部の存在よりも先行する。いいショットが撮れたからといって、いい映画ができるわけではない。『最も危険な遊戯』での、悪者の車を松田優作がいつまでも追い続けるという現実に不可能な事態が映画ではなぜか自然に見える。その自然さは、システムの要請が生み出した自然さなのではないだろうか。松田優作はこの映画の主人公であり、主人公が絵になるならそれはどんな不可能なことでも自然な流れなのだというジャンル映画特有のシステムに忠実だからだ。悪者が隠れている三階建てのビルに拳銃を構えて突入する松田優作の美しさも、それはカメラマンのテクニックもあるのだろうけど、長回しというカメラの機能が生み出した美しさだと思う。録画のスイッチをオンにして後はひたすら松田優作を追い続けるカメラの動きは、カメラマンの決めた構図の美しさを超えて、カメラが人を追い続けるということだけで映像に緊張感を与える。それはカメラが動くことそれ自体の驚きと美しさなのではないだろうか。個性的な俳優や脚本家のセリフ、監督の美意識で映像が成り立つのではなく、カメラの機能が映像を成り立たせる。俳優はスタートがかかったらただ動き、脚本家はストーリーの面白さよりも映像の進行を優先させ、監督はスタートとストップの掛け声をかける。映像に必要なのはそのような機能だけではないだろうか。

テンポとキーを決めればミュージシャンは勝手に演奏し始める。どんなジャンルの音楽を演奏するかで各自が弾くフレーズは、そこで自動的に決定される。ロックならこんなフレーズ、ジャズならこうと、それらのフレーズが無意識に浮かんで、指板の上を勝手に指が動く。その姿は、彼らミュージシャンが主体的に演奏を引っ張っているのではなく、ジャンルが彼らを引っ張っているように見える。彼らの無意識下に蓄積されたフレーズがジャンルの要請によって呼び出される。ジャンルが彼らの無意識を呼び出し、その呼び出された無意識によって彼らは動かされる。ジャンルとはシステムであり、そのシステムが人を動かす。彼らは主体的に演奏しているのではなく、ジャンルというシステムの力によって演奏をさせられている。ミュージシャンに求められているのは、その人の個性なのではなく、機械のように正確にいつまでもテンポとリズムをキープできるかどうかなのだ。システムは個性を要求しない。システムにとって個性は律動の邪魔であって、流れるように動くこと、そのために個性は抹消されなければならない。それは音楽における人間の部品化であり、システムが進行するためには、人間は喜んで音楽の部品にならなければならないだろう。

Vシネマ俳優たちのほとんどお約束事のような演技は、俳優の部品化であって、Vシネマのシステムに俳優の個性は必要とされていない。黒沢清のVシネマ『勝手にしやがれ!!』での哀川翔や前田耕陽は、遠景の向こうで走っているだけで、顔のアップはあまり使用されていなかった。遠くで点のように見える彼らが走ったり暴れたりしているだけで、誰が何をしているのかも分からなかった。そこに俳優の個性はどこにもない。Vシネマのシステム特有のお約束事だけで進行している。俳優が走り、暴れている姿が映っていればそれだけで映像は面白いという『勝手にしやがれ!!』は、電車の通過を何時間でも見ていられる幼児の視線に近いような気がする。映画の中で電車が走っているのを見るだけでゾクゾクするとある評論家が書いていたが、映像は積極的に人間の視線を幼児化するのではないだろうか。音楽を律動させるには、音を細かく刻むように感じることだ。音を4拍子で

感じるか、8拍子で感じるか、16拍子で感じるかというように、リズムを細かく感じることで律動感が生まれる。それは音の細分化であり、フィルム映画が1秒間を24コマで切り刻むのは、その方が動きを映し出すのに最適だと判断されたからだろう。細かく刻むことで動きを出すこの二つのメディアは、切り刻むことで、現実の運動とは微妙に違う動きを生み出す。1/24秒に切り刻まれたコマは基本的に静止している。けれどそれは写真のように一枚として独立して成立しているのではなく、映像という連続の中に配置されることではじめて成立する。1/24コマはつねに全体の流れの中で成立しているわけであって、その流れから独立して存在することができない。映画の一コマを取り出してもそれが映画にとって何の関係もないように、切り刻まれたコマは、システムの連続性と不可分なのだ。切り刻まれたコマは連続の中でしか存在しないだろう。1/24コマや個々の音が映像や音楽を決定する重要な要素なのではなく、それらを連続して動かすシステムが重要なのだ。静止画の集合が映像になるのではなく、静止画の集合が動くことではじめて映像が成立する。映画や音楽では、システムの連続する動きが、コマや音よりも前に存在している。聞こえる部分だけではなく、聞こえない部分を含むことで音楽が成立するのではないだろうか。人間の耳の可聴範囲外の音や拍子と拍子の間、リズムギターやベースライン、バスドラ、スネアやハットの間に存在する微細な隙間が音楽を成立させるのだと思う。連続的に流れる時間の中のすべてに音符がぎっしりと詰まっているのではなく、必ずそこには隙間が存在する。その隙間が音楽を律動させるのではないだろうか。音楽の連続性は、音と隙間の繰り返しによって動く。譜面上では静止しているように見える音符に律動を与えるには、音だけではなく、隙間が必要なのだ。映像にそんな音楽に値するような隙間が存在するのだろうか。映像け切れ目なくショットが続いているように見える。1/24コマずつ動くフィルム映画では、1/24秒毎に目に見えない微妙なフィルムラインが現れる。人間の肉眼がフィルムラインの切れ目を認識できないから、隙間なしで動いているように見える。1/24コマで撮られた

人間の動きは、実は微妙に不自然なもので、それを自然に感じられるように見えるのは、肉眼の機能が不完全だからだと思う。現実の世界ではありえない不自然な1/24コマの動きが、映画で自然に見えるのは、現実の再現を映画は要求していないからだ。現実を再現しようとするフィルム映画は、写した対象を1/24コマ毎に分割する。分割されたことで、写っているものと見えないフィルムラインが交互に現れ、映像を進行させる。それは現実の動きとはまるで違う過程を通過して現れる動きだ。現実の動きと映画の動きには微細な差異が存在し、それはもう一つの現実なのかもしれない。

　肉眼で捉えた現実の動きが本当の動きなのかといえば、それはどうなのだろう。肉眼の動きは対象をジャストに捉えているのだろうか。対象が確認されるには、瞳から角膜そして脳という時間の過程が必要になる。そこに若干の遅延が発生するのではないだろうか。本当の現実を見ることは人間にはできないのではないだろうか。瞳や角膜は人間にとって、認識を遅滞させるバイアスでしかないのではと思う。1/24コマで上映される映像の不自然さや遅滞が発生する肉眼には、現実をジャストに捉えることができない。そこには遅延と隙間がつねに生み出される。フレームの外の現実は映像には写らない。けれどフレームの外の現実は写っていなくても、それは確かに存在していた現実であって、写っていないそのような現実を抱え込むことで成立するのが、映像なのではないだろうか。写ることと写っていないことのせめぎ合い。写っていないものが、写っているものを決定する。映像は内部だけで成立するのではなく、外の存在も含むことで成立するのではないだろうか。外部のない内部が存在しないように、フレームの存在を前提として成立するする映像には、写っていない外部の存在が必要なのだ。すべてを撮りきることができないというカメラの機能的な限界がフレームの外部を発見する。写っていない外部の現実が、映像を駆動させているのではないだろうか。シュトックハウゼンが言うように、映像もまたスタートとストップだけで成り立つのかもしれない。カメラのボタンを押すと録画が始まり、もう一度そのボタンを押すと録画が終わる。スタートとストッ

プという機能以外に映像に必要なものは何もない。システムの骨組みがそこに透けて見える。映像にあるのはシステムだけだ。Vシネマのようなシステム化された映像でさえ、はじまればストーリーを追ってしまい、終わりが近づけばなぜか少しドキドキしたりする。スタートすればいい悪いも関係なく巻き込んでしまうのが映像なのだと思う。画像が動いているだけで映像はもうそれだけでいいのだろう。Vシネマはつまらないと思いつつも、画面に何か動いているものが写っているというだけで目が離せなくなる。それならストーリーの役割というのは何だろう。ルーティン化されたVシネマのストーリーに、なぜ人はドキドキしてしまうのだろうか。お約束事だと分かっているはずの『昭和残侠伝』シリーズにおけるラストでの高倉健と池部良の殴り込みに、なぜあんなにも興奮するのだろう。ルーティン化され、システム化されればされるほど映像は面白くなる。ルーティン化されることで見ている人間は映像に対して何も考えなくなる。何も考えなくなれば、幼児のように何かが動いているだけで興奮するようになる。映像にとって思考は敵なのかもしれない。ただ見ているだけで面白いという姿勢に賛同する人間は、思考と敵対するだろう。「Dead-Stick Landing」は、エンジンやプロペラの停止状態を指示する言葉で、　エンジンが止まれば、飛行機は飛ぶという持続を停止させられる。機械的な持続を停止させられた飛行機は、持続から放り投げられ、空中に孤立させられる。飛行の運動から取り残された飛行機は、ゆっくりと地上に向かって下降していく。運がよければどこか平原のような場所に不時着できるだろう。けれどそれは運であって、どこに不時着するかは誰にも決定できない。どこか安全な場所に不時着できるかもしれないし、海のような茫洋とした場所で誰にも知られないまま飛行機ごと沈んでいくこともあるだろう。けれどそれは終わりではない。エンジンの停止は持続の停止ではない。地面か海に不時着した飛行機はそこでゆっくりと錆びつきながらも、錆びていくという運動の持続の中で存在する。エンジンやプロペラが停止しても、だからそれは本当の意味での停止ではない。どこかに不時着して、そこで錆びつきジャンク化していくことは

停止でも終わりでもなく、それもまた持続する運動なのだ。飛行機は持続の中で存在する。持続が飛行機より先に存在し、飛行機の存在を決定する。飛行機は単体で成立しているのではなく、持続することではじめて成立が可能になる。停止もまた一つの持続の開始であり、墜落して不時着に失敗しても持続は止まらない。死んで土の中に帰ることで、人間ならそこで自然の円環的な持続のサイクルに回帰する。持続は無限だ。錆びついてジャンク化していくことも持続の流れであるなら、破壊されても海の中に沈んでいても、飛行機はあり続けることになる。持続が飛行機の存在を決定するなら、持続が続く限り飛行機はどんなにジャンク化されても存在し続ける。海の波にさらわれた機体がどこかの陸上にたどり着く。ばらばらになった飛行機の部品が陸上にたどり着いても、それを見つけた人間にとってそれはただの意味不明なものでしかなく、それはそこに届いただけのものだ。ただそこに届くだけの意味不明な部品が送られる。不時着というのは宛先不明で送る郵便のようなものではないだろうか。『Dead-Stick Landing』は、誰かに見せようという映像でありながらも、その誰かは特定できない。特定できない誰か、誰だか分からない誰かに向けて作られている。宛先は不明で、どこに届くかも分からない。それはだから不時着のようなものだと思う。

Essay 02

Cinematic time is a product of various montage techniques including cutaway shots and cutting an action. These techniques deliberately cut time in reality into pieces, reassemble them, and create a drama. This is basically a fictional time; numerous shots are connected to construct a fiction. Montage is a key technique to achieve this. On the contrary, in one scene/single, long tracking shots, filmmakers cannot manipulate time as much as they want. The long take tends to be restrained by time, space, and place in reality. Does this bring films closer to theatrical production or documentation of reality?

The sense of time in long takes is closer to that in our real life, compared with time as edited by montages. In Theodoros Angelopoulos's *The Travelling Players,* six years' passage of time was crammed into a long take lasting twelve minutes. It is, of course, fiction but has a flow of time close to that in reality. This one scene/one shot had the effect of blurring the boundary between fiction and reality giving both fictive and realistic impressions. Long takes — uninterrupted shots without a single cut — fixate a flow of time of, say, three minutes, exactly the same length of time the camera ran for. In this sense, the time in long takes is realistic, which is different to the montaged time.

Montage enables manipulation of time; however, the long take approaches time differently. It brings a raw, realistic time into films, and thus disturbs their fictionality. Films, safely protected inside a rampart of fiction, are thus released from con-

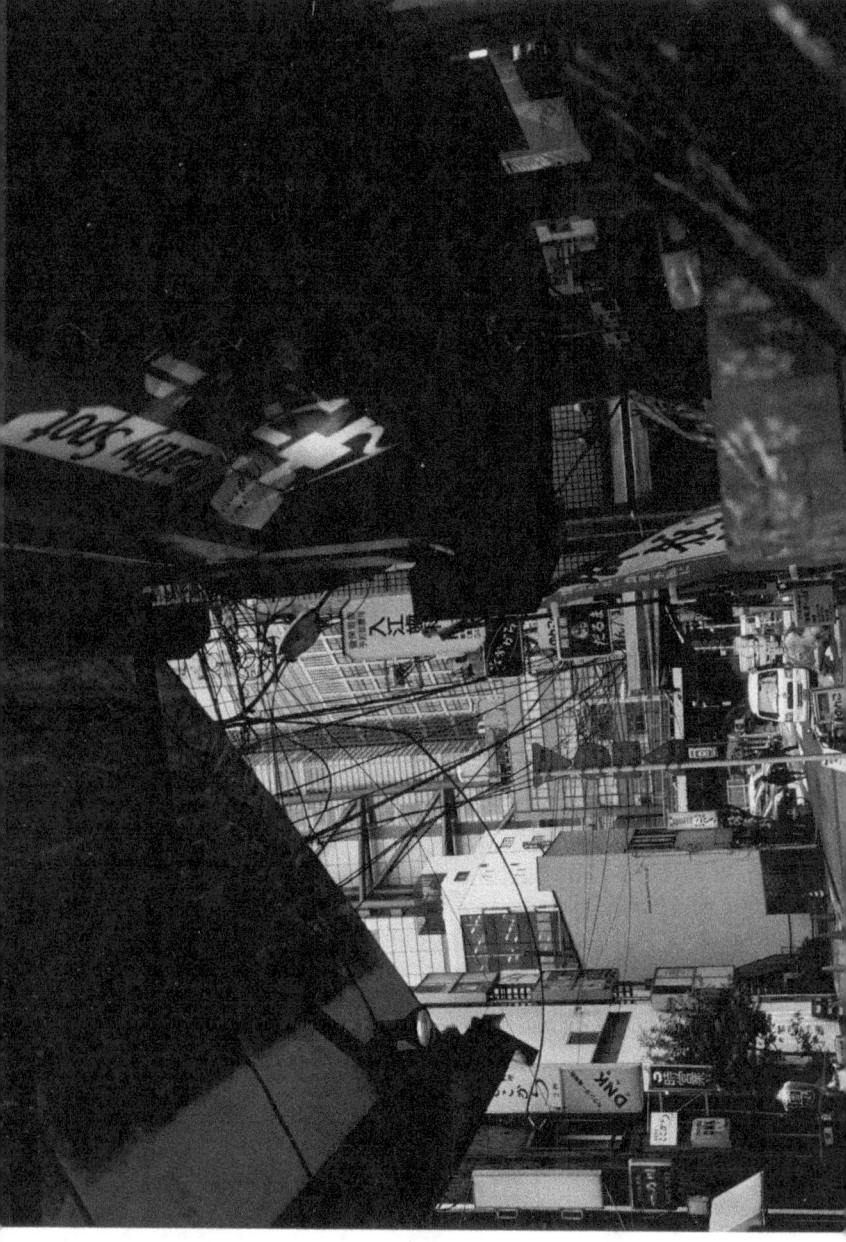

finement in their own world and forced to confront reality. The long take creates a chaotic perception in which both film and reality are blended together.

The camera frames a part of reality, detaches it from actual time, and transforms it into non-temporal being. The subjects thus framed and frozen by the camera become fixed onto a film, and a projector motor gives motion to them. This is how time commences in films; this cinematic time, realized by still images and a projector, is basically automated and mechanical. Shots put together flow from a projector automatically. The montage completely destroys the irreversibility of actual time; by cutting and pasting it arbitrarily rearranges reality, ignoring the actual temporal flow. Photographs freeze time and transform it into something retrievable. The montage readily rearranges time and fabricates a false impression as if all the images have emerged in real time. Using these techniques, monotonous, mechanical time, automatically divided into twenty-four frames per second, is transformed into a spectacle.

However, do films really need these fabricated spectacles? This is rather an extreme example, but in Andy Warhol's films, nothing happens. The camera is fixed on the ground and it just captures a sleeping man or the Empire State Building; it just documents a passage of time. Warhol's films make me feel as if I have become a factory worker who works on an assembly line and watches a conveyor belt moving all day. Is cinematic time comparable to this kind of tedious, industrial sense of time that is like a conveyor belt? In the sense that the critic Atsushi Sasaki described Warhol's films as "watchmen of boredom," it is a kind of film where people watch a projector operating continuously. This kind of industrial boredom and monotony is probably the essence of films. In a projection room, the heart of a cinema, a large projector sits in the middle; the audience seriously stares at images projected onto a screen. Cinema is an inhuman, machine-dominated space; its audience somewhat reminds me of workers in Fordist factories who are enslaved by machines.

Warhol uses long takes quite often; I assume his long take shots also aimed at challenging fictionality by bringing a crude reality into films. Actual life is always boring, and the film, a technology based on automated mechanical time, is also basically a boring medium. It involves a kind of boredom found in Fordist factories; the only job left for humans in highly automated environments is to watch machines move. It is a nightmarish boredom — humans being subordinated to machines. When filmmakers cannot stand this boredom, I reckon they transform images into a spectacle using montage techniques, etc.; however, some filmmakers are possessed by this nightmarish boredom and Warhol was definitely one of them. Another example was Eugène Atget who took pictures at the same location over and over again until he died. (Berenice Abbott also said that if possible, she wanted to take pictures of New York until she died. Do many photographers like monotonous repetition?)

Were they possessed by this tedious repetition? It was Kraftwerk that first showed us the pleasure of monotonous mechanical repetition. People were possessed by this band because they showed them the pleasure of humans being incorporated into a rhythm box and led them to a realm where humans and machines are fused together. In this realm, humans are not the masters of machines and machines do not enslave humans as in alienation theory, either. The boundary between humans and machines, or between reality and films, is obscure. Under these circumstances, artists find it difficult to maintain their identity. When they are uncertain as to whether the media they are working with is fictional or realistic, it is not easy to control their positionality. In fact, Kraftwerk on stage did nothing but press the buttons of the synthesizer. When the role of artists is thus fragile and unstable, the camera's recording function becomes effective. Warhol's *Sleep* is heavily dependent on the recording function of the camera; rather, we should call it a film that specializes only in recording.

When shooting videos or photographs, you sometimes lose the thread of what you are doing. The awareness that you are conducting a shooting gradually fades. Your perception becomes obscure, thinking, who is taking the pictures, the camera or me? Or landscapes? You are not sure whether you are actually looking at reality or seeing it back through a viewfinder. I sometimes think that the world existed from the beginning as a visual image. The relationship between images and reality becomes reversed; people take pictures not because reality exists, but reality emerges because the camera captures it. Or, any reality you experience seems like a photo. Reality is probably already a photograph; we capture this photo-like reality with a camera as if duplicating it. When you shoot, there is always a feeling that the perspective of the world — the relationship between subjects and objects has been inverted.

Some people criticize Warhol's *Sleep* saying it needs editing or it just presents reality as it is; however, I rather appreciate this extraordinary film without the slightest fictionality. It is a sheer product of the camera as a recording device; *Sleep* is a materialist film that is genuinely motivated by the mechanical functions of the camera. Warhol's film basically lacks artistic subjectivity, but what significance does this have in films anyway? In my opinion, artistic subjectivity conceals the mechanical monotony that is the essence of films. Modern society transforms everyday life into an event obliterating its boredom; likewise, the film, a product of modern technology, creates a spectacle covering up the boredom of technology under the name of drama and artistic subjectivity.

The camera documents everything it is pointed at; this is almost a synonym of violence. It captures literally everything without making a distinction between misery and happiness. The camera does not feel self-restraint or hesitation; nothing stops it from recording. I believe filmmakers bring artistic subjectivity or drama into films in order to conceal this violence of the recording camera; this is how they try to domesticate such violence. However, *Sleep* does its best to expose this violence. The footage of a man sleeping for five hours and twenty minutes cannot fabricate fantasies or fiction. What we see is the cruelty of the camera that documents reality as it is.

Out of the studio system in the 1950s appeared film directors who took no notice of artistic subjectivity and worked silently on assigned projects (there was no such thing as artistic subjec-

tivity in films first of all). They resembled skilled laborers working on an assembly line; as a result of the studio system, films
resembled a Fordist factory. The film-as-entertainment retains a
boredom that originates in modern technology, and filmmakers
accepted this as their fate. They showed no interest in artistic
subjectivity or creation of drama; renouncing these decorative
aspects, they confronted the sheer violence of the camera. The
camera that documents everything must have excited them. The
desire to film must have taken priority over their artistic subjectivity and drama. Otherwise, you cannot explain why they spent
an incredible amount of time and effort preparing for actual
shooting, while only a limited time was given for script writing.

In the 1950s, the genre movie was still hot in Japan. Many
filmmakers adopted the principles that were typical of each
genre; hundreds of films of the same genre were produced each
year. When filmmakers are loyal to the principles of genre movies and keep repeating them, the narrative system ceases to
function and a monotonous, material texture of films gradually
emerges. They tried to create on screen a materialist world; like
in Warhol's work, these films avoid affecting language, narrative or reason, and the films exist as material substance. Kenji
Misumi's *Satan's Sword* is interesting because of the constrained
body movements of Raizō Ichikawa who becomes blind and
disabled, and the texture of water in the flood scene (For some
reason, a flood hits the peak of a high-altitude mountain). The
attraction of mass-produced samurai dramas lies in the tedious
pleasure of repeatedly watching films with a highly clichéd style.
This pleasure is different from what you experience when you
are in the midst of suspended narrative. It resembles what the
audience experiences in *Sleep*: the pleasure of staring at a flow-
ing film strip. The audience's focus gradually shifts to the mechanical automatism of the camera, which records twenty-four
frames per second, and the material texture of the films. There is
an expression that film is a textural art, not a visual art; I suspect
people say so because the coarse texture of films reminds them
of materiality. The textural experience in films derives from an

attitude of finding pleasure in the materiality of films, rather than in its dramatic aspect.

I suspect that a primary concern of filmmakers who mass-produced B movies in the '50s was not pursuing artistic inspiration or stories. They instinctively knew that accurate mechanical functions and the scientific knowledge for handling films and photographic papers are more important than artistic themes. The narrative ceases to function as similar stories are repeated in hundreds of films made each year. Actors appear as meaningless forms unrelated to narrative — I suspect the directors in the '50s thought this was how films should be. They must have been more concerned with the violent aspects of recording cameras and the tedious materiality of films; their interest in these basic components of filmmaking was far greater than that in fictions made by montage. In other words, they were more serious about the details of pictures than in making dramas. They were so meticulous about how they showed detailed images that they changed light settings for individual shots and tinted each leaf, for example, with different colors to create a contrast between them. This is inconceivable in the production of television dramas, but they were adherent to detail because they considered films to be material as well as textural art. Their enthusiasm becomes evident in realistic details including sets, props, location, and space, not in imaginary stories. They created out of reality a so-called tedious material spectacle. The filmmakers in the '50s, who were not willing to hide the boredom of material reality, would probably appreciate Warhol's tediousness.

The boredom in Warhol films could resonate with the minimalism of factory images in Yasujirō Ozu's films (he is said to have kept walking eight hours a day for about three months to find the location), or the shots of an empty staircase and daughter's room in *Late Autumn*. They both project tedious materiality onto the screen.

Ozu, who insisted on prioritising cinematic perspective over reality — he couldn't accept the fact that the size of beer bottles placed in the foreground and background is the same — resembled in my view a factory manager who strictly controls products. He treated props and actors' bodies almost in the same way as industrial products; for him, humans only existed for visual effect. Additionally, the forms in Ozu's films are concrete and solid, but never abstract. For example, paper screens, window frames, and wardrobes in the background are arranged for visual effects, but still retain their materiality. Ozu's films present the outlines of subjects that are as precise as industrial goods; however, they do not abandon individual concreteness and avoid abstract aesthetics.

These filmmakers declared their loyalty to machines: cameras, recorders, and projectors, not to stories. Humans do not play a central role in their filmmaking. For them, filmmaking was an unconditional affirmation of the shameless violence of recording cameras and silent acceptance of the ruthless materiality of films and cameras. They paid homage to the tediousness of these mechanical devices.

Sleep is purely motivated by the recording function of the camera; there is no hint of fiction. However, as you watch, there is a moment in this nonfiction film when the boundary between reality and fiction blurs. The actual reality documented by the camera, a man sleeping for eight hours, suddenly looks obscure for some reason. When I saw the news footage about the explosion of a hijacked airplane in *Red Army/PFLP: Declaration of World War,* it also seemed somewhat fictional. Watching the footage of the explosion gave a far stronger sense of reality than witnessing a real explosion. You were struck by the strange feeling that reality and fiction had been reversed. What we acknowledge as reality — is it already a fiction, or do films blur the boundary between them?

The film blurs the boundary between reality and fiction, and bridges these spheres. And probably what we acknowledge as reality does not really exist; we only have its "image." If that is the case, we can say the film is a medium that captures this "image," rather than reproducing reality as it is. The naked human eye frames reality, which does not exist *a priori*; reality cannot exist without being framed by our eyes. Therefore, what we see is probably a mere fiction. It is the nature of the human eye that it cannot really experience reality without framing. In this sense, we are destined to live in a world of inverted perspective.

Even the film *Sleep,* said to be extremely boring, is not completely free of the danger of becoming a spectacle. A cat suddenly appears and this transforms the monotonous footage into a spectacle. The cat emerges, walks across the screen and disappears. A similar example is found in the action scenes in Tai Kato's films; several samurai brandishing swords enter and exit the screen as they fight. The camera frame divides reality into two spheres — inside (fictional sphere) and outside (reality) its scope. This interplay between fiction and reality creates a cinematic spectacle; the binary spheres of inside and outside screens emerge as the audience's attention is drawn toward what lies beyond the camera. This creates dynamic movement in films.

The cat that walks across Warhol's camera and the group of samurai in Kato's films both look equally vibrant. Their movement across the camera brings dynamic action into the film. It is a property of film that subjects can move into and out of the screen. If a camera only captures people moving within its frame, I would not call it a film. Their movements across the screen draw our attention to what lies beyond. This external reality is perhaps nothing but another image in a Bergsonian sense but at least it pluralizes the images seen on the screen. The framing leads the audience's attention to a plurality of cinematic images. This seems somewhat similar to a long-take technique which injects real time and disrupts fictional time in films. Therefore, we can say that framing pluralizes reality; the role of the camera is not to confine subjects or reality into a single frame and pursue some aesthetic goal. Framing serves to bring to a head conflicting elements in films; it creates a site of dialectical struggle where fiction and reality, fiction and another fiction compete with each other.

The one scene/one shot technique frequently inserted in Shinji Sōmai's *Shonben Raidā* develops a vague sense of time; actual time embedded in cinematic duration disturbs the fictionality of film. This effect dismisses the linear time framework central to narrative films where time always proceeds toward a climax. No ending is necessary for *Shonben Raidā*; it evokes a sense of suspension where we don't know when or how the film will end. The notion of time depicted in this film is more primitive than the modern, linear sense of time. It does not flow like a river running from upstream to downstream; it is subtle and wavering where the stagnant motion somewhat resembles a marsh (Aleksandr Sokurov's *Spiritual Voices* had a long take that showed us this stagnant time, which reminded me of catfish living at the bottom of a marsh).

The encircling, primitive time in *Shonben Raidā* is not due to the Japanese narrative structure *kishotenketsu** typically found in banal films. There is no dramatic scene in this film; using long takes and long shots, it just shows a distant view of people milling around. The sense of time here is completely different from cinematic time fabricated to flow in a linear fashion toward a climax. In *Shonben Raidā*, long-take shots frequently show characters moving into and out of the frame. The well-known example is a scene in which several characters run and chase each other on logs floating on a reservoir at a timber yard. They easily cross the boundary between fictional space (inside the camera frame) and reality (outside the camera frame), which creates an impression of fictional time and reality being gradually fused together. What lies outside the camera scope is, of course, invisible, but it constantly leads the audience's attention toward the external reality. And the crude, slow, actual time gained by long takes disrupts the linear flow of time. Long takes in this film give the audience pleasure as if time has been endlessly extended. This pleasure is distinct from the thrill gained by fast editing often used in recent films — probably recent films cannot accommodate this slow passage of time. For those who are used to fast editing, long-take shots lasting more than three minutes may seem extraordinarily dull; however, film is a medium that embraces opposite extremes — fabricated speed gained by fast editing and slow reality gained by long takes. Another example is the opening scene in Orson Welles's *Touch of Evil*, in which a

---

*   See translator's note on p. 61.

long take lasting more than three minutes creates the suspense that explosives might blow up at any minute. The audience is thrilled as this suspense proceeds slowly. Orson Welles was a director who could work with both extremes: fictitious rapidity and realistic slow speed. He did not sacrifice reality to creating cinematic fiction; he achieved it by bridging fiction and reality, and synchronizing fictional and realistic time. The long take is thus effective in slowing down the passage of time in films.

Framing creates a boundary between what lies inside and outside the scope of the camera, and subjects are frozen in the moment they are photographed. Photographs that have captured a suspended moment trace this suspended time inscribed in themselves, toward the past instead of toward the future. Suspension and retrogression: the camera creates these movements. Time in real life is, at the moment it is photographed, suspended and stored as the past. From the moment the camera has captured its subjects, they are confined to the past. In this way, the camera constantly transforms the present into the past immediate history. Photographic time is retrogressive: it constantly transforms the present into a trace; it constantly resets the reference point from which to look back at the present. Photography, which can only recollect the past, is in mourning for the lost present. It keeps offering a silent prayer to the present, feeling remorse and adhering to it. Therefore, photographers are like chief mourners who bid farewell to the present and subjects photographed. Photography certainly creates countless farewells. In order to say goodbye to both the present and subjects, pictures are taken. Photographers are powerless in this. I feel that what we actually do is keep hosting a memorial service. Photographers are in a state of indefinite mourning.

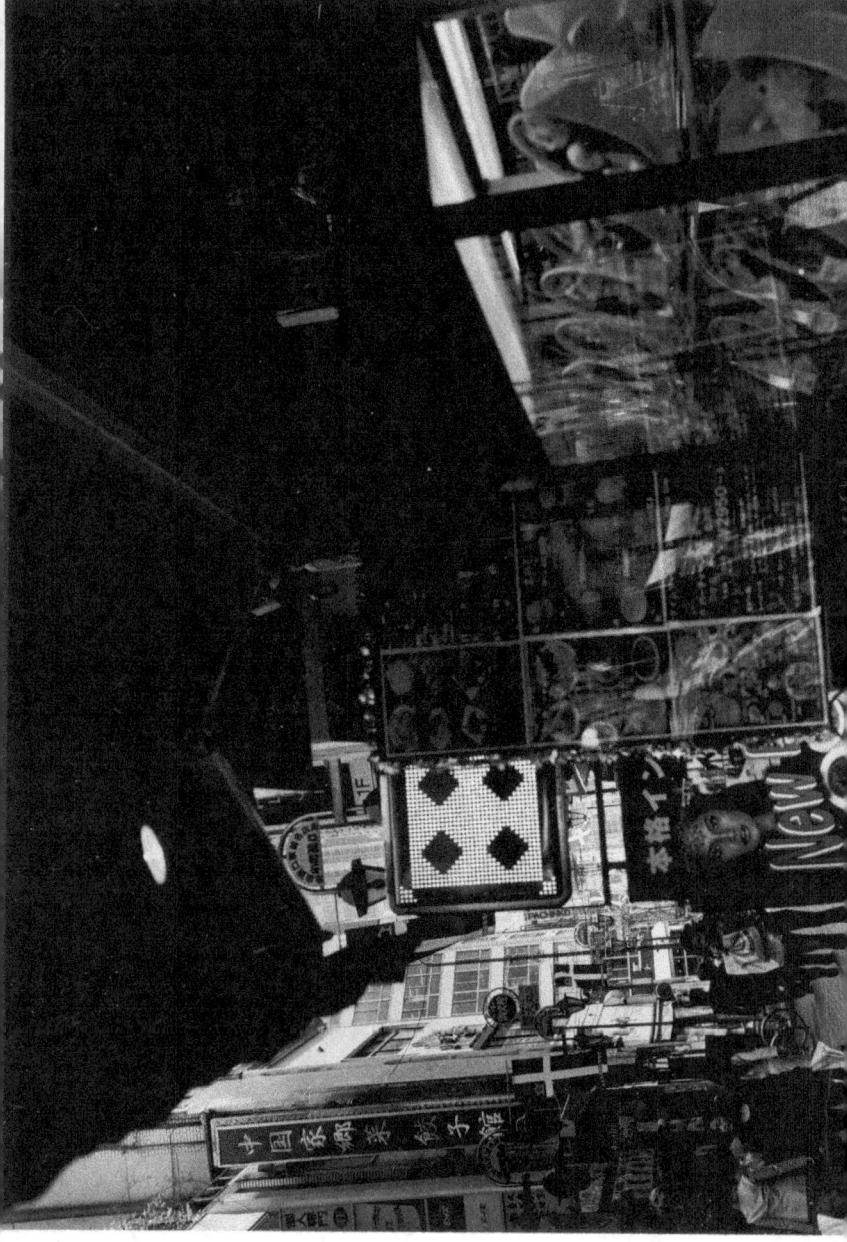

エッセイ02

カットバック、アクションつなぎ等々の多様な技法を駆使したモンタージュが生み出す映画の時間は、ドラマを成立させるために遡行する現実の時間を任意に切り刻み、つなぎ直します。それは基本的にフィクションの時間だと思うのです。無数のカットがつながれることで、虚構の物語を成立させる。そんなモンタージュの技法は、映画という虚構の世界を成立させるための重要な技法だと思うのです。それに対してワンシーン・ワンカットの長廻しは、モンタージュほど時間を好き勝手に操作できない。どちらかといえば現実の時間や空間や場所に拘束されがちです。それは映画をもっと演劇の領域か、現実の記録の領域に近づけてしまうのでしょうか。

　長廻しの時間はモンタージュ技法であらわされる時間と違って、もっと現実の生の時間の領域に近いと思います。アンゲロプロスの『旅芸人の記録』では、十二分間のワンシーン・ワンカットで六年間の時間経過を強引にあらわしていましたが、カットのつなぎ合わせで表出されるモンタージュの時間と違い、その十二分間は現実の生の十二分間の時間感覚に近いので、何だか嘘っぽいけれどリアリティーがあるという、虚構と現実が混濁するようなショットでした。それはフィクションなのですが、時間の流れ方が現実の流れ方に近い。カットを割らないでカメラを廻し続ける長廻しは、例えば三分間カメラを廻し続けたら、三分間の現実の時間の流れがフィルムの中

に定着される。そういう意味ではモンタージュが生み出す時間とは、まったく真逆の現実の時間だと思うのです。

　モンタージュは時間の操作を可能にしますが、廻し続けられたその三分間の長廻しは現実に経過した三分間の生の現実の時間でして、モンタージュが生み出したフィクションの時間ではない。長廻しはだからフィクションとしての映画の中に、生の現実の時間を導入することではないでしょうか。フィクションとしての映画の時間に、リアルな現実の時間を導入することで、長廻しは映画のフィクションに対して亀裂を入れることなのではないでしょうか。モンタージュによって成立する映画のフィクションに対して、現実を導入することでフィクションの城壁の中で守られている映画に亀裂を生じさせる。映画を映画だけの世界に囲い込むのではなく、映画を現実の世界と地続きの関係に持ち込むのです。映画の中に現実を、現実の世界に映画を浸透させていく渾然一体とした感覚を長廻しはあらわそうとします。

　現実のある一部を囲い込むカメラのフレームは、囲い込んだ対象から現実の時間を簒奪（さんだつ）するでしょう。対象から時間を奪い、無時間的な存在に転化させます。そしてフレームによって切り取られ、停止させられた対象がフィルムに定着されることで今度は、映写機のモーターで停止させられた対象が動き始める。それが映画の時間の始まりなのですが、そんな映画の時間は基本的に静止した映像を映写機で動かすことで生み出された機械の時間です。映写機によって、つなぎ合わされたカットが自動的に流れ出す。現実の時間が持つ不可逆性を根底から突き動かすのがモンタージュです。現実の時間の流れに逆らって、それはカメラによって切り取られた現実を、好き勝手に貼付け、再構成し直すのです。写真が時間を凍結することで、時間を過去に戻ることが可能な、逆行可能の時間に転化します。モンタージュは時間を自由に組み替え、すべての映像が今 現在にあらわれたかのような虚構の現前性を強調します。それらの技法を駆使することで、二十四分の一という自動化された単調な機械の時間が、スペクタクルな時間に変貌するのです。

　けれど映画にそんなスペクタクルな現前性が必要なのでしょうか。少し極端な例ですが、例えばウォーホルの映画は何も起こりません。眠っている男やエンパイア・ステート・ビルディングをカメラが据え置きのまま写しているだけです。現実の時間がただ経過していくだけの映画です。それは何だかベルトコンベアーをずうっと眺めている、流れ作業に従事している工員のような気分になります。映画の時間はそんなベルトコンベアーに代表されるような、インダストリアルで退屈なものなのでしょうか。ウォーホルの映画を"退屈の監視人"だと佐々木敦が書いていましたが、映写機という機械が正常に動いていることを監視する。そんなインダストリアルで単調な退屈こそが映画の本質なのかもしれません。映写機という大きな機械が中央に鎮座している映写室を中心にして成立する映画館の空間は、人間ではなく機械が中心であり、機械が写し出す映像を真剣にみんなが見ている姿は、機械に支配された空間であり、それは何だかフォード式の工場で働いている機械に牛耳られた工員の姿とよく似ているような気がします。

　ウォーホルも長廻しを多用する映像作家ですが、彼の長廻しもまた、映画の虚構に対して生の現実を映画の中に導入することだったと思うのです。そして生の現実というのはつねに退屈なのですが、自動化された機械の時間が前提となって成立する映画もまた、基本的には退屈なメディアだと思うのです。高度に機械化された工場での人間のやる仕事といえば、その機械の動きを見張っているだけです。そんなフォード式工場の持つ固有の退屈さを映画もまた内包している。それは人間が機械に従わざるを得ない悪夢のような退屈さです。その退屈さに耐えきれなくなったときにモンタージュ等々の技法を使って映像をスペクタクル化するのだと思いますが、ときにはその悪夢のような退屈さに取り憑かれた映像作家もいるのです。ウォーホルもその内の一人なのでしょうが、アジェも同じ場所を飽きることなく、何度も死ぬまで撮り続けていました（ベレニス・アボットもできることなら、死ぬまでニューヨークを撮りたかったと言っていました。写真家というのは単調な繰り返しを好む人が多いのでしょうか）。

　彼らは退屈な反復に取り憑かれたのでしょうか。機械の単調な反復が快感だと最初に提示したのがクラフトワークだと思うのですが、リズムボックスという機械に人間が合わせていくことで、人間が機械化する快感だけではなく、それは人間と機械の領域が地続きになってしまう面白さに取り憑かれたのではないでしょうか。人間が機械に対して主ではないし、かといって疎外論のように人間が機械の従になるわけでもない。機械と人間の境界が曖昧になるのです。それは現実の世界と映画の境界が曖昧になっていくような感覚と似ているのではないでしょうか。機械と人間、虚構と現実の境界が曖昧になっていくとき、その場に居合わせた作家的主体もまた自己のアイデンティティーをそこで維持し続けるのは難しいでしょう。虚構なのか現実なのか判断不可能なメディアに対して、主体の位置を確保するのは困難なことだと思うのです。現にクラフトワークはステージの上では、シンセサイザーのスイッチを押す以外に能動的なことは何もしていなかった。そんな風に作家的主体があやふやになって消滅しようとする瞬間に現われるのが、カメラの記録機能なのだと思います。『眠る男』はカメラの記録機能に徹底的に依存した映画です。むしろ記録機能しかない映画とでも呼ぶべき映画だと思います。

　写真撮影もそうですが、撮影を続けていると自分が撮っているという意識が怪しくなる。撮影において自分がイニシアティヴを握っているという感覚がだんだん崩壊していきます。自分が撮っているのか、機械が撮っているのか、または風景に撮らされているのか。現実を見ているのか、ファインダーに写ったものを見ているのか、そんな境界が曖昧になり易い。ある意味では、世界は最初から映像化されているのかと思うときもあります。映像と現実の関係が逆転してくる。現実があるからその現実を写真に撮るのではなく、写真に撮ったからその現実が立ち現われてきたのではないか。またはどんな現実も写真のように見えてしまう。現実はすでに写真なのかもしれない。だから写真のような現実をもう一度まるで複写するかのように撮

影する。主体と客体としての世界とのパースペクティヴな関係が逆立ちしているような気が、撮影にはつきまとうのです。

　ウォーホルの『眠る男』に対して、撮りっぱなしだとか、現実をそのまま写しているだけだという批判がありますが、けれどフィクション性の欠片もない映画というのもすごい映画だと思います。カメラの記録機能だけで作られているわけですよね。それは機械の機能に忠実に作った映画でして、映画の下部構造たるカメラの存在を前面に打ち出す唯物論的な映画です。ひたすら機械の機能に忠実に撮る彼の映画は、作家的主体が欠落したままです。けれど映画においての作家性というのは一体どんな機能を担うのでしょうか。作家性は結局 映画の本質を担う機械の退屈さを覆い隠すために機能するのではないでしょうか。近代社会が退屈さを隠蔽して日常をイヴェント化したように、近代テクノロジーと相似的な関係にある映画もそのテクノロジーの退屈を、ドラマや作家性の名において隠蔽し、スペクタクル化しょうとしているのではないでしょうか。

　レンズを向ければすべてを記録してしまうカメラの記録性は、ほとんど暴力と同義です。悲惨なものも、楽しげなものもすべて分け隔てなく記録してしまう。カメラの記録機能には自重や反省という言葉がありません。何の躊躇もなくどんどん撮ってしまう。映像に作家性やドラマという性格を刻印しようとするのは、そんなカメラの記録機能が持つ暴力性を隠蔽させるためなのではないでしょうか。ほうっておけば何でも撮ってしまうカメラに対して、作家性やドラマという人間性を加味することで、その暴力性を飼い馴らそうとしているのです。『眠る男』はそんな記録機能の暴力性を最大限に剥き出しにします。カメラを五時間二十分眠る男に向け続けることによってあらわれるただの眠っている男には、ファンタジーやフィクションが捏造する夢がない。そこにあるのは、カメラは目の前の現実をただ写すという無慈悲な記録機能だけがあらわれるのです。

　五十年代の撮影所システムは映画から作家性を追放して、言われた企画を黙々とこなす（映画には最初から作家性なんて存在しませんでした）

。ベルトコンベアーの流れ作業に従事する熟練された工具のような監督を排出しました。撮影所システムの制度は、映画を限りなくフォード式の工場システムと近似させます。それは娯楽としての映画の裏に存在する近代テクノロジーが支配している退屈さであり、彼ら監督たちはそんな退屈さを文句一つ言わずに引き受けるのです。彼らは作家的主体性や、ドラマを完成させた達成感なんて興味も持ちません。そういった作家性やドラマという装飾を破棄して、剥き出しのカメラの暴力性を受け止めるのです。彼らはものがどこまでも写ってしまうカメラに熱狂していたのではないでしょうか。ともかく画面を作りたいという欲望が作家性やドラマよりも先に存在していたのではないでしょうか。脚本作りの淡白さに対して、画面作りへの手間ひまのかけかたは、スケジュールの日程を考えても異常です。

　五十年代の映画状況はジャンルがまだ活性化している状況でした。ジャンル固有の法則で映画を撮る。年間に何百本もの同じジャンル映画を撮り続ける。忠実にジャンルを遵守し反復し続けることでそれは、物語の説話体系が意味をなさなくなり、やがて単調なフィルムの物質性が顔をあらわすでしょう。彼らは物語という言語体系や、理解に訴えかけるのではなく、ウォーホルさながらにスクリーンの上をフィルムという物質が機械的に流れるだけでいいのではないかという唯物的な世界をあらわそうとするでしょう。三隅研次の『大菩薩峠』が面白いのは内容ではなく、目が見えなくなり、体も不自由になった市川雷蔵の身体の束縛された動きや、洪水（標高の高い山頂に、何故か洪水が来るのです）がフィルムであらわれたときの水の物質感です。大量生産された時代劇の面白さは、この先何が起こるか分からない的な物語の快楽ではなく、無内容に形式化された映像を反復して見続けるという退屈さに快楽や面白さを感じるようになる。それはフィルムが無内容にただスクリーンを流れ続けることに快楽を感じる『眠る男』のような物質的経験です。一秒間に二十四分の一コマで動くカメラの機械的な自動性や、フィルムの物質性に快楽の焦点が移っていくのです。よく映画は視覚ではなく触覚芸術だという言われ方がされますが、それはフィル

ムのざらつく感じが触覚性を喚起させるので、そういう風に言われるのでし
ょう。映画の触覚的経験は映画をドラマではなく、フィルムという物質的側
面で快楽を感じるということなのです。

　写真を成立させるのに必要なことが作家的主体性ではなく、正確に動
く機械の機能性や、フィルムや印画紙を正しく扱うための科学的知識や
物質性であるように、大量にB級映画を排出していた五十年代の監督も
また、作家的主体や物語に重点を置いていたのではないと思うのです。
年間に何百本も撮られ続けることで、ジャンルの反復が生み出す物語の説
話機能の停止。物語が有効に機能せず、カメラの記録機能が役者を無意
味なフォルムに成り果てさせる。そんな映画の姿を肯定していたのではない
でしょうか。それはモンタージュの生み出す虚構性ではなく、カメラやフィ
ルムという映画表現の下部構造が生み出した、記録機能の暴力性と、フィ
ルムの退屈な物質性を愛していたのではないでしょうか。

　彼らはドラマを作ることよりも、画面の細部をどうするかに夢中だっ
た。テレビドラマでは考えられないことですが、彼らはワンカット毎に照明
を変え続け、コントラストをつけるためには木の葉っぱ一枚一枚に色を塗
り続けるそんな手間暇を惜しまないぐらいに画面にこだわっていたのです。
そんな映像の細部にこだわるといのは、映像を物質としてまた、触覚芸術
として考えていたからでしょう。ストーリーの観念性ではなく、セットや、小
道具や、場所や、空間という現実の細部にこだわる。それは現実が生み出
した退屈な物質的スペクタクルです。現実の物質的な退屈さを隠そうともし
ない五十年代の監督達は、ウォーホル的な退屈さを肯定するでしょう。

　小津安二郎の撮る工場の外観(その工場の風景を探すために、三ヶ月ぐ
らい毎日八時間歩き続けたそうです)のミニマル性や、『秋日和』での誰も
いない階段や娘の部屋のショットは、意外にウォーホル的な退屈さと共鳴し
ているのかもしれません。それは物質的な退屈さが画面に露呈することの
共鳴です。

　テーブルに置かれた手前と、後方のビール瓶が同じ高さになるという現実のパースペクティヴを拒否して、映画的パースペクティヴを要求した小津安二郎は、まるで工場製品を完璧に管理する製造責任者のようです。工場製品として小道具や役者の身体を見ていた小津安二郎は、人間をフォルムとして見ます。そしてフォルムでありながらも、小津は対象を抽象化しない。対象はフォルムに還元されながらも、それは抽象化されたフォルムではなく、抽象化に抗い続け、具体性を手放さない頑強なフォルムなのです。背景の障子や、窓枠、たんすがフォルム的に再配置されながらも、その物の物質性は手放さない。工業製品のようなフォルムでありながらも、個別的具体性を放棄しない小津安二郎の映画は、フォルムの持つ抽象的な美学の領域には決して回収されないのです。

　彼らは物語ではなく、カメラや、録音機や、映写機という機械に対して忠誠を誓ったのです。映画とは人間が作るものでも、人間を撮るものでもない。記録機能の破廉恥な暴力性を無条件に肯定し、フィルムやカメラの無慈悲な物質性を無言で受け入れることです。それは物質固有の退屈さを賛美し続けることなのではないでしょうか。

　『眠る男』はただカメラの録画機能に忠実なだけで、そこにはフィクションの欠片もありません。けれど見ているうちに、何だかそれは現実なのかフィクションなのか分からなくなる瞬間があります。本当に寝ている人間を八時間写しているだけのノンフィクションの映画なのですが、たとえ本当の現実を撮っていても、映像は何故だか知りませんが、写した対象を曖昧にさせる力があります。『赤軍-PFLP　世界戦争宣言』でのハイジャックした飛行機が爆発するニュースフィルムの映像を見たとき、なんだかフィクションのように感じました。それは現実にその爆破現場を見るよりも、映像を見る方がリアリティーを感じる。現実とフィクションが逆転する奇妙なパースペクティヴ感におそわれるのです。わたし達が認識する現実というのはそれ自体がすでにフィクションなのか、それとも映像は現実とフィクションの領域を曖昧にするのでしょうか。

　映像は現実とフィクションの境界を曖昧にさせます。映像と現実は地続きなのです。そしてわたし達の認識できる現実は、リアルな現実ではなく"もう一つのイマージュ"なのかもしれません。すると映画は現実を再現したイマージュではなく、イマージュを写したイマージュなのではないでしょうか。イマージュの二重化が映画なのでしょうか。人間の肉眼自体が一つのフレームなのであり、現実が最初にあるのではなく、わたし達の目前には現実よりも、フレームが先行して存在しているのではないでしょうか。フレームを通して現実を見る。それはだからつねに虚構しか見ていないのかもしれない。フレームを通さなければ現実をまともに見ることができないのが人間の肉眼なのではないでしょうか。そういう意味ではわたし達は最初から倒立したパースペクティヴの世界の中で生きているのです。

　退屈の極みと言われる『眠る男』もスペクタクルから完全に自由にはなれません。途中に現れる猫の存在が単調な『眠る男』に対してスペクタクルを与えるのです。フレームを横切るようにして現れる猫の存在は、フレームの外から表われ、画面の真ん中を横切り、フレームの外に消えていく。加藤泰の映画にも何人もの侍が対決し、刀を振りかざしながら、フレームを出たり入ったりするアクションシーンがありますが、フレームの存在が映画に画面内と画面外という二つの領域を生み出します。それは虚構の領域としての画面内と、現実の領域としてのフレーム外という分断を導入します。虚構と現実が行ったり来たりすることが、映画が本来的に持っているスペクタクル性なのではないでしょうか。画面の中に収まりきるのではなく、画面の外を想起させることで、画面に内と外という二重の領域を出現させるのです。画面の二重化が映画に運動を生み出すのではないでしょうか。

　ウォーホルの画面を横切る猫は、加藤泰の映画の侍たちと同じくらいアクション感を感じさせます。フレームを横切るというその運動が、映画にアクションを与えたのです。フレームの内と外を出入りすることができるのは、映画だけです。画面内にいる人間の動きをただ撮っているだけでは映画にならない。フレームを横切ること。映画にはフレームの外があるので

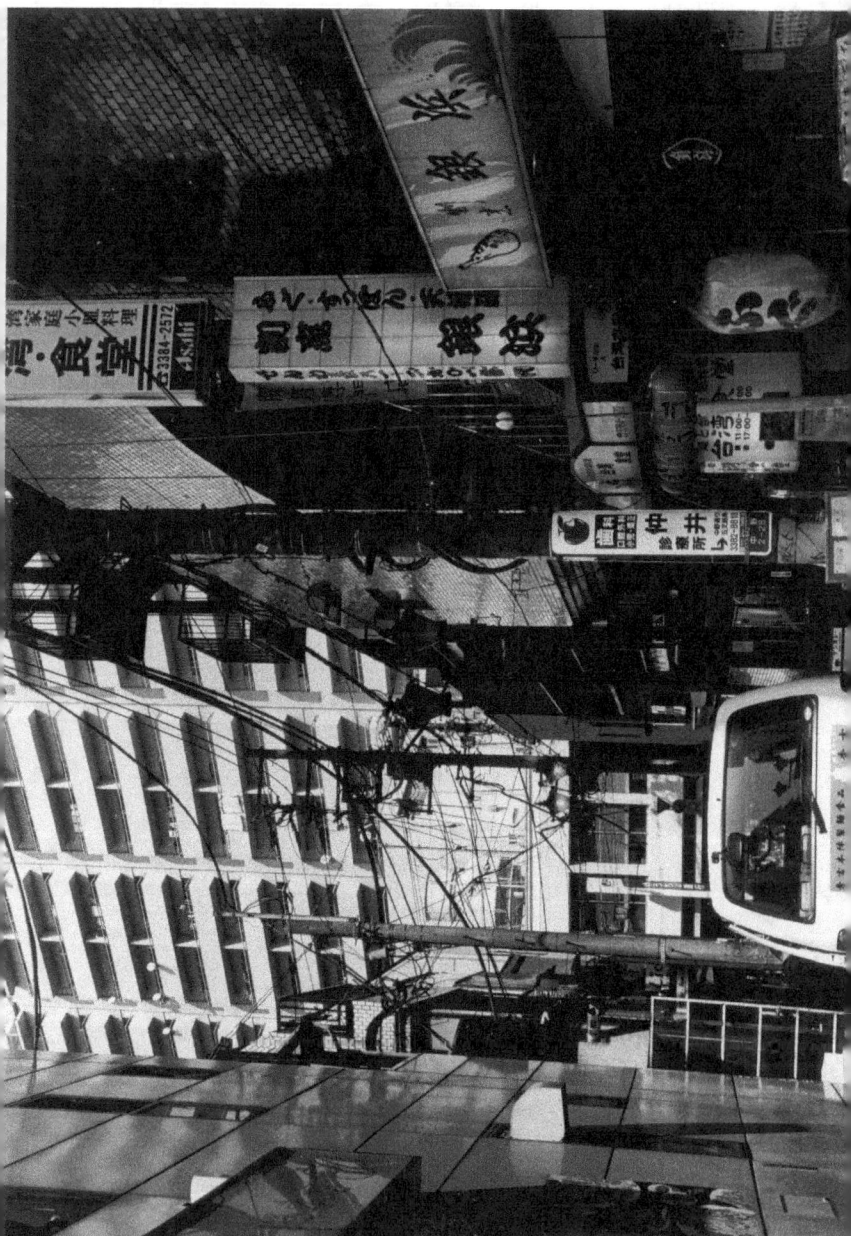

す。そのフレーム外の現実もベルグソン的に言えば、もう一つのイマージュなのかもしれませんが、少なくともフレームの存在は、単数でしかない画面＝イマージュを複数化することに成功したのです。長廻しの技法が虚構としての映画の時間に、現実の時間を対立させることで映画のフィクショナルな時間を分断したように、フレームの存在が単数として成立する映画の画面を複数化したのです。フレームはだから対象を一つの枠の中に収め込んで美学化する装置ではない。現実のある部分を切り取って一つの枠に収斂するのではなく、現実を複数化するための装置なのです。それはつねに対立を呼び込むための装置なのです。虚構と現実、または虚構ともう一つの虚構を対立させるための階級闘争の場を出現させるのがフレームの役割なのだと思います。

『ションベン・ライダー』（相米慎二）の全編にわたるワンシーン・ワンカットの長廻しを見ていると、フィクションという壁に守られていた映画の時間に、現実の生の時間が入り込むことで、映画のフィクション性が揺れ動き、時間の感覚が曖昧になる。その揺れ動く曖昧さが、劇映画が要請するクライマックスに向かって直線的に進行する物語の時間を棄却するのです。終わるような、終わらないような宙づりの感覚をおぼえさせる『ションベン・ライダー』に結末なんて必要ではないのです。『ションベン・ライダー』の要請する時間は、直線的に流れるという近代的な時間ではなくて、もっと原始的な時間なのではないでしょうか。それは川の流れのように上流から下流に向けて遡行する時間ではなく、沼地のように動いているのか動いていないのか分からない（ソクーロフの『精神（こころ）の声』が沼に棲息する鯰のような、そんな遅滞した時間を感じさせる長廻しでしたね）、微妙に揺れ動く時間のような気がします。

円環するような原始的な時間を持つ『ションベン・ライダー』の時間は、凡庸な映画の起承転結の時間では収斂できません。劇的なシーンが何もなく、ただ人物がロングショットの長廻しで画面の中に小さく蠢いているだけの映画ですが、それは起承転結に代表されるようなクライマックスに向け

て時間が直線的に流れるという偽造された映画の時間とは、無縁な時間でした。木場の貯水湖に浮かぶ材木の上を走りながら、追いかけ合うシーンを筆頭に、フレームの中を人物が出たり入ったりするだけの映画なのですが、それはフレームの中という虚構の世界と、フレームの外という現実の世界が分断されたことで互いの領域を行き来できる。そのことが内と外を連続させ、虚構の時間と現実の時間が混濁してくる。フレームの外は当然見えませんが、フレーム外の現実をつねに想起させ続けます。そしてクライマックスに向けた直線の時間に収斂させるのではなく、長廻し特有の現実の生の時間、もったりとした時間が映画の時間を遅滞化させる。時間がいつまでも続くような『ションベン・ライダー』の長廻しは、スピーディーなカット割りで得られる壮快感ではなく、いつまでも時間が引き延ばされていくような快感をおぼえます。最近の映画の早過ぎるカット割りは、この時間の遅滞化に耐えられないのでしょう。三分以上の長廻しは、スピーディーなカット割りから見れば異常なぐらいに鈍いのでしょうが、映画はカット割りという虚構の速度と、長廻しという現実の鈍さが同居しているメディアなのだと思います。オーソン・ウェルズの『黒い罠』のトップシーンでの爆弾が破裂するかもしれないという状況設定の中での三分間強の長廻しは、その長廻しの現実の速度が表象する鈍さにはらはらするのです。オーソン・ウェルズは虚構の速度と現実の鈍さを行き来できた監督なのだと思います。それは現実を排除することで映画的虚構を成立させるのではなく、現実と地続きに連続化することで、両者の時間をシンクロさせながら映画的虚構を成立させたのだと思いますし、速度に対して遅滞を導入するのが長廻しなのではないかと思います。

　フレーム外とフレーム内という二つの領域を生み出したフレームは、さらに写した対象の現実の時間を凍結します。凍結することで停止された無時間の写真。そして凍結されたことで痕跡化された写真は、未来ではなく過去に向かって逆行し続ける。停止と逆行。そんな二つの領域をカメラのフレームが生み出すのです。現実の時間は写されたその瞬間に

強制的に停止させられ、過去の領域に貯蔵されます。映像は写したその瞬間から対象を過去の領域に送りこむのです。それは現在をつねに過去化させる。現在を過去に刷新する。写真の時間は逆行的な時間です。過去に向かって遡及していく写真の時間は、つねに現在を痕跡化するでしょう。現在を回顧する基点として設定し直すのです。過去を振り返り続けることしかできない写真は現在に対して、つねに喪に服し続けているのです。現在に対してそれは黙祷し続けることであり、後悔し続けることであり、拘泥し続けることです。写真家とはだから現在と対象に対して、喪主的な立場に立ち続けることであり、永久に告別を執り行う存在ではないでしょうか。無数のさようならを写真は、繰り返し生み出し続けるでしょう。現在と対象に対してさようならを言うためにシャッターは切られ続ける。写真家は現在と対象に対してさようならしか言えない無力な存在なのです。わたし達にできることは、喪の儀式を執り続けることだけではないでしょうか。無期限の喪中に服し続けるのが写真家だと思うのです。

Interview

The Plaubel Makina camera encounters the city through your hands, mind, and body. Looking at your images, I have the feeling that the city itself is there in order to reveal and determine the interior structures, functions, and advantages of the camera. You seem to use the exterior world including streets, bicycles, cars, people, and cityscapes to reveal the internal, visceral quality and structure of the camera. For me, the internal dynamics of the Makina become the real subject of your images. The cityscape is not the real subject; it is more like a pretext or an excuse to explicate the camera's structure.

You can immediately tell that your black and white images of the 1990s are shot with the Makina. There is a dehumanized, mechanical feeling. Your pictures, even the black and white analogue film images, seem to have this quality. This sense of de-humanization seems completely new in the history of photography, especially street, urban photography. Can we also say you have taken an approach that is completely opposite to paintings?

Photographers don't have direct contact with their subjects. The camera always mediates what you see. In order to make contact with subjects, you look into a viewfinder first, and there they appear; the encounter takes place through a viewfinder. So, for me, images appear through the camera. As you said, I look at the subjects through the Plaubel Makina's interior structure; what interests me are the streets that you see through the camera, not real streets. As you say, it is this interior structure that is the important issue for me.

I've always been interested in the framing and composition of camera shots. I am more interested in how the image is framed within a square shape than in the actual substance of the photo. Also, moving images cannot be made without framing and composition. In *Sho o Suteyo, Machi e Deyō* (*Throw Away Your Books, Rally in the Streets*), Shuji Terayama made his protagonist shout, "What are you doing? Nothing starts when you sit like that in the darkness of the cinema. Screens are always empty." I suppose he did it to question the structure or system of cinema, but my feeling was that you can't do this by provoking the audience through the images shown, from *inside*. Images cannot be re-imagined unless you create shots with an alternative framing and composition: they're the basic elements that enable the creation of moving images. And you can't completely re-invent them, but you can come very close to doing so. That's how I think.

I like films made by Peter Kubelka and Michael Snow, the so-called structural films. They don't show the kind of images that you see in ordinary films. They present the basic components of filmmaking including photographic film, cameras, and projectors. They question the structure of images rather than the stories or images themselves. I watched these films a lot when I was in my twenties, so it must be from their influence that I'm more interested in the structure of the image rather than the image in isolation.

I don't have a particular interest in the city of Tokyo. I don't shoot looking for stories about the city. I happen to live there, so I can easily shoot there; I don't have to take the trouble to travel somewhere else. I just shoot in Tokyo because it's convenient; I can do so whenever I have the urge.

When I started photography, I was more interested in how to shoot than what to shoot. Cityscapes framed into 6×7 format interested me more than what was there in the city. I get more excited about images of Tokyo framed into 6×7 than the city itself. Streets, bicycles, cars, and people — I have no interest in what these things imply. For example, I don't wipe dust off negatives; even if dust blurs the expressions on people's faces or the words written on signboards, it doesn't bother me at all. What I think is rather more important is that the dust can expose the materiality of film. Streets, bicycles, cars, and people are, as you say, a means to reveal the structure, framing, and composition of the camera, and also the materiality of film.

I find the framing and composition of camera shots interesting because they divide the world into two: what is shown and not shown in pictures, what is visible and invisible. For example, Mao Zedong discussed idealist dialectics that divide one into two, not making two into one, against Marxism's dialectical materialism that eventually subsumes two conflicting ideas into one. Contradictions are found in everything. They are essentially involved in the nature of things — that's Mao's theory. Conflicting ideas always exist, and thesis and antithesis keep fighting without reaching synthesis, which differs from the dialectics of thesis–antithesis–synthesis that subsume the opposites on a higher level. In Mao's dialectics, which lack the higher dimension of synthesis, conflict and struggle endlessly continue. This is Mao's revolutionary theory and even after the revolution succeeded, it demanded that people purge spies and enemies of the working class who were supposed to exist everywhere.

The movements to purge lackeys of capitalism and anti-revolutionaries during the Cultural Revolution in the 1960s kept the society in a state of contradiction and transformed Mao's theory into a reality. Mao said that the enemies of the working class exist eternally, even after the birth of a socialist regime. Constantly searching for the enemy is to keep dividing one into two. It endlessly creates contradictions, and even when the conflict of class has been negated by the establishment of a socialist regime, further divisions will be introduced. Did Mao consider increasing contradictions, divisions, and conflicts to be the essence of dialectical materialism? Reading this, Mao's theory reminds me of photography.

Mao imagined permanent revolution as the ideal model of revolution, and the Cultural Revolution led by him was a revolutionary movement eternally moving without stalling. Just like Mao's dialectics, the camera constantly divides the world; it is endlessly divided into the visible and the invisible, which multiply. These two spheres remain torn apart, never being reintegrated into one.

Shooting images amplifies the invisible, I think. The act of shooting to visualize the world more deeply makes it even more invisible. The desire of photography to fix the world onto a sheet of photographic paper creates countless worlds that cannot be captured. That is a de-visualization of the world. Photographs drag people into a more opaque, invisible world rather than offering clear visions.

If painters generally deal with the substance of images, I would say I am different from them as I am more concerned with structures. Since childhood, I've wondered why some people draw figurative paintings when there are cameras, which are more convenient. I wondered why they choose such a time-consuming method, when cameras take less than a second to capture things. This was how I thought as a child without much knowledge about paintings, being ignorant about the individual touch of painters, but I still feel a bit like that. The individuality or distinctive character of the artist doesn't interest me. Art critics in Japan often think photography is beyond their understanding because unlike paintings it doesn't show the photographer's individual character. But from my point of view, I found it harder to understand why the artist's individual qualities are so overrated. I don't understand why art should be evaluated in terms of the unique traits of the artist.

I suppose these individual characters were accidentally made possible by structures? Structure precedes the artist's individual identity and individualities are determined by structures, not the other way round. It is the history of art and structures that determine and create the personal qualities of painters and photographers. That's why I am interested in the structures that establish the individual qualities of artists, but care very little about individuality itself.

I wonder when this tendency started, when people started to show more interest in artists rather than what they express. Perhaps photography tried to obliterate the artist as the centre of focus. Pictures taken in Eugène Atget's era, especially documentary photographs by Maxime du Camp, for instance — they almost all look similar. But they are not boring at all. You can concentrate on the pictures without being distracted by the existence of the artist.

Talking about human figures and bodies in film and video, looking at your video work, I've always thought that your treatment of the human form is very interesting. You seem to use these images to generate a kind of pure "internal movement and noise" within the picture. On the other hand, you sometimes approach them in a more conventional way. Have you changed the way you film humans?

For example, in your early Super 8mm films, you sometimes portrayed your own image. This created an interesting feeling because the image of you (and the room you were in) gave some information related to the artist (yourself) and his surroundings. In one Super 8mm film, we can even see a woman lying on the floor of a room and saying "bye-bye" looking into the Super 8mm camera. This element was very innovative for experimental films.

How important is autobiography in your video work? For example, why do your videos include traces and scenes of your wife's artwork? Why do you sometimes bring interior, private spaces into your films? What do public and private images mean to you? Are there political meanings or intentions in the distinction between the public and private?

It was at the end of the 1990s that I started shooting *Everyday XXX* with an 8mm video camera. Watching the footage I shot on the street later, perhaps because the sounds recorded by the

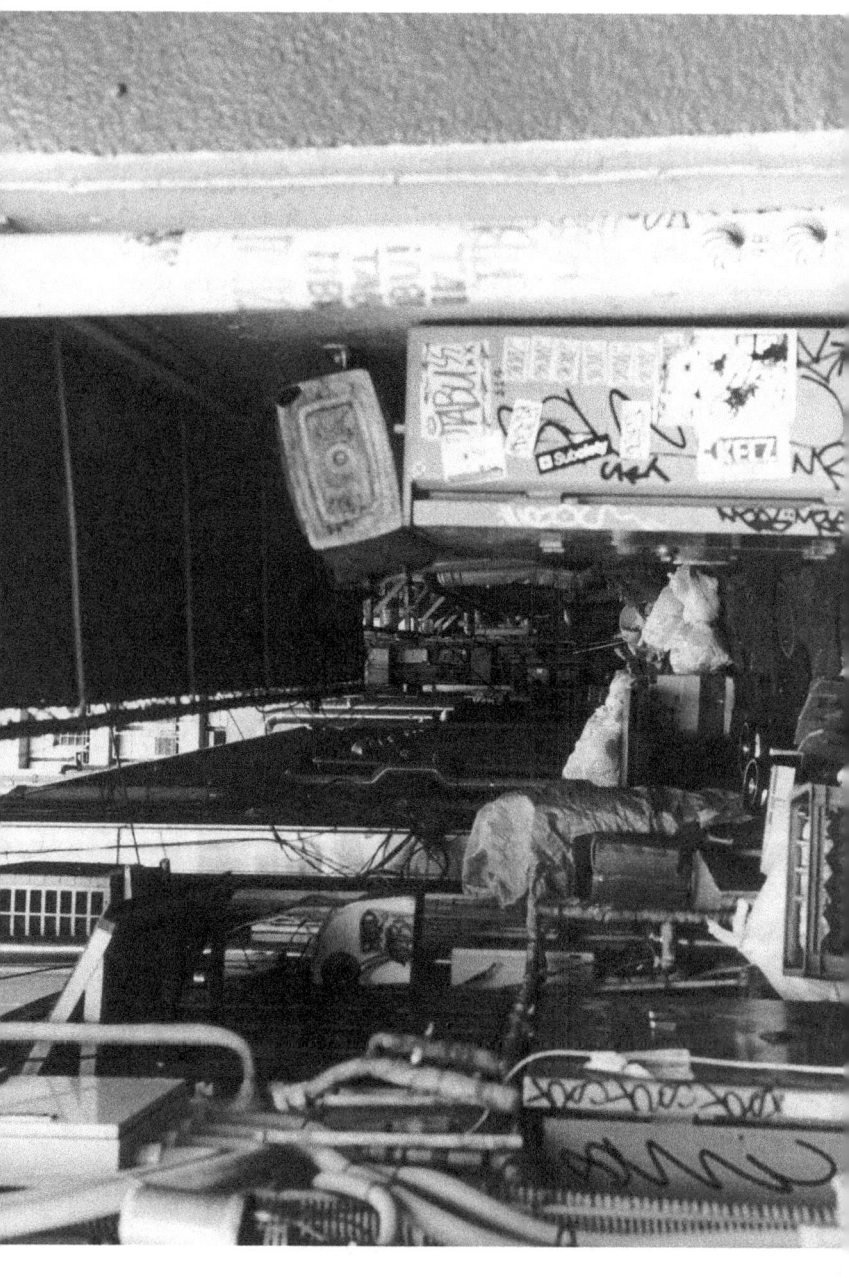

video camera were very loud, the people and cars in the images became pronounced in terms of noise. 8mm video cameras have an automatic, simultaneous sound recording function. Listening to the recorded sounds, I discovered how noisy Tokyo was. That's how I started becoming interested in the sounds recorded by the camera. In those days, I took short shots lasting about 0.5 to 1 second and accumulated them. As they were short, the recorded sounds were also short and they sounded very abstract. It had the feeling of Pierre Schaeffer's *musique concrète* that used concrete sound materials to create music.

The 8mm video camera was for me a noise generator, rather than a camera. I almost felt it made howling noises generated by amplified electric guitars. I wasn't thinking much about what to shoot, I just wanted to fractionate reality by making intermittent shots.

I had no interest in editing then. There wasn't enough equipment, and I just enjoyed filming at random. I discovered the environment I lived in, and this discovery was different from what I had experienced with black and white photos.

You pointed out that I sometimes approach human beings and bodies in a more conventional way. I think this is because I've adopted long-take shots in addition to short, fragmented ones. I started doing this because although my personal taste tends toward the fragmented cutting techniques that appear in works such as Stan Brakhage's *Dog Star Man,* Hitoshi Nomura's *Dec.1973–Oct.1974* or *the Brownian Motion of Eyesight,* and Jonas Mekas's works. I was also interested in films using long-take shots as in Masao Adachi's *A.K.A. Serial Killer,* James Benning's *El Valley Centro,* and Marguerite Duras's *Son nom de Venise dans Calcutta desert.* My new work *Life Is a Gift* was made by combining these two elements.

In *Dead Stick Landing,* I intended to show each shot carefully, which was a different approach from the previous videos I made. Therefore, each shot is long. You can say this approach is more conventional.

I'll give you an example from *Life Is a Gift.* Holding the camera close to the monitor set up on a shop window: images flow on the monitor, displaying the reflections of people and the street overlapping with the *real* people walking on the street — and all these images look fused together. This is a very unique video effect. The humans who appear in advertisements on the monitor, the reflection of pedestrians in the window, and actual people walking — all become equivalent when seen through the camera. I have no interest in reproducing reality in films; things which happen to be captured by the camera are all equivalent images. Cars, buildings, and human beings — everything takes on a similar value in terms of image.

I want to show the reality of the image; I don't want to reproduce a verisimilitude of reality through the image. Moving pictures acquire a unique sense of reality by transforming existing human beings into images. Images create a different reality. I sometimes approach human beings and bodies in a more conventional way, not to attempt to reproduce reality, but to express a sense of reality inherent in the image itself. That's why fairly long-take shots were necessary.

Looking at my long-take shots that last more than 30 seconds, viewers become curious about the movements of people in the foreground or that of cars in the background. Their sight starts to wander around and visual perception gets more complicated. Short shots continuously overwhelm viewers with the impression of afterimages retained on their retina, while long-take shots make them eager to scrutinize what is shown in the picture. I adopted long-take shots because I thought if you keep overwhelming the audience, they become passive; I wanted to encourage their active engagement. By bringing two contradictory elements, passivity and activeness, into one video, I intended to create perceptual tension between these two kinds of shot. It's not exactly like Mao's dialectic, but it's like the dynamics created by the conflict between contradictory values.

It's not my goal to reproduce a verisimilitude of reality through video, so I try to make self-contained entities. Relying on objects in real life, you'll never reach the dynamism inherent in the images themselves. But by introducing short- and long-take shots, contradictory elements collide and differentiate from each other, and thus videos acquire autonomous movements. I think this is possible. In this way, the tension between shots is brought about by moving pictures' internal structures, rather than relying on external elements, and its internal integrity is maintained. The reality of images is approachable only through this kind of process.

I studied at Image Forum, a school for experimental film in Japan, 32 years ago. In the Japanese experimental film scene in those days, Takashi Ito's structural film *SPACY* attracted much interest. But it was unpopular among my classmates; they kind of thought such structural films were self-referential and had no future. People's interest was much more focused on Shirouyasu Suzuki's diary films or private films confessing personal problems. Being influenced by this, I also thought of making a film out of my personal, daily life, but I was never attracted to the idea of diary films or private films that focused on the limited, private realm. Both private and public elements, once they are shown in films, are processed as equivalent images. Isn't it then difficult to distinguish them? Jonas Mekas's diary films showed the filmmaker's social reality as a Lithuanian refugee and nullified the commonly believed supposition that diary films only deal with limited, private topics. An individual exists in relation to others within a social network and there are no individuals whose existence is limited to the private sphere. Individuals thus lead a socialized existence, and there is no point distinguishing between the private and the public.

The subject matter depicted in films can be anything. I just want to work with the camera; this feeling is stronger than the desire to shoot specific subjects. Everyday life materials are often shown in my work because I had a sudden urge to shoot with the camera. It wasn't that I witnessed something extraordinary happening and decided to shoot — objects give me an excuse to work with the camera.

Hiroko Komatsu's work appears in my videos, I inserted it thinking it would connect well with other shots. I don't see videos semantically; her work and streetscapes don't suit well in terms of meaning. I see videos as series of images. If the shots connect as images, the semantic relationships don't matter. That's my attitude.

My videos are edited in such a way that private and public spaces are intertwined. I don't have a clear concept before filming, but if there is a consistent element, it's that I walk intensely. Since I started photography, I've been thinking that the creation of videos is only possible by walking. Even if you haven't come up with an idea, you can shoot something by walking. This concept of shooting while walking makes private and public spaces equivalent, in the sense that both are places I frequent.

You asked a question about autobiographical elements in my works. I think my videos are made up of accumulations of the experiences of walking around — walking is to experience places. I don't direct or stage scenes, so in that sense, I can say autobiographical or empirical elements are strongly reflected in my work.

To repeat, there is no border between the public and private in videos. No border between images and reality, either; it's in the nature of videos to invalidate such borders. They rip meanings away from spaces and whether they are private or public doesn't make a difference. Every shot is equivalent.

People tend to think social and political structures create the public while private spaces are detached from this, which is not true. For example, families function in capitalist society as factories to reproduce labor, and in this sense, the private is inseparable from the production process in capitalism. Isn't it impossible to distinguish between the public and private in these terms? The belief that free, private space exists is a trick propagated by capitalist society. People eat and sleep in order to reproduce labor, and even recreation and relaxation are incorporated as a part of the production process of capital. We are cogs in a wheel that operates 24 hours. Both public and private spaces are controlled by the logic of capital.

How important is post-production in your video work? Have you ever worked in collaboration with editors? How much time do you take to complete a video? What was the process of creation and editing of *Elvis the Positive Thinking Pelvis* and *Dead Stick Landing*?

Elvis the Positive Thinking Pelvis and *Dead Stick Landing* were made to some extent in collaboration with editors. My previous videos were unedited and I didn't know how to edit digitally, so I needed their advice. Shots in my previous work were extremely short — so it might've been the influence of collaboration with editors — these works are composed of fairly longish shots. They have an easy, comfortable feeling, which is very beautiful; there is no structural disruption, either. These are the differences from my previous work. The roughness diminished and delicate sensations inherent in my videos emerged. When working with others, an unexpected part of yourself will be discovered. I am being repetitive, but when making work that is unedited, you can't avoid the constraints of actual temporal contexts and so unedited images tend to have a monotonous rhythm. By introducing editing, shots are released from actual temporal contexts, and editing gives a more complex rhythm: you can connect shots that have different rhythms. But it doesn't mean I've given up on non-editing. I've been thinking of making one like that again. The excitement you feel when shooting material for non-edited work — it's a strange feeling of tension that's incomparable. You can't feel the same exultation when preparing material for edited works.

I spend about a month or two on shooting and editing. I want to create in quantity rather than spend too much time on each work. Degree of perfection is of lesser importance than presenting up-to-date feelings. I'm interested in Godard's agitation-propaganda films in the 1970s or more recently Jonas Mekas's "365 Day Project" — works that seemingly capture the contemporary spirit of the times.

> Can you talk more about sound and music? Is it possible to apply punk to image makings? What is punk for you? What is punk in photography, today?

Punk is an attitude, said Sex Pistols manager Malcolm McLaren. Punk has nothing to do with issues of performing technique; it's an attitude. It raises the question of how you commit yourself to the world.

Punk declared that performance techniques don't matter and welcomed musicians who couldn't play any instruments. Listening to their music played with off-key guitars, I came to realize that the instrument was not there only to be played according to the Western scale. Anything goes — that's punk, and through it I discovered plural perspectives, that there were scales other than the Western ones. This discovery was a big shock, because until then I'd only played regular scales on a properly tuned guitar. I discovered that things have multiple viewpoints. For example, the drummer of the British band AMM — this was not a punk band, though — didn't play the drums but just rubbed the surface of snare drums and cymbals with his sticks, which was very beautiful. It taught me that there are no rules in playing instruments.

In addition, punk was groundbreaking because it linked itself to the history of underground music in the 1960s and '70s. Artists spoke in interviews about the influence of the Stooges, MC5 and Velvet Underground. I was surprised that they were forthright about their historical connection with earlier musicians while many rock bands overemphasized their originality. I learned that music is created within a historical dimension, and since then, I've started listening to different kinds of music. It's important to associate yourself with history. When I started photography, I was always thinking about how to link myself to the history of photography, how to interpret it.

To your question "is it possible to apply punk to image-making?" I would think it is possible and also necessary because punk is anger. Expression with no fundamental anger doesn't interest me. As a teenage punk listener, I was constantly angry, and perhaps I still am. There are too many things you feel enraged about living in Japan. In that sense, I am still a punk.

Rock in the late '70s had already become conventionalized. Rock musicians' anti-establishment statements and behavior sounded to me like a mere commercial attitude. Musicians like Boston and Journey (they were called industrial rock in Japan) and music produced in studios after rehearsals had become mainstream. It was a capitalization of rock. After the success of Fleetwood Mac and the Eagles, 10-million-record sales became average, so the bourgeoisie took the chance to develop it as a new industry and customized it into a business. Hippie bands that were singing revolution in the late '60s like Chicago and The Doobie Brothers were the first to industrialize. I remember it was around that time the American revolutionary Jerry Rubin adapted to these conditions and built his reputation as a businessman.

Punk music after the Sex Pistols had already become commercial and smelt of money, but New York punk musicians such as Johnny Thunders, Richard Hell, Suicide, and The Dead Boys were all wonderful. When Johnny Thunders played "Pipeline," all the instruments had atonal, off-key, and inaccurate rhythm. Their bad technique didn't bother me. I rather felt it was more real than rock played perfectly. They deviated from convention; everyone was sick and tired of over-produced rock.

A lot of Japanese punk bands had members wearing nazi swastika armbands and I asked them why. I remember their explanation was the older, hippie generation was offended by them. Hippie band musicians who were older than me used to do boring MC (master of ceremonies) performances on stage, saying "Everyone, drink beer and enjoy" before starting. I used to wonder why I had to enjoy or relax while living in such an insipid era. There was even a band that asked the audience from the stage, "Do you love each other?" I was fed up with love, peace, and the kind of society advocated by hippies. What they called love was nothing more than being exploited to make profits. Armbands with swastikas seemed more cool than these tedious MCs with their stale clichés. Hippies did business with "love." Compared with their love and peace, punks' hate and war sounded more authentic. Their armbands with swastika symbols showed anger and destructive power against the existing order. If they had destructive attitudes against the reality we lived in, being nazis or communists didn't seem so bad to me.

Everything had become too formalized — I had that feeling, and I guess I wasn't the only one. The Ministry of Education organized rock concerts and the Beatles' songs were adopted in school textbooks. Rock had become rapidly commercialized and bands that had raged against the world disappeared one after the other. The disco I was playing in with my band used to be a place where people took toluene and become really wild. But disco music gradually took over and people preferred dancing all together to predetermined steps rather than taking narcotics and going wild by themselves. Even in a place like discos where people got rid of frustrations from their daily life, formalized, homogeneous steps, anduniformity were forced upon us.

Yoshio Hayakawa, a member of the rock band Jacks once said that he had so many things to say or sing that he had no spare time to gain performance skills. I read his comment as he just wanted to start singing as soon as possible, so he didn't have time to practice. Jacks' performances were insane and their music was on the brink of collapse, but it was because they rejected singing and performance skills acquired through practice. Hayakawa's attitude was to speak with his own words despite being immature. The urge for singing was stronger than the fear of being considered inadequate. Isn't this irrepressible nature — in other words, the spirit of punk — important?

The invention of digital photography allowed anyone to take pictures. Acquisition of skills is no longer necessary. If you want to express something, you can immediately do it. The same is true about music that is nowadays largely played by computers. One of the reasons why I started photography was that I thought it wouldn't take much time to acquire technique. If you aimed at mastering skills, you would soon be old. Now when the technologies are highly developed, you need to have a punkish, alternative sensibility rather than trying to become a virtuoso.

In the text written for your photo book *Ectoplasm Profiling,* you used the word "communist." I felt this word functioned as the most powerful, controversial sign in the whole book. What's the meaning of this word for you? What's the role of ideology when you create artworks especially in the aesthetic choices you make? What's the meaning of "communism" to you?

Every revolutionary is condemned to death, said Sergei Nechaev, and it was Vladimir Lenin's words that revolutionaries are "the dead on holiday" (they are destined to die). The goal of communist society was the extinction of nation, ethnicity, and class. And according to Lenin, the communist party anticipated a world in which all these values would disappear and it would achieve, in advance, the society yet to come. Nechaev's comment introduced above implied that revolutionaries, already being dead, were prepared for their death. What Nechaev and Lenin tried to say was that the communist party, as both revolutionary and vanguard party, anticipated its death or disappearance, and that it materialized these values in the present reality.

Photographic art transforms existing objects into "things of the past." The moment objects are photographed they become remnants of the past. This is a principle of photography. Therefore, the things you see in pictures testify to their non-existence. Isn't photography the art that demonstrates the non-existence of photographed objects? Photographs record the existence of things in the past and also materialize their non-existence. As communists materialize the death of self or nation, photography materializes the disappearance of objects. Materialization of death or non-existence — this is what the communist and photographer share in common, I think.

Photography fits naturally with the idea of death or non-existence. Doesn't the art that captures "something which existed in the past, and is no longer there," resemble a ghost? It takes existing beings toward nirvana. If revolutionaries are the dead on holiday, revolution is a call from the dead. Likewise, photography is a call from the world of the dead. Revolution and pho-

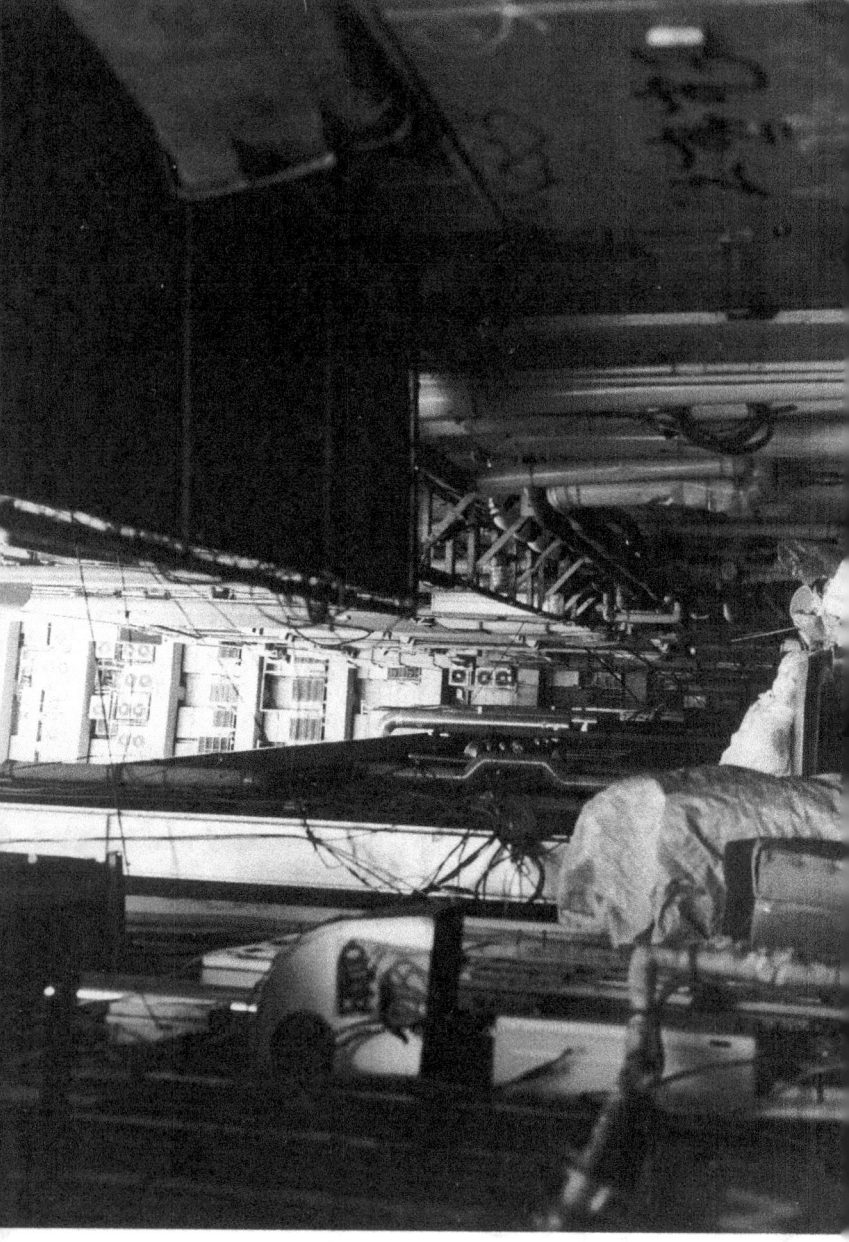

tography approximate to death or non-existence: photographs that imprint the trace of non-existing objects resemble death, or in particular, corpses. Corpses, too, exist while they materialize the absence of their owners.

When the Russian Social Democratic Labour Party split up, the leftist group led by Lenin was the minority, but he named his own group Bolshevik, the majority. The name came, I guess, from their pride that despite the numbers they represented they were the true proletariat. But if you literally interpret the word "majority," the real majority of human beings are the dead, not the living. The existence of the dead might have occurred unconsciously to Lenin's mind, and so he compared revolutionaries with the dead on holiday. For Lenin, the proletariat could have been a class of the dead. If revolutionaries were really destined to die, the seizure of power that the Bolsheviks sought would mean that power was gained by dead or ghostly figures. Existing communists anticipate their own death — this is exactly the same as the principle of photography that turns everything photographed into corpses.

Aesthetics are always determined by existing ideologies. There are no genuinely beautiful things. Our perception of beauty is always influenced by ideology and thus we feel beauty looking at something.

Photographers have their own styles. Through each individual form of expression they reveal how they see the world. For photographers-to-be, establishing a style is the first challenge that they have to deal with. Photographers always demonstrate their attitude of being-in-the-world, so once their style is established, it's not easy to change. Some photographers constantly change their style, but I don't agree with that.

Having your own style is to doubt what the media defines as beautiful. Consider the idea of beauty propagated by the media, for example, cherry blossoms and Mount Fuji in Japan; landscapes are treated as aesthetically attractive, consumable objects and brought under the umbrella of commercialism. This kind of aesthetic covertly supports the ideology of capitalism, so artists who choose their own style should be critical of this kind of ideology.

Looking at Parisian landscapes, some people are genuinely moved and say they look exactly the same as in tourist photos. But this happens because they are deeply influenced by the images created for advertising before actually seeing the place. It's a brainwashed view. And the role of tourist pictures is to conceal the real Paris that has economic, ethnic, religious conflicts behind a veil of beauty; therefore, tourist pictures side with bourgeois ideology. Having your own style doesn't mean unconditional affirmation of beauty, but to resist beauty manipulated by ideology.

What Walter Benjamin meant by the term "the politicization of aesthetics" was at the core of communist art. Communists must scrutinize all aesthetics and examine the ideologies hidden behind them. Every aesthetic conceals an ideology; without it, aesthetics can't exist.

For example, Italian Futurism declared that war was beautiful which meant an affirmation of modern technology. Airplanes and artillery invented by new technologies glorified war — the atomic bomb was an extreme example. These weapons of mass destruction were handled by remote control, so soldiers could avoid witnessing their enemies. Also these weapons created by modern technologies were very photogenic. Their attractive appearances in photographs or films were essential for the wars that occurred from the twentieth century onward. Photogenic images were necessary to conceal bourgeois ideology existing behind war.

Photography doesn't represent beauty; it is a medium that captures perspectives that enable beauty. It shows the structures that beauty is based upon, the milieux in which beauty is fulfilled. I don't usually use close-up techniques because they obscure the context in which objects exist. Here is a beautiful flower, and if you get closer to it, taking a nice photo is of course easy. But the beauty of this picture is made possible by the environment where the flower blooms, which is not shown. For example, if this flower were in Auschwitz, it wouldn't be simple to say this flower was beautiful. Close-ups are effective in capturing beautiful images because they conceal the contexts that objects are surrounded by.

As Karl Marx said, communism is a process, not a goal to be achieved, and there is no end point in my photographs and videos. All my work remains in process and is never completed. If there is a completion, it will only occur on my death.

The urban landscape became the greatest subject in Masao Adachi's film *A.K.A. Serial Killer.* Has the work of Adachi ever inspired your video work? Is it still possible to use landscape as an ideology? Can landscape photography become a new frontier of political photography? How do you think contemporary urban landscape influences people's behavior? Is there a link between photography, landscape, and even crime? Do photography and terrorism share something in common?

I saw *A.K.A. Serial Killer* when I was twenty. No stories, no actors — I was surprised to know that you could make films only with landscape images. This film relied on sheer imagination about the landscapes that Norio Nagayama, the executed prisoner, might have seen, and it must have been the power of the images that conveyed such a strong sense of reality. Films can be made only with images, without stories or words. The details of the backstreet landscapes in Aomori and the field of sunflowers and apples shot through a taxi windscreen overwhelmed me. I was convinced then that you just need details in film, nothing else.

I came to know later that *A.K.A. Serial Killer* was made based on Masao Matsuda's landscape theory (*fūkei-ron*). Unlike prior political documentary films, it has no emotional or humanistic elements. The music by Masahiko Togashi and Mototeru Takagi has a rather sentimental touch, but basically the film aims to dismiss emotion and humanism from the screen.

Matsuda, the producer of this film wrote, "It was because landscapes were conceived more than anything else as "the power" that confronts us. Norio Nagayama must have fired his gun in order to tear those landscapes apart. The power of the state would boldly destroy them and build instead, the Tōmei Expressway, for example. At the very moment we enjoy a pleasant drive, "the power captures us and the landscape puts us under a spell." In capitalist society, everything is transformed into a monotonous landscape; Nagayama's anger that he could only express by committing crimes was no exception. So if you fight against this capitalist ideology through emotion, your struggle will be easily absorbed and dissipated in the landscape. In Japan in the 1960s, emotional approaches were accepted as relatively mainstream. In order to theoretically justify the armed demonstrations, confronting the shields of riot police with planks of wood or iron pipes, people defended themselves saying, "We project our ourselves onto the shields of the riot police." It was common in those days that political thinking took an emotional form; the existentialist questions concerning protesters' selves were crucial in dealing with political tasks. Emotions were nothing but a social construction created by environments or systems. This way of confronting power only results in being swallowed up by that power. The struggle that is motivated by emotion in capitalist society will be consumed by the system.

A.K.A. Serial Killer captured inhuman landscapes that reminded me of life after death. The landscapes in the film reject any hint of a humanistic approach. Details of the landscape are accumulated so that this film reveals a world where people have been expelled. Matsuda wrote that emotions are detached from political struggle and only landscape remains. This was said as a criticism of the inhumanity of capitalist society, but it also describes the essence of film. As capitalism has transformed people into the commodity we call the labour force, film has turned human beings into a mere detail of landscape.

A.K.A. Serial Killer portrayed landscape in a way alienated from human emotion or feeling. As a landscape film, this work is still stimulating; landscape films or photography still have some potential, I think.

In Tokyo, the moment you exit from a ticket barrier, you are exposed to a flood of product commercials displayed on monitor screens everywhere. On trains you hear endless lectures about approved behavior: please offer your seat to disabled passengers; if you find someone who is in trouble, help them, etc. If you live in a society like this, it must impact your consciousness in several ways.

At rail stations, you hear announcements all day saying that the safety of passengers is prioritized. You hear this type of nonsense so often that you end up feeling irritated whenever you hear the word "safety." Train announcements euphemize "violence" into "trouble between passengers," and "suicide" into "fatal accident." This phenomenon is connected with the very Japanese notion that public transport should always offer pleasant, comfortable service — an idea that I call leisure fascism. There are small monitor screens in every train carriage and they endlessly play silly footage that exhorts people to have fun. If people are constantly exposed to such phoney messages all the time, they end up going mad. If you switch on the TV, you'll see a flood of product commercials that encourage you to seek a better quality of life. At rail stations you are forced to endure droning monologues telling you the importance of passenger safety and mutual help, while on the street you constantly receive the message that human happiness in capitalist society is achieved by continually buying things. No wonder crime occurs frequently. If you look at the number of advertising signboards in my pictures, nobody would want to live in such a place.

Terrorism, photography, and films are all deeply related on a fundamental level. The principle of terrorism is to take the minimum action in order to create maximum fear. This reminds me of the early film technology called phantasmagoria that cast a strong light onto a film and enlarged images projected through a lens onto screens. Or rather, terrorism is a kind of phantasmagoria, don't you think? As WalterBenjamin used the principle of phantasmagoria to explain the experience of the arcades in

Paris, terrorism can also be associated with the magical effects of phantasmagoria. A fear of terrorism is the fear of illusions created by terrorists. Recently in Japan, every time North Korea launches a missile, alerts are issued on TV telling people to hide inside large buildings, or the train network stops because of the emergency. The Japanese media is trying to create a phantasmagorical terror out of North Korean missiles. This is ideological manipulation by the Japanese government which approves of the United States' policies toward North Korea.

The reflections created by photographs are not real. By framing objects, photographs produce something different from the original. Reconstructing the framed reality thus creates some kind of phantasm. For example, Tokyo is not all chaotic as you see in my pictures; there are tidier, nicer places, too. But an intensive shoot of these chaotic places allows me to reach an alternative sense of reality. This sense of reality, which is different from the actual Tokyo, resembles the phantasms that terrorists create. The fact that they are actually phantasms gives images a strangely intensified sense of reality. Amplified images acquire a stronger sense of reality. Terrorism, photography, and films all have phantasmagorical aspects in common. Also, terrorists manipulate violence and information. In order to effectively notify people of their activity, they choose the best sites for their publicity and repeatedly carry out suicide bombings or hijacks. This resembles the way that capitalism advertises products. We are under the onslaught of commercial terrorism on a daily basis.

For terrorists, phantasmagorical images are nothing but a means to achieve the goal of raising fear around the world. On the other hand, photographers and filmmakers are haunted by amplified images seen in the phantasmagoria. For them, the images are a goal, not a means; they end up living within the images they have created rather than in reality. Terrorists may also use images as their means, but they will eventually become drowned in them. But both photographers and terrorists are haunted by images.

You said you have done only a few exhibitions in Japan but many in Europe. As a European, I consider your work to be some of the most rigorous and important that has appeared since the conceptual Becher School. Reflecting on the potential influence of your work (including your writing, not only your photographs and videos), I feel that your contribution to photography is actually far more significant than the Becher School itself: 1) Your black and white photos introduced the concept of visual noise and accumulation of information into photography, and achieved a completely new way of composition and relation to space. For photographers, space and framing cannot be related in the same way after seeing your black and white images of Tokyo. 2) You invented a totally new approach to video. Your video work questions the nature of narration with a completely new direction and dimension. 3) *Z-Trash Diary* explored a further dimension in image-making. Thus, you explored new, powerful possibilities in at least three ways using different media.

If your contribution to the history of photography becomes more acknowledged, what changes do you think will occur in image making in the future and people's awareness of photography? What makes an image contemporary? What is a contemporary image, for you? Does the concept of contemporary image mean anything to you, or not?

I consider photography to be an essentially *punctum*-like medium to use Roland Barthes's term. Excessive details that resist simple coded messages accumulate and create photographs. In Japan, since the nuclear accident and the Tōhoku earthquake, photography has been treated predominantly as a tool to document and convey social messages. If my work were to be more acknowledged, people would pay more attention to the excessive details in pictures that have been disregarded, and understand an alternative mode of photography that goes beyond social codes. Photographs are more than messages or illustrations conveniently added for the purpose of explanation.

Images are illusions. They have no substance; that's why they attract us with a strange fascination. Only when images are tied to social codes and become convincingly real, can you relate images and the contemporary. Social codes transform images into equivalence with illustrations, something explainable. If you look at images as a reflection of the real, you fail to notice their phantasmagorical fascination and fetishisms. Images are incomprehensible. They remain unknown forever and fascinate us.

Languages and currencies, just like photographs, offer images. Things that are real lie beyond the reach of humans. Without images, people can't access objects. What emerges through an image is reality. We are trapped in a sea of images and there is no escape.

In order to understand contemporary life, images are thus necessary. But straightforward understanding is not easy, because images always accompany phantasmagorical illusions and bias. There is no image that you can easily share with others; we all perceive them differently. People conceive contemporary life differently. Understanding the contemporary is not as simple as considering it through the simple term "contemporary image." In addition, images are also produced by ideological manipulation. If fascists and communists both see contemporary Japan, I'm sure they will hold completely opposite views. If such an image universally understood in the population exists, it must be one controlled by capitalist society.

How did you meet Takuma Nakahira? How was it like to film him in Osaka? What is the most important lesson that young photographers can learn from him? What is his heritage for photographers of younger generations?

I have known Takuma Nakahira's work since I was a student. His pictures were good, but his writing also fascinated me. They were rather Kafkaesque, saying what was important for photography was not "I" but the world, and so I was deeply impressed.

When I went to film him in Osaka, I thought his posture holding the camera was very sculptural. It reminded me of Alberto Giacometti's sculptures.

Japanese photography is often very autobiographical. Artists who work in "I-photography" (*shi-shashin*) often don't understand that our identity is a social construction. There is no identity that precedes our existence, whereas people tend to think that we are able to determine our identity on our own. Nakahira's photos have a potential power to destabilize this kind of idea in which our identity is something innate and inevitable. His photos and texts make us believe that our existence consists of the world and we are merely its component.

Nakahira's approach has not yet fully influenced young Japanese photographers, I think. The influence of emotional pictures such as Daido Moriyama's seems to be stronger. Many people still think that photographers' aesthetics should be predominant.

What about the political background of your generation? Do you think your generation has some common political background? In your life and creative aspect, how has your political awareness developed over the years? How did you become a political individual? How long did it take? Would you have different political views if you were not an artist?

The people of my generation have a strong bourgeois sense of humanism. On March 11, 2011, the Tōhoku (or Northeastern Japan) earthquake damaged the nuclear power plants. Northern Japan had been a domestic colony where the former farmers mobilized from the region were used to provide a steady supply of proletarian labor for industry. The bourgeoisie had deliberately created a social and economic gap in the society so that they could pursue their profits by taking advantage of this situation. Unlike Western Japan, where commercial centres are scattered around, the Tōhoku district had a geographical disadvantage as there was no other trade partner than Tokyo. The power balance between the regions was obvious; Tōhoku was

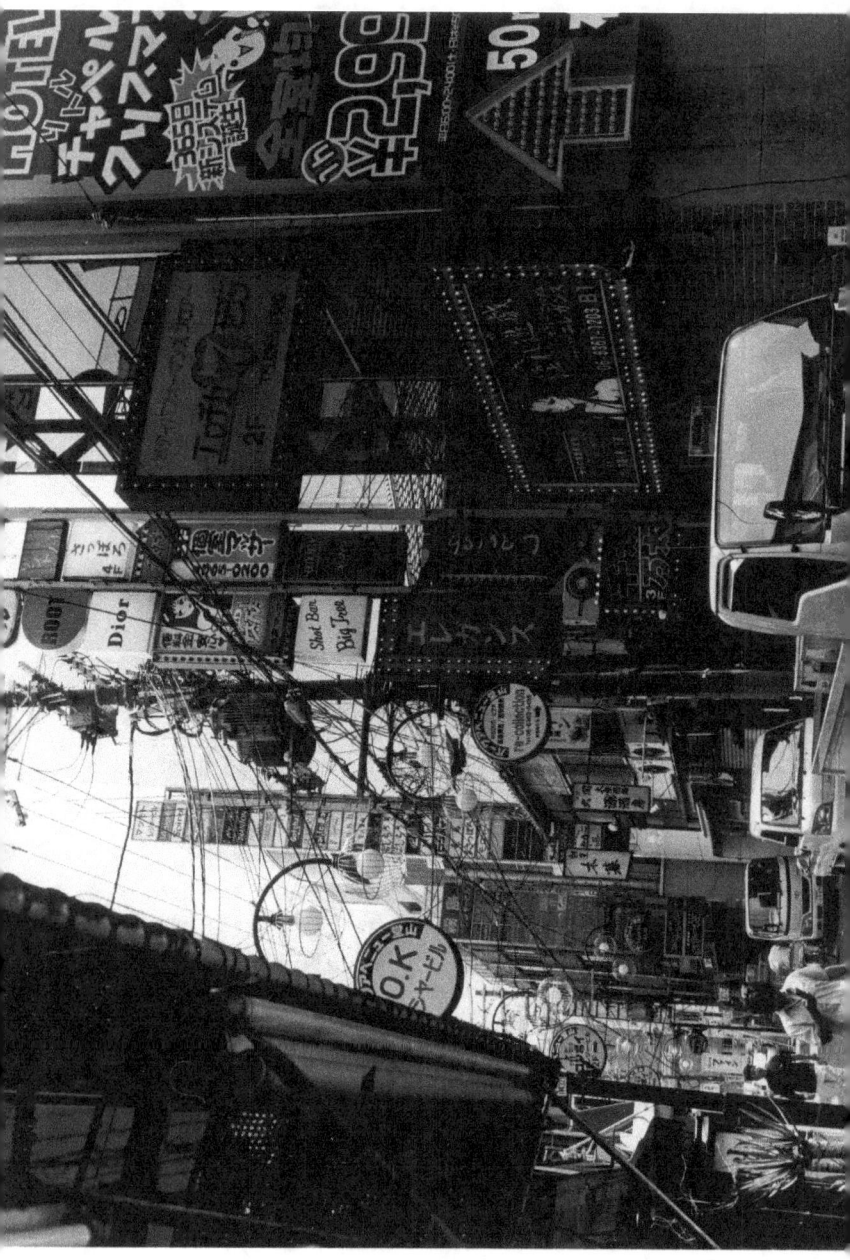

destined to be colonized by Tokyo. My guess is, probably the difference in agricultural systems — double-crop and single-crop farming — also had an impact, but the economic relationship between Tokyo and Tōhoku was obviously unequal.

Tōhoku used to be an agricultural region. During the Meiji Restoration the Japanese government mobilized native farmers into a workforce for the industrializing society. In order to secure the labor necessary for industry, they destroyed farming communities and the farmers who used to be deeply connected to their land became penniless proletarian workers. Tōhoku was thus treated as a labor pool. When capitalists moved to Southeast Asia to exploit cheaper labor there, Tōhoku was deserted and the poverty remained. In the 1970s the politicians of the Liberal Democratic Party (LDP) tried to redistribute wealth into Tōhoku and other areas, and invested taxpayers' money into the development and improvement of the infrastructure of the region. The nuclear power plants were also introduced into Tōhoku under the same pretext: redistribution of wealth and revitalization of the region. It provided the best chance for the Tōhoku area, because local areas could receive huge subsidies from the government and a major electricity company.

The comfortable lives of people in Tokyo have been built on this sacrifice. The LDP government introduced risky nuclear power plants into Tōhoku under plausible pretexts, but when the disaster hit the area, nobody worried about the structural problems of capitalist society. They just chanted hypocritical slogans such as "Go, Tōhoku!" or "Let's be united!" I personally think the destruction of the Fukushima Daiichi Nuclear Power Station and the widespread diffusion of radioactivity in Japan was Tōhoku's revenge, a kind of curse, for being colonized over the years. When the reactors exploded, many people determined to leave the country to protect their families. But I thought how dare they do so after having had the benefits of a comfortable life made possible by Tōhoku's sacrifice. The prosperity of Japan had been brought about by the exploitation of domestic colonies and the Third World. After exploiting them for so many years, you want to survive the radioactivity? I don't really understand.

I almost wondered what else was left for Japanese people except being exposed to radiation as their fate.

There are some people among the artists of my generation whom I think share my political background, and their attitudes are also anti-humanistic. Bourgeois humanism conceals all political issues. However, many photographers, the best known example being the members of Magnum Photos, are motivated by their humanistic convictions. So I think that not many artists share my political view.

I'm from a minority class in Japan, so for me, politics and private life have always been inseparable. Quite a few people in this country reflect on art, private life, and politics as separate issues, but I really don't get it. Perhaps they do this because in Japan the truth is often made invisible under euphemistic expressions. For example, "salaried workers" were once called "salaried slaves" in newspapers. I think this latter phrase is very accurate but this expression is now politically incorrect. The word "working class" is no longer in use; we have all become "citizens." This word "citizen" has made me feel uncomfortable since my childhood. It sounds too flat. From the word "working class" you can imagine real working people, but the word "citizen" sounds too abstract to actually feel their existence. My generation grew up in an environment where the essence of things wasn't twisted by such deceitful phrases. This kind of linguistic environment has cultivated my political awareness over the years.

If I were not an artist, my political awareness would still be the same. If I suddenly became a millionaire or something, it might change, but I doubt it. It's not easy to abandon the values you grew up with even when the environment changes.

On slides: *Elvis the Positive Thinking Pelvis* can be considered an interesting, complex approach to slide screenings. You also did some exhibitions using slides in the past. How important are slides for you? How did you develop the idea of slide exhibitions? What is the difference between using slides and videos?

I did a slide exhibition at a gallery in Ginza a few years ago. I used twenty slide projectors put randomly on the floor and projected images onto the ceiling and the walls. I did a performance there, too: I shot the portraits of the visitors who had paid 5,000 yen with a Polaroid camera. Until then, my photographs had been displayed in galleries almost all in the same way — 60×50-sized pictures were shown on the walls in vertical lines of 4 pictures each. So this slide exhibition gave a very spectacular impression.

When I was invited to screen my slides, I intuitively felt I didn't want to use digital projectors. The analogue feel you get from slide projectors seemed to be more attractive. I just thought it would be nice to hear their rattle when changing slides one after the other, but I wasn't feeling nostalgic for film photos. The projectors constantly rattle flashing lights on and off at the venue — I thought it would be a beautiful sight.

I want to show my videos in the same way. I'm thinking of bringing several video projectors to a venue and projecting images.

I like the expanded cinema that was in vogue from the 1960s to the '70s in experimental film circles. They used multiple projectors to show images on a screen, or did loop screenings. For example, in Annabel Nicolson's *Reel Time* holes were punched into the reel of film using a sewing machine. Takahiko Iimura's *Dead Movie* used two projectors — one with a black film leader looped and another operating with transparent celluloid aimed at each other. This type of film installation interests me; you could say I was never tempted to make film installations without them.

Thinking back, the slides in those days had a bit of a nostalgic feeling but by using digital videos, such sentimentality can probably be avoided. Kenneth Anger named his box set of films *Magick Lantern Cycle*. I also consider my videos to be magic and am hoping to create the lantern-like atmosphere that slides have.

Digital videos differ from slides in being the latest technology and are therefore more inhuman. They have an inorganic feeling. But at the same time, the latest technology is the very thing that creates magic. The latest technology does this, I think; just like electric guitars in the '50s, the latest technology then, exposed the voodoo magic of African American blues music. Mellotrons or analogue synthesizers, the latest invention in the '70s also, involved something ethereal. I remember how the Beatles used a mellotron in "Strawberry Fields Forever"; it was very magical. Videos have a new power which is different to the nostalgic associations of slides.

Hiroko Komatsu kindly told me she felt something ghostly in my videos. I believe a magic lantern-like eeriness dwells in the latest technology.

What is it like using an LCD screen instead of a viewfinder? What kind of digital cameras do you use, and how do you choose them? What is the biggest limitation of digital cameras?

I still haven't gotten used to LCD display. Unlike the viewfinder on film cameras, you can't look through it and become one with the camera. I always feel somewhat uncomfortable when I use it. But it may work better that way. The LCD display makes me feel that I'm operating the camera, not taking pictures. I don't feel I'm a photographer; I become the operator of the camera.

I'm using a Ricoh GR digital camera. Someone in charge of GR asked me to use it as part of a sales promotion. Recently I have also used an iPhone camera; the zoom function is handy. I'm thinking of making something with iPhone video footage, probably around next year.

I had a wonderful opportunity to see for the first time in many years, films by Michael Snow, James Benning, Toshio Matsumoto, Takashi Ito, and Jun'ichi Okuyama. They still inspire me. Film has a depth in its frames, and strong texture, which is lacking in digital videos. In short, digital videos are lighter in texture and their pictures are also flatter than film.

However, digital videos are easy to edit and have greater advantage in terms of cost. I use two hours of footage to make a piece of work that lasts about twenty minutes. If I used film, it would cost a lot more.

Digital video definitely has a lighter, flatter texture than film, but this lightness can be its advantage. The cost issue could be involved, but Frederick Wiseman and James Benning have also shifted to digital.

A limitation of digital video is that the image is so clear that it only creates a flat impression. The material texture found in analogue film images is also absent. This is the limitation of digital videos, but I repeat again, it can also be its positive point.

The train in the Lumière brothers' *The Arrival of a Train at La Ciotat* is not real, nor material, either. It's an enlarged image produced on the screen by a projection of light. Although people knew it was only an image, they panicked and ran away, probably because they sensed a materiality different from real trains — for example, particles of film appeared with the image of the advancing train. The audience would have seen enlarged film particles on the screen for the first time. They could have felt that these particles or even the film itself was going to attack them.

Compared to this kind of experience, digital images are just too clear. They look clearer than reality because the grainy texture is eliminated in digital videos images? Is it possible to express the film texture we found in *The Arrival of a Train at La Ciotat* in digital?

To create grainy texture using media that don't have this materiality…. I am interested in the material texture of cameras and film, which are excluded in digital videos. Digital media seek a purer reproduction of reality and therefore won't accept the "impurities" of film cameras. The abnormally strong urge for accurate reproduction of reality, as seen in the inventions of 4K and 8K cameras, denies noise and materiality. The images captured by 4K or 8K cameras are no longer a reproduction of reality; reality can't be this clear, flat, or beautiful.

The beauty of digital cameras resembles an image of heaven I used to have as a child. Beautiful images floating in flat space…. Can digital videos resemble ghosts? Ghosts scare people because they appear in the real world without having a material base. The possibility of digital videos, if there is such a thing, lies in a ghostliness of this kind.

And if some kind of materiality could take place in digital videos, it would be ghostly. We know ghosts have no material substance, but we cannot help perceiving them anyway. No matter how much you search, you won't be able to find them. The less your chance of finding something, the more you look for it. Its sheer absence makes you seek an alternative materiality. The despair of not being able to find materiality in digital video will create a new materiality for it, I think.

Additionally, you can manipulate prints and create some effects to stimulate viewers' emotional responses to black and white photographs, but if you try the same thing with digital pictures, the results will be a joke. Emotional effects added to digital photos often end in awkward results; digital technology is not compatible with human emotion. However, this kind of inhuman quality is very attractive for me.

> Reading *Ectoplasm Profiling,* I had the feeling that your writing is slightly similar to painting. It made me think of paintings by Tsuyoshi Higashijima, for example. Have you ever used paintings? Are you interested in painting at all?

In Tsuyoshi Higashijima's paintings, line and plane elements collide and integrate within a picture. My texts are certainly chaotic and not easily resolved into a structuralized view. Higashijima seems to be a painter who attaches great importance to conflicting elements in paintings, while my texts and especially photographs and films also contain multiple discrepancies. Perhaps you can say conflicts are maintained without aiming at sublation in my texts, photographs, and films. In that sense, you are right to reference Higashijima's work by reading my texts.

I've never tried to bring painting-like effects into my black and white photographs. You may find unintentional effects, though. For instance, the foreign press once wrote that my streetscape pictures with electric wires all over the place resembled Jackson Pollock. Paintings certainly interest me, but the method that I intentionally brought into my photographs is that of film. The electric wires that look like scratched wounds come from the unconscious influence of the experimental filmmaker Stan Brakhage, and it's through Yasujirō Ozu's influence that I capture things layered against the background.

I adopted a method from painting in *Ectoplasm Profiling*, in which photographed objects are out of focus and blurred, creating an abstract feeling. All my black and white pictures are clear, sharply focused, but in this photo book I used a completely new approach. To put it simply, I wanted to introduce brush stroke-like ambiguity. *Ectoplasm Profiling* was made under the influence of collage or paintings.

My black and white photo books present each picture separately, but in *Ectoplasm Profiling* I wanted to combine multiple images with words. Various textured papers were used because I wanted viewers to experience different sensations of touch as they go through the book.

I usually check the results of digital photos shot by Ricoh GR at increased playback speed, probably played at around 0.5. The things that have been captured don't interest me much — I just like looking at a series of pictures at a faster rate like time-release films. *Ectoplasm Profiling* was made to reproduce this kind of images that reverberate on the retina.

Just before I made *Ectoplasm Profiling*, I had a chance to see the Francis Bacon exhibition in Tokyo. The images of human figures he painted: their outlines melted and metamorphosed into something else — this inspired me. I wanted to create a hazy, disquiet ambience that foreshadows objects which manifest themselves on the retina. So I decided to insert texts between photographs and make collage effects.

Ectoplasm Profiling didn't receive positive reviews in Japan, by the way. Probably because people here only saw me as a black and white photographer and they didn't get its concept of collage. It was kind of ignored completely.

How do you create texts? Do you start from an idea or does the process generate itself during writing? How did you write the text in *Ectoplasm Profiling*? Have you ever been interested in Gozo Yoshimasu's writings?

The process of writing generates the texts. I don't arrange my thoughts before I write. Sitting in front of the computer, my hands naturally move. It's a bit shaman-like; I even think so myself. But when I try to arrange my thoughts and output, my hands suddenly freeze. The same thing happens when I talk. In earlier days, I used to talk looking at notes on which I scribbled what to say, but it didn't work well. One day I stood on the stage without preparing and I could talk well. Maybe I'm shaman-like by nature?

The texts in *Ectoplasm Profiling* were also written in the same way. In 1972, there was an extreme leftist group called the United Red Army in Japan, rather like the Italian Red Brigade. When I was writing the texts for *Ectoplasm Profiling,* I was reading a book about them. So those texts were written under its influence. The United Red Army eventually declined after the lynching of group members and a gunfight with the police. Its leader Tsuneo Mori, during the interrogation of one member who was alleged to have committed espionage, thrust an ice pick into the suspect's heart saying, "If you are a real communist, you won't die." The man obviously died, but Mori concluded that he was a spy because a real communist couldn't possibly die. I read this and was very surprised to know that Mori believed that communists could transcend death.

As André Bazin wrote, photography is the detaching of objects — as if photographs are treated with preservative and given immortal life — exceeding the duration of time destined for any organic life. By being detached from moments in actual life, photographed objects gain a kind of immortality. Isn't this, in other words, transcending the death ordained for all living things?

Mori might have thought communists have immortal flesh. I guess for him communists existed in a non-human form; he didn't see them as organic and alive. He conceived communists as people who were transformed into some kind of different matter. In Dostoyevsky's *Demons,* Kirillov, who was modelled after Sergey Nechayev, said: "Go beyond death, that's the new human being." For Nechayev, who wrote that revolutionaries are people who are sentenced to death, revolutionaries were already dead and therefore death was nothing to be feared. And those who are not scared of death are not human but only organic substance. To have immortal flesh is to transcend death, so I think communist is another term that denotes something material.

Communists transform human beings who have an organic body into something more durable. As a pseudonym Stalin means "iron man"; communists were willing to become physically non-human. Aren't they similar to photographers whose job is to fixate real world objects onto photographic paper? As Mori struck the ice pick through the heart of one of his fellow members and expected him to overcome death, photographs detach objects from organic time duration and give them eternal life. In other words, their job is to pronounce organic life to be dead.

I wrote the texts in *Ectoplasm Profiling* based on my notion about the connection between photographers and communists. The former detach photographed objects from the organic cycle of time, provide preservative treatment, and give them eternal life, while the latter aim at the inorganic materiality that transcends death under the belief that real communists won't die.

Gōzō Yoshimasu's writings are good, but I prefer his pictures. His double-exposure method is epoch-making. He left films he once used for many years, and when a suitable time arrived, took them out and used them again. The fact that when he reuses films, he doesn't remember what he previously used them for, surprised me very much. I was interested in his indifference to what he had once photographed.

Yoshimasu's photographs don't record subjects; they seem to capture the traces of relationships between the artist and subjects. Therefore, his pictures strongly imprint the existence of the artist himself. Just as Jonas Mekas's films can only be categorized as Mekas's, the same is true with Yoshimasu's photographs and films.

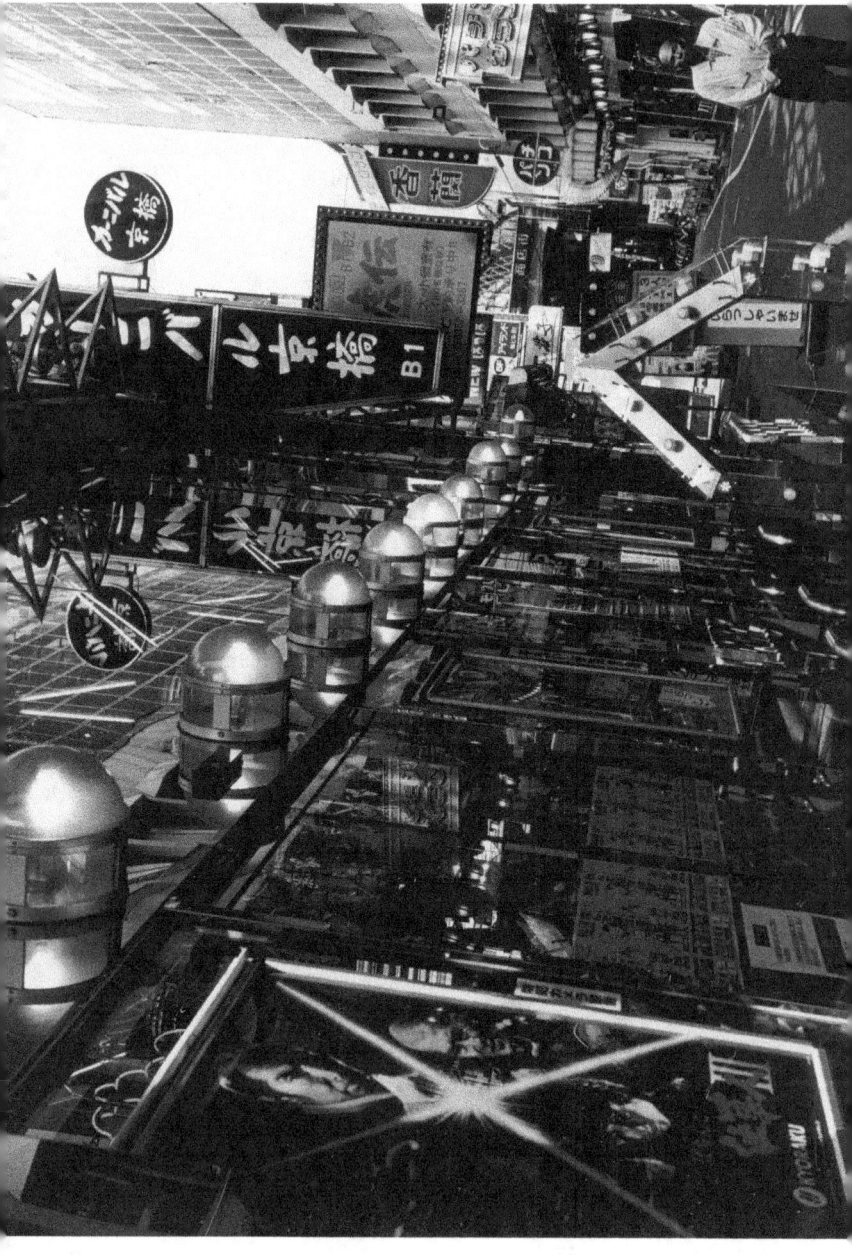

Breaking the rules of narration, subverting narration, can also be a way of making political art to some degree. TV commercials mostly use a relatively standard narrative and symbolic format. Taking an anti-narrative approach is also a political choice. Do you think of *Ectoplasm Profiling* as an anti-narrative book? Do you think that the video *Everyday XXX* and the book *Ectoplasm Profiling* share something in common, in terms of narrative style?

Film narrative has never interested me; *Ectoplasm Profiling* is an anti-narrative photo book. Photographs and films shouldn't be a slave to stories. Excessive detail in images can't be subordinated to the narrative. Accumulation of detail creates photographs, and photographs subordinated to narrative become illustrations. Around the time I started photography, I saw Ed van der Elsken's photo book shot in Paris, and the overly strong narrative that pervaded the book irritated me. The sheer details of the pictures were made invisible — it was just an explanation of young adults who were influenced by existentialism, hanging out on Saint-Germain-des-Prés. Are narratives necessary in photographs or films? Why? Subjects are shown — that's all you need.

Ethnicity, religion, class, and nation — all these are fictions. And they are very well constructed. But if you are a communist who wants to abolish these things, you have to take an anti-narrative approach. That's because these values are invented fictions.

My photographs and films are very minimal. I intended this because I thought it would reduce the risk of forging narratives in my work. When my retrospective exhibition is held in the years ahead, the venue will be filled with photographs that look more or less the same: similar type of pictures continuing from the entrance up until the exit. There will be no space for stories there.

We live surrounded by narratives. From the old ones like ethnicity and religion to those invented in the 20th century like humanism, class, and nation — many such constructions surround us. They precede our consciousness, function as super-concepts, and direct our lives. We don't tell stories; stories make us tell them. You may think you speak voluntarily, but in truth stories make you speak. Plus, they are so banal that anybody can understand. People enthusiastically tell these banal narratives as if they invented them. Repeating stories is to become their slave. People don't tell them from any kind of free will: the stories haunt them, but they tell them as if they were original. Stories thus find people who by telling, establish their identity in a community. When they're repeatedly told, the old, banal narratives create a sense of solidarity between people.

Communities are built on consensus; for example, if someone says, "This is A," everyone in the community including myself should be able to understand it. The fact that everybody can understand it is important. Photographs and films refuse to be understood by everyone, but communities are based on mutual understanding between the constituent members. Therefore, those who belong to a community hold the same ideas, feel satisfied in sharing the same thoughts with other members, and seek friendship and affirm identity there.

Stories or narratives are a device to establish mutual understanding. People believe this can help circulate the same thoughts among members of the community. Subverting stories is to see reality without the help of this device. If you look at reality without stories, you'll realize it actually consists of details that are beyond our understanding.

When people tell nationalistic stories, they assume we all naturally love the country we are born in. People consider love of one's country to be an inborn human condition although it is a fiction. These stories are taken for granted without good reason and then circulated. Communist artists who stand for abolishing nation and class should keep saying no to such narratives.

Montage is a technique that uses human nature to find meanings in combined images. In *Everyday XXX* and *Ectoplasm Profiling,* I intended to keep the shots disconnected; it's an anti-montage technique in which disconnected shots don't produce meanings. Shots next to each other just adjoin without any significance. Montage creates the illusion that disconnected images are connected; on the other hand, in both my works, disconnected images are placed next to each other — however they are unconnected. *Everyday XXX* was also made with this anti-narrative sensibility.

Have you ever planned to print *Z-Trash Diary* in book format? Or will it always be online material? Why did you decide to show your pictures on the Internet?

I'd like to publish *Z-Trash Diary* as a book, but I assume no Japanese publisher would be interested. Is there any Italian publisher that might be interested, do you think?

Z-Trash Diary would probably be a book similar to *Ectoplasm Profiling,* but the collage element would be stronger, I imagine. I am interested in collage, which in my opinion is what photography essentially is. The streetscapes of Tokyo made by patchy construction and random city planning that I shoot, look like collage work. My black and white pictures are usually displayed directly on the walls and I'm well aware of the connections in collage.

To your question "Will it always be online material?," not necessarily so. *Z-Trash Diary* happened to be online because there was nowhere else to show it. Plus, I thought that pictures taken by digital camera looked better seen through computer monitors. But digital printing technology has improved these days; I could probably show them in good print form now. My frustration about showing work on the Internet is that I can only show one picture at a time. I'd like to expand *Ectoplasm Profiling* by adding some video work and doing an exhibition.

In addition, *Z-Trash Diary* has a feeling of showing unselected pictures — a bit like showing contact prints of film photos. So some of them were rejects, some of them look obscure. My black and white photos are carefully selected, but those in *Z-Trash Diary* are different, they are more randomly chosen. But if you keep on posting both rejected and successful pictures on the Internet, the distinction between good and bad photos becomes unclear. You'll never know what is good and bad. I sometimes doubt the criteria of selecting pictures.

Looking at film photos taken a while ago, those pictures you thought were failures and you didn't show immediately after shooting, can sometimes look very good with the passage of time. A mysterious phenomenon. The more time goes by, the more interesting all pictures become. Is this a distinct quality of photography? If so, can good or bad photos really exist?

When developed prints are left inside a file box for several years, something different may be added to them. Photographic art is said to capture moments, but perhaps what has already been photographed, matures.

Wolfgang Tillmans said he was obsessed with creating "new" car images. Someone said to me that Takashi Homma created a "new vision," although I personally don't agree. A lot of photography critics are obsessed with what comes next in photography, as if we can witness a never-ending change and mutation process. In your case, you say that photography has nothing to do with becoming new or renewing critical ideas toward an idealistic future. In Italy, very naive critics and photographers exist who still think that black and white is old and colour is new. Why do people and society still need images and poets?

Nothing is older than the desire to see and experience something new. Constantly looking for new things is a most conservative psychology. For example, think of the history of photography; has photography achieved any progress since Atget? A progressive view of history that believes art must "progress" is a trap of modern society.

People who always seek something new in art, in short, consider art to be a consumer commodity. Consumption always requires new products. Capitalist society demands that we look for something new, fresh. Consumers, too, they probably feel themselves somewhat renewed by buying new products. Capitalist society has produced a kind of shopping addiction among people on a daily basis; they are convinced that they can renew their identity by consuming.

People who seek new modes of art resemble shopping-addicted patients who always have to keep buying new things. They never confront artwork properly. In capitalist society, art is treated as a series of accessories anyway. Most people see or talk about art in order to improve their image. They don't like art, they just love being involved with it. That's why they pursue new things.

I've been taking the same kind of pictures for over twenty years so people often think I'm a conservative photographer. When I showed *Ectoplasm Profiling,* people told me I had challenged something new, but nothing had changed from my previous black and white photos in terms of my method that focused on details of urban landscape. I like repetition. I am the type of person who finds pleasure in repeating routines.

It was Lou Reed who deplored the immaturity of contemporary poets by singing "The poets they studied rules of verse" in the song "Sweet Jane." This phrase makes sense when you look at the advertising slogans that flourish in Japan. The title of my video that I showed last year, *Life Is a Gift,* was taken from the Isetan department store's advertising campaign at Christmas promotion time. It's an empty slogan that has no other message than to encourage people to buy Christmas gifts at Isetan. Nowadays advertising agencies have become like poets in Japan. The Japanese rock band Zunou Keisatsu translated Hermann Hesse's poem "Leb wohl, Frau Welt" in their song "Farewell, Mrs. World" and sang: "The world lies in junk/ We used to love it so much/ Now Death no longer/ Scares us that much/ The world always gave us love and tears/ But we have no dream about your magic any more." And the lyrics continue: "We are fed up with your weeping and laughter" and they say farewell to Mrs. World. We need poets because the world has become a rubbish dump. But poets in capitalist society can no longer admire Mrs. World who was once beautiful. As you wrote, Marco, people are "obsessed with creating 'new' car images." The magic of capitalist society has already gone. What's the point of contributing new images to the world or offering beautiful poems? The magic which can turn junk into gold (the lyrics above) has failed.

I think photographs are closer to prose than poetry. The function of the camera is practical; it just captures objects. Photographs have no meaning. They just show objects and lack further meaning. Because of this nonsense-ness, viewers are able to perceive various meanings. In this sense, we can say that photography encourages an allegorical way of seeing.

When you look at a photo, your eyes move as they capture its content. They keep flicking right and left trying to capture adjacent objects. Observing photographs thus essentially involves an optical movement that perceives adjoining things; the viewers shift their gaze vertically and horizontally.

Human beings cannot live without images, as I wrote earlier. I have a wish to one day go beyond the world of images and make direct contact with reality. However, images stand there as a material wall and prevent us from apprehending it. Many people live under the illusion that they are in direct contact with reality. For example, you go to the woods on a sunny day, see green leaves and think them beautiful. You think them beautiful because of the image you have in your mind about these leaves. The leaves themselves actually exist beyond the judgment of whether they're beautiful or not.

However, this realm where the adjective "beautiful" is no longer inevitable is approachable in photographs. Adjectives are almost an enemy of photography; once some adjectives are attached to images, this can create the worst type of aesthetics. Adjectives interpret images with words, which kills their own dynamics. If images inevitably exist as the reality in which people live, they should possess some material substance. Photographs strip all adjectives from the scene and present an image in material terms. The materialization of images. The important thing is to regain the material aspect, saying no to adjectives that try to represent their meanings.

Questions by Marco Mazzi (July 30, 2017)
Answers by Osamu Kanemura (September 1, 2017)

インタビュー

　ブラウベル・マキナの広角レンズがあなたの手や心身をとおして都市と出遭います。あなたのイメージをみていると、都市そのものはマキナの「内面的構造、機能、利点」を見きわめ、明らかにするために存在している、という感じを抱きます。街、自転車、車、人びと、街の景観といった外的世界は、このカメラのもつ内面的、内臓感覚的な性質、構造を明らかにするために用いられているように思われるのです。私にとっては、マキナのもつ内面的な力作用こそが、あなたのつくるイメージの真の被写体です。街の景観は真の被写体であるというよりも、カメラの構造を分析するための口実のようなものです。

　あなたの90年代のモノクロ写真がマキナで撮影されたものであることはすぐにわかります。非人間的な感覚、機械を思わせる感覚があるのです。あなたの写真には、白黒の動画作品においてさえも、機械的、非人間的な感触があるように思います。この非人間的な感覚は、写真史のなかで、とくに都市や街をとらえた写真の歴史においては、完全に新しいものであるように思われます。あなたのアプローチは絵画とは正反対のものであるとも言えるのでしょうか。

写真家は直接対象と接するわけではありません。写真家と対象の間には、必ずカメラが介入します。対象に接するには、カメラのファインダーを最初にまず覗き、ファインダーの中に対象が現れる。対象との出会いは、カメラのファインダーを通して行われます。だからわたしにとって対象の世界は、カメラを介在して現れるのです。マルコさんのいうように、マキナの「内面的構造」を通してわたしは対象を見ている。わたしが興味を持つのは、実際の街よりもカメラを通して現れる街です。

　カメラを通して現れる街に興味があるというのは、カメラの「内面的構造」を経由して現れた街に興味があるということですから、マルコさんのいうように、カメラの「内面的構造」は、わたしにとって重要な問題です。

　わたしはいつもフォーマットに興味がありました。写っているイメージよりも、イメージを四角く囲んでいるフォーマットに興味があるのです。フォーマットがあるから映像は成り立つ。寺山修司の『書を捨てよ町へ出よう』は、映像の制度を破壊するためだったのでしょうか、"何してんだよ。映画館の暗闇の中で、そうやって腰掛けてたって、何にも始まんないよ。スクリーンはいつも空っぽなんだよ"と主人公に叫ばせていましたが、わたしはそのようにイメージの中で挑発しても映像の構造や制度は壊れないのではと思っていました。カメラのフォーマットを壊さない限り、映像は壊れない。フォーマットが映像を成立させるためのぎりぎりの臨界点です。そしてフォーマットを壊すことはできませんが、臨界点ぎりぎりにまで近づくことはできるのではないか。そういう意識でカメラのフォーマットを考えています。

　わたしはペーター・クーベルカやマイケル・スノウの映像が好きです。構造映画といわれている映像です。それらの映像は通常の映画のようなイメージは持っていません。フィルムやカメラや映写機のメカニズムという映画の基本的なシステムを提示している映画です。物語やイメージよりも映像の構造を問題にしている映画ですね。それらの映像を二十代のときに集中的に見ていたので、イメージよりも構造の方に興味を持ってしまうのは、それらの映画の影響なのでしょう。

　わたしは東京という街に特別の興味はありません。街の物語を求めて東京を撮影しているわけではありません。たまたまそこに住んでいるので、どこかにわざわざ撮影に行かなくてもすぐに撮れます。撮りたいと思ったらすぐに撮れるから東京を撮っているだけです。

　写真を始めた頃は、何を撮るかよりも、いかに撮るかということに興味がありました。東京という街の内容よりも、6×7のフォーマットに切り取られた東京の街に興味がありました。実際の東京の街よりも、東京の街が6×7のフォーマットに切り取られ、写されたイメージに興奮します。街、自転車、車、人々、それが何を意味するのかということに、わたしは興味がありません。例えばネガに埃が付いていてもわたしはそれを払ったりしません。埃によって人の顔なり、看板の言葉なりが見えづらくなっても、わたしにとってそれはどうでもいいことです。むしろそれによってフィルムの存在が画面に露呈することの方が重要です。街、自転車、車、人々は、マルコさんのいうようにカメラの構造やフォーマット、フィルムの物質性を浮かび上がらせるための口実でしかありません。

　わたしがカメラのフォーマットを面白いと思うのは、現実の世界がフォーマットに切り取られたことで写ったものと写らないもの、見えるものと見えないものの二つに世界を分断してしまうことです。

　例えば対立する二つのものが最終的に一つのものに止揚されるコミュニストの唯物論的弁証法に対して、毛沢東は二つが一つになるのではなく、一つを二つに分断するのがコミュニストの正しい弁証法だと言いました。全ての物事には矛盾が存在している。物事の本質には矛盾がつねに存在しているということが、毛沢東の一分為二の論理です。対立する二つのものが物事の中につねに存在するのであり、それらを一段高いレベルで止揚させる正-反-合の弁証法ではなく、二つの対立物が合に行き着くことがないまま正-反が互いに争い続ける。合という高次のレベルが存在しない毛沢東の弁証法は、無限に対立と闘争が続く。それが毛沢東の革命理論であり、

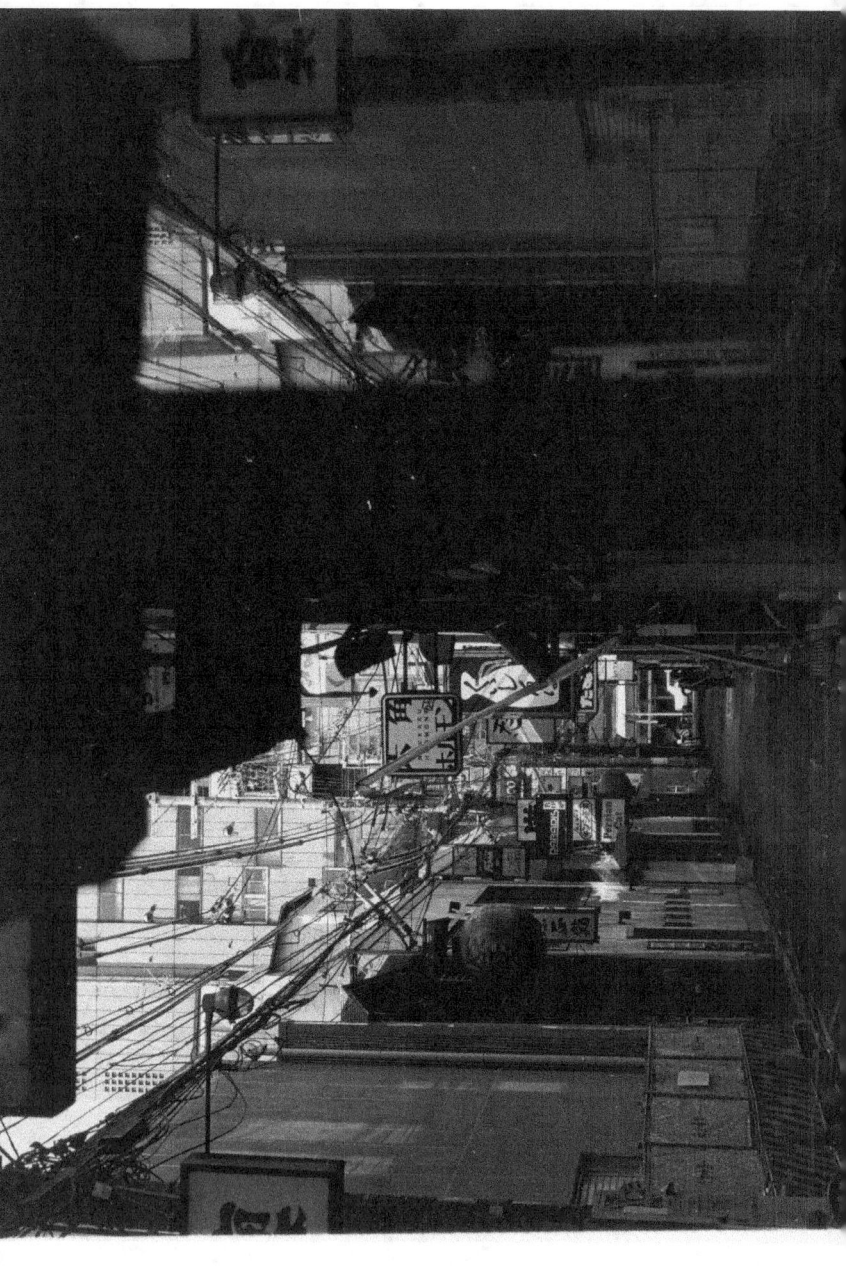

革命が成功した後も、あらゆる場所に存在するはずのスパイや階級敵の摘発を人々に対して要求するのです。

　資本の走狗を摘発する運動や、60年代の文化大革命における反革命摘発運動は、社会をつねに矛盾の状態に置いておくという毛沢東理論の現実化です。毛沢東は、階級の敵は永久に存在し、社会主義政権になってもそれは存在し続けると言いました。敵を探し続けることは、一をつねに二に分断し続けることです。それはいつまでも矛盾を作り続けることであり、社会主義政権成立という階級の矛盾が止揚されたときでさえも、更にそこに分裂を持ち込もうとする。矛盾と分裂と対立の増殖が、唯物論的弁証法の本質だと毛沢東は考えたのでしょうか。わたしはそれを読んで、一を二に割り続ける毛沢東の思想は、写真と似ているのではと思いました。

　毛沢東のイメージする革命の理想像は多分永久革命だと思いますが、彼の指導した文化大革命は、まさに着地点のないまま永続に動き続ける革命運動でした。毛沢東の考える弁証法のように、カメラのフォーマットはいつまでも世界を分断し続けます。写る世界と見える世界、写らない世界と見えない世界の両者に分断され増幅し続ける。その二つの領域は一つに止揚されることがなく、いつまでも二つの領域に引き裂かれたまま放置されるのです。

　撮影することは、見える世界よりも、見えない世界の方をより増幅させることではないでしょうか。世界を更に可視化しようとする撮影行為が、世界をますます不可視化する。世界を一枚の印画紙の中に定着させたいという写真の欲望は、定着されなかった世界を無数に生み出すのです。それは世界の不可視化であり、写真は世界をクリアにするのではなく、より不明瞭な盲目の世界に引きずり込もうとするのです。

　絵画がイメージを問題にしているなら、わたしは構造を問題にしているので、イメージを追求している絵画とは、自分はやはり違うのではないかと思います。

　わたしは子供の頃から世の中にはカメラという便利なものがあるの
に、具象画を描いている人がいるのを不思議に思っていました。カメラ
なら一秒もかからずに対象を捉えられるのに、何故わざわざ手間のかかる
ことをしているのだろうと思っていたのです。絵画についての知識がなかっ
た子供の頃の話ですから、画家によるタッチの個性とかが分からなくてそう
思っていたのですが、今でもそんな気持ちが多少あります。わたしは人間
の個性や癖に興味がない。日本の美術評論家は、写真は絵画と違って作
家の個性が見えてこないので分からないという人が多いのですが、わたし
は個性を中心に考える美術評論家の考えの方がよく分からなかった。どうし
てそんなに個性が必要なのか、個性を基準に芸術を考えるという考え方そ
のものがよく分からないのです。

　個性というのは構造が作ってしまったものではないでしょうか。構造より
も前に主体的な個性が存在していて、その個性が構造を作るのではなく、
個性よりも先に構造が先行して存在し、個性は先行された構造によって決
定される。絵画なら絵画の、写真なら写真の歴史や構造が画家や写真家
の個性を作り決定するのです。だからわたしは、表現者の個性を成立させ
る構造には興味がありますが、表現者の個性そのものにはほとんど興味が
ありません。

　いつの時代からなのでしょう。表現されたものよりも、それを表現した
人間に興味が持たれ始めたのは。写真はむしろそのような人間を抹消しよ
うとしたのではないでしょうか。アジェの時代の頃の写真、特にマクシム・
デュ・カンのようなドキュメンタリー系の写真を見ると、ほとんどみんな同じ
ように見える。けれどそれが退屈かといえば、そんなことはない。むしろ
表現者の存在が気にならないで、見ていて画面に集中できます。

　映像やヴィデオにおける人間の姿、身体について。

　あなたのヴィデオ作品をみて、人間の存在、身体の扱い方がとても興味深いと感じてきました。それらは純粋な「内的運動やノイズを発生させるもの」として用いられているように思います。一方、人間の存在や身体がより「伝統的な方法」で扱われることもあります。人間を記録する方法に何らかの変化があったのでしょうか?

　例えば、初期のスーパー8mmの作品では、あなた自身の姿や身体が映し出されていますが、これは興味深い感覚をつくりだします。あなた自身のイメージ(それから、あなたのいる部屋のイメージ)が、アーティスト本人とそれを取り囲むものについての情報を与えるからです。あるスーパー8mmの映像では、部屋の床に横たわり、カメラにむかって「バイバイ」と言う女性の姿さえ見えます。このような要素(「バイバイ」と言う女の子)は、実験映画においては斬新なものです。

　あなたのヴィデオ作品において、自伝的要素はどのような重要性をもちますか?例えば、あなたのヴィデオには、どうして奥様の作品の痕跡や光景が出てくるのでしょう?映像作品のなかに内面的、私的な空間が持ち込まれることがあるのはなぜですか?あなたにとって、公的、あるいは私的なイメージとは何を意味しますか?公的、あるいは私的な領域の区別に関して、政治的な意味や意図はあるのでしょうか?

8ミリヴィデオで撮り始めた『Everyday XXX』は、90年代の終わりの頃だったと思います。久しぶりに街で撮った自分の映像を見たら、ヴィデオカメラに録音されている街の音がうるさくて、その影響でしょうか、写っている人や車がノイズのように見えました。8ミリヴィデオカメラは自動的に同時録音されます。その録音された音を聞いていたら、東京はこんなにもうるさいのかという発見がありました。それでカメラに録音された音に興味を持ち始めたのです。そのときのわたしの撮り方は、0,5秒から1秒ぐらいの短いショットを積み重ねていく撮り方だったのですが、ショットが短いので、

録音された音も短く、とても抽象的な音になりました。具体音で音楽を作るピエール・シェフェールのミュージック・コンクレートのような感じがしましたね。

8ミリヴィデオカメラはわたしにとってそれはノイズ発生機のようでした。カメラというよりも、アンプで増幅されたエレキギターが発生させるハウリングのような気がしました。具体的に何を写すかというよりも、途切れ途切れに撮ることで、現実をひたすら断片化したかったのです。

そのときは編集に興味がなかったですね。編集環境が整っていなかったし、無造作にただ撮っているのが面白かった。自分はこんな環境に住んでいるのだという、わたしの撮ったモノクロ写真とは違う発見がそこにありました。

マルコさんのいう「人間の存在や身体がより"伝統的な方法"で扱われる」のは、細かいショットだけで映像を構成するだけではなく、長回しの方法をわたしが取り入れ始めたからだと思います。何故そのような方法を採用したのかというと、わたしはスタン・ブラッケージの『ドッグ・スター・マン』や野村仁の『Dec.1973–Oct.1974又は 視覚のブラウン運動』やジョナス・メカスのような細かいカット割りが好きなのですが、『略称・連続射殺魔』やジェームス・ベニングの『セントラル・ヴァレー』、マルグリット・デュラスの『ヴェネチア時代の彼女の名前』などの長回しの映像にも興味を持っていました。わたしの新作『Lif is a Gift』はそれら二つの要素を折衷して作ったものです。

『Dead Stick Landing』は、それ以前のわたしの映像と違って、じっくりと一つのショットを見せようとしています。そのために一つ一つのショットが長い。その長回し的なところが、伝統的な方法に見えるのかもしれません。

『Life is a Gift』の例ですが、ショーウィンドウに設置されているモニターにカメラを近づけて撮影すると、モニターに流れている映像のイメージとモニターの画面に反射している人間や街のイメージと路上を歩く実際の中に人間が重なって、溶け込んでいるように見える。それは映像特有の世界です。広告映像のモニターの中に映っている人間と画面に反射してイメー

ジ化された人間と、実際に歩いている人間はカメラの中では同じイメージだとわたしは思います。わたしは現実のリアリティーを映像で再現することに興味がありません。写ってしまったものは全てイメージでしかない。映像は全てをイメージ化する。車も建物も人間もそのような意味で、みんな同じイメージになるのです。

　現実のリアリティーを映像で再現したいのではなく、イメージそのものが持つリアリティーが欲しいのです。映像は現実に存在する人間を、イメージに転化させることで、映像特有のリアリティーを獲得します。イメージというのは、わたしはもう一つの現実だと思います。「人間の存在や身体がより"伝統的な方法"で扱われる」のは、現実のリアリティーを再現するためではなく、イメージのリアリティーを表すためです。そのためにある程度の長回し的な映像を導入することが必要だと思いました。

　30秒以上あるわたしの長回しのショットを見ていると、手前の人の動きや、後ろの車の動きとかが気になり、視線が画面のあちこちに動き始め、画面が複雑化していきます。短いショットを見ているときは網膜に残った残像の印象で圧倒されたまま画面が続いていく感じですが、長回しのショットは見る人がショットの中に何が映っているのか見ようという気にさせます。圧倒させているだけだと見ている人間が受動的な態度でしか見なくなるので、もう少し見ている人の能動性を喚起させようと思い、長回しのショットを取り入れました。受動性と能動性という矛盾した領域を一本の映像の中に同居させることで、ショットに新しい動きを出させたかったのです。毛沢東の弁証法ではないですが、相反するもの同士の対立が物事を動かす源です。現実のリアリティーの再現を目指しているわけではないわたしにとって、映像はそれそのものとして成立させなければいけない。現実の対象に寄りかかっているだけでは、イメージのリアリティーを獲得することができません。細かいショットと長回しのショットという、相反する要素を映像の中に導入することは、相反する要素がぶつかり合って差異化運動が起こり、そのことで初めて映像が映像だけで動き出す。そのようなこと

が可能ではないかと考えています。映像の内部に導入された矛盾と差異の動きでショットが動きだすことは、外部の力を借りないで映像の内部の構造だけで動くことであり、それが映像の自己運動です。そのような映像の自立性を通して、初めてイメージそのもののリアリティーが獲得できるのではないかと思いました。

　わたしがイメージフォーラムという日本の実験映画の学校に行ったのは、今から32年前でした。その頃の日本の実験映画は伊藤高志の『スペーシー』という構造映画が話題を呼んでいたのですが、当時のイメージフォーラムの学生は、そのような構造映画は自己言及的で未来がない、という雰囲気で人気がなかった。むしろ鈴木志郎康の日記映画や、個人的な悩みを告白する個人映画という映画にみんなの興味が集中していました。その影響で、わたしも身の回りの日常を撮ろうと思ったのですが、決して私的な領域に限定されただけの日記映画や個人映画を撮りたいとは思わなかった。私的な領域も公的な領域も映像に写ってしまえば、すべて同じイメージとして処理されます。映像の中で両者の明確な区分けをすることは、難しいのではないでしょうか。ジョナス・メカスの日記映画が、リトアニアからの亡命者メカスという社会性を露わにしたことで、私的領域に限定されるジャンルだと思われていた日記映画の境界線を無効にしました。個人というのは社会的な網の中で他者と関係することで存在するのであって、私的な領域だけに存在する個人というのは存在しません。そのような社会化された個人に、私的な領域も公的な領域もないのではとわたしは思います。

　映像に写っている対象は、わたしはなんでもいいと思っています。何かが撮りたいというよりも、ただカメラを回したいという気持ちが強いのです。日常をよく写しているのは、カメラを回したくなる衝動が突然湧いてきたからで、日常の何か素晴らしい瞬間が目の前に起きて、それを撮ろうと思ったわけではありません。対象というのは、わたしにとってカメラを回すための口実です。

　わたしの映像の中に小松浩子さんの作品が出てきますが、それは他の
ショットとうまくつながると思い、入れてみました。わたしは映像を意味で
見ていません。意味でつなげていけば、彼女の作品と街の光景が合うわ
けがない。画面で見ているのです。画面としてつながるなら、意味としてつ
ながらなくても構わないというのがわたしの立場です。

　わたしの映像は私的な空間や公的な空間をごちゃまぜにして編集してい
ます。きっちりとコンセプトを決めて映像を作ることを、わたしはしません
が、けれど、もしわたしに映像のコンセプトらしきものがあるとしたら、ただ
ひたすら歩くことです。わたしは映像というのは歩かなければ撮れないもの
だと、写真を始める頃からずうっと思っていました。何もアイデアが浮かば
なくても、歩いていれば何かが撮れるのです。歩いて撮るのがコンセプト
ですから、私的な空間も公的な空間も歩いた場所という意味では同じ空間
になります。

　マルコさんがわたしの映像の中での自伝的要素について質問されてい
ますが、歩くということは、自分がその場所を経験することですから、わた
しの映像はそのような経験の積み重ねで成り立っていると思うのです。演出
したり、作ったりしているわけではないので、その意味では自伝的要素と
いうか、体験的要素が強く反映されていると思います。

　繰り返しになりますが、映像の中では公的、私的の境界線はありま
せん。イメージと現実の境界もないと思います。そのような境界線を無効
にしてしまうのが映像なのではないかと思っています。その場所が公的な
空間なのか、私的な空間なのかという空間の意味を剥ぎ取ってしまうのが
映像です。公的な空間も私的な空間も映像の中では差がない。すべての
ショットは等価です。

　公的な空間は社会的、政治的な構造で成り立っているけれど、私的空
間はそのような構造から切り離されていると思っている人がたくさんいます
が、例えば資本主義社会下での家族空間は、労働力再生産工場として機
能しているわけで、その意味では私的空間は、全て資本主義社会の生産

過程に組み込まれています。そのような社会状況下で公的空間と私的空間を区分けすることは不可能ではないでしょうか。自由できままな私的な空間が存在するというのは、資本主義社会の宣伝によるトリックです。食べることや、眠ることは、労働力再生産のためであり、気晴らしに遊んだり、リラックスしたりすることですら、資本の生産過程の一部に組み込まれている。わたし達は24時間稼働している機械の歯車の一部なのです。公的空間も私的空間も資本の論理によって貫かれているのです。

あなたのヴィデオ作品において、ポスト・プロダクションの重要性とはどのようなものですか?映像編集者と一緒に仕事をしたことはありますか?ひとつのヴィデオを完成させるのに、どのくらいの時間がかかりますか?「Elvis the Positive Thinking Pelvis」と「Dead Stick Landing」の製作・編集の作業過程はどのようなものでしたか?

「Elvis the Positive Thinking Pelvis」と「Dead Stick Landing」。その二つの作品は映像編集者とある程度一緒に作りました。それまでは無編集で作っていたし、デジタルの編集というのはどういうものかわたしは分からなかったので、相談しながら作りました。それまでわたしの映像はショットが極端に短かったのですが、映像編集者と相談しながら作った影響でしょうか、自分としては割合長めのショットで構成しました。ゆっくりとした感じで作られているので、とても美しく感じます。構成にも破綻がない。そこが今までのわたしの作品と違うところだと思います。荒っぽさは後退しましたが、わたしの映像が持っているデリケートな感覚が表れたと思います。人と一緒に作業をすると自分の意外な一面が表れるものです。

　前にも書きましたが、無編集で作品を作ると、どうしても現実の時間の文脈から逃れられない。編集を導入すると、現実の時間の文脈からショットが自由になれますし、無編集だと映像のテンポが単調になりやすい。編

集作業を取り入れると、極端に速いテンポからいきなり遅く動くショットをつなぎ合わせたりとかができるので、テンポに複雑さがでると思います。けれど無編集の方法をわたしは捨てたわけではありません。今もまた無編集で作ってみようかと思っています。無編集を前提にした撮影は、妙に緊張感があり、気持ちも高ぶります。その高揚感は、編集を前提とした撮影では感じられない高揚感です。

撮影と編集でだいたい一ヶ月か二ヶ月ぐらいで作ります。わたしは時間をかけてじっくりと作品を作るよりも、とりあえず量産していきたいと思っています。完成度よりもup to dateな感覚を重要視したい。ゴダールが70年代に撮っていたアジテーション・プロパガンダの映像や、最近ではジョナス・メカスの365日プロジェクトとか、時代と並行して走っていくような映像に興味があります。

音や音楽について、もう少し話してくださいますか?イメージをつくる仕事にパンクを応用することは可能でしょうか?あなたにとってパンクとは何ですか?今日の写真におけるパンクとはいかなるものでしょう?

パンクというのはアチチュードだとセックス・ピストルズのマネージャーのマルコム・マルクレンが言いました。パンクは演奏技術の問題ではないのです。アチチュードです。世界に対してどのように態度を表明するのかという問題です。

パンクは、演奏技術はどうでもいいと宣言したことで、演奏ができないミュージシャンもミュージシャンに含めました。チューニングされていないギターで演奏する彼らの音楽を聴いて、西洋音階をきちんと弾くためにだけギターは存在しているわけではないということが分かりました。何をしてもいいのだというのがパンクであって、西洋の作った音階以外にもスケールがあるのだという、複数的な視点の発見がパンクだったのです。それまで

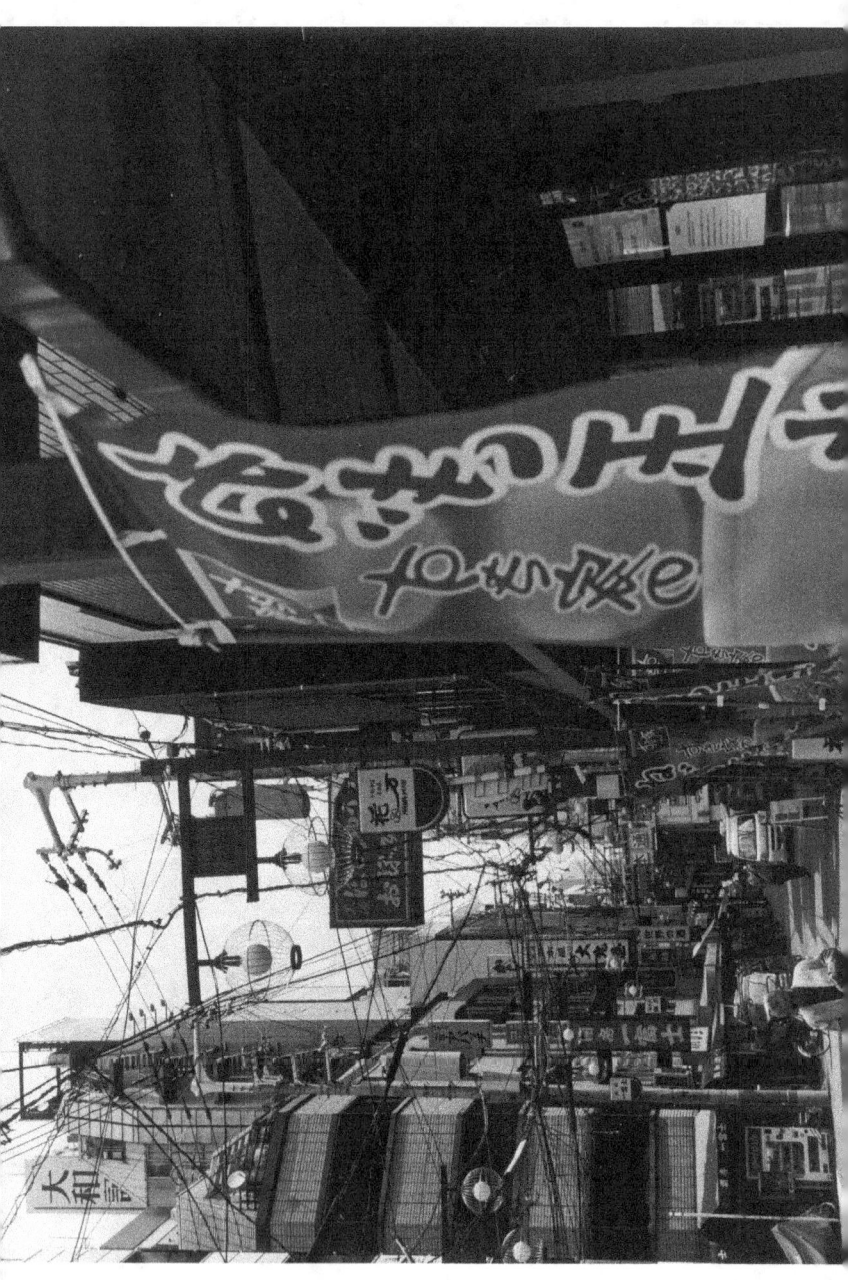

わたしは、きちんとチューニングされた楽器で、決められたスケールでし
かギターを弾いたことがなかったので、それは大きなショックでした。物
事というのは、一つの視点ではなく、複数の視点で成り立っているのだと
思ったのです。例えばこのバンドはパンクバンドではないのですが、イギリ
スのAMMというバンドのドラマーは、ドラムを叩かないで、ひたすらスネ
アの皮やシンバルの表面をスティックで擦っているだけだったのですが、そ
れがとても美しかった。楽器に約束事はないのだと知りました。

　それとパンクが画期的だったのは、60年代や70年代のアンダーグラウン
ド音楽の歴史に自分達の音楽を連結させたことだと思います。彼らはイン
タヴューでStoogesやMC5やVelvet Undergroundの影響について語りまし
た。自分達の独自性ばかりを喧伝するロックバンドが多い時代に、歴史の
中で繋がっていることを公にしたことにも驚きました。音楽というのは、歴
史の持続の中で生まれるのだと知り、それからですね、色々な音楽を聴き
始めたのは。歴史に連結するというのは重要です。わたしは写真を始めた
頃は、どんな写真の歴史に自分を連結させるのか、過去の写真史をどう
いう風に解釈するのか、いつも考えていました。

　「イメージをつくる仕事にパンクを応用することは可能でしょうか?」とい
う質問ですが、パンクというのは怒りですから、わたしは可能だと思うし、
それは必要なことだとも思います。表現の根底に怒りのないものにわたしは
興味がありません。パンクを聴いていた十代の頃のわたしは、いつも怒っ
ていたような気がしますし、それはたぶん今もそうです。日本に住んでいる
と腹が立つことはいっぱいあり過ぎます。そういう意味では、わたしは今で
もパンクです。

　70年代後半のロックは既に様式化されていました。ロック・ミュージシャ
ンの反体制的な言動は、わたしには商売上の口上にしか聞こえませんでし
た。BostonやJourney(それらのロックを日本では産業ロックと呼んでいま
した)のように、きちんとリサーチしてからスタジオに入って音楽を作るミュー
ジシャンが主流になってきました。ロックの資本主義化です。フリードウッド

マックやEagles以降、レコードが一千万枚ぐらい売れるのが普通になって
きたので、ブルジョワは新しい産業としてロックをビジネス様にカスタマイズ
し始めたのです。シカゴとかドゥービー・ブラザーズとか、60年代の末に革
命を歌っていたその手のヒッピー系のバンドが、いち早く産業化していきま
した。アメリカの革命家で有名だったジェリー・ルーヴィンも、その頃ぐらい
からですか、実業家で名を成し始めたのを覚えています。

　セックス・ピストルズ以降のパンクは、すでに商業主義的でお金の匂い
がしましたが、ニューヨーク・パンクのジョニー・サンダースやリチャード・
ヘル、スーサイド、デッド・ボーイズとかみんな素敵でした。"パイプライン"
を演奏していたジョニー・サンダースは、全員チューニングは狂ってい
て、キーも合ってないし、テンポも合っていなかった。けれど完成したロッ
クの様式を聴かされるよりも、わたしは下手でもいいから様式から逸脱して
いるものにリアリティーを感じます。ロックの様式には、みんなうんざりして
いたのです。

　日本のパンクバンドは、ナチスの鉤十字の腕章を付けている人が多か
ったのですが、その理由を聞くと、自分達の上の世代、ヒッピー世代が
それを見ると怒るからだと言っていたのを思い出します。演奏が始まる前
に、ステージ上のミュージシャンが、"みんな、ビールでも飲んでエンジョ
イしてくれ"とつまらないMCを喋るのが、わたし達より上のヒッピー系のバ
ンドでした。なんでこんなつまらない時代に、エンジョイとかリラックスし
なければいけないのかとよく思っていました。ステージ上から"愛し合って
いるかい?"と呼びかけるバンドもありましたね。ヒッピーが語る愛や平和や
社会にうんざりしていたのです。彼らの言う愛や平和なんて、ビジネス上
のコンテンツでしかない。その手のMCを聞かされるよりも、確かに鉤十字
の腕章の方がかっこいいと思いました。ヒッピーのMCは様式的にしか聞
こえなかった。彼らの言うLoveは商売です。Love&Peaceよりも、パンク
の言うHate&Warの方がリアリティーを持っていたのです。LoveやPeaceよ
りも、鉤十字の腕章の方が現状に対する怒りや破壊力を持っていました。

現状に対して破壊的なアチチュードを持っているものなら、ナチスでもコミュニストでもわたしはどちらでもいいと思いました。

みんな様式化されていく。そんな感覚がわたしにはありましたし、そう思っていた人は多かったのではないでしょうか。文部省主催のロックコンサートが行われたり、教科書にビートルズの曲が採用されたり、ロックは急速に商業主義に変質していき、世の中にともかく腹が立つという感覚を持ったバンドは、どんどん消えて行ったような気がします。わたしが演奏していたディスコは、みんなトルエンを吸って大暴れする場所だったのですが、段々とアメリカの黒人のディスコ・ミュージックが主流になり、トルエンを吸って一人で大暴れするよりも、みんなで決まったステップを踏むというスタイルが好まれるようになりました。日常のフラストレーションを発散する場所としてのディスコでも、みんなと同じステップを踏むという様式と均質を強要されるようになったのです。

ジャックスというロックバンドの早川義夫が言っていたのですが、言いたいや歌いたいことがたくさんあったので、演奏技術を獲得してから歌うなんていう時間の余裕がなかった。ともかくすぐに歌いたかったから、練習する時間がなかったという発言を読んだことがあります。ジャックスの演奏は滅茶苦茶で破綻寸前の音楽なのですが、それは演奏技術を教わってから歌ったり、演奏したりという学習で習得した技術で演奏することを拒否した結果でした。未熟でも自前の言葉で喋ろうというのが早川義夫の考えだと思うのです。人に下手だと言われてもいいから、ともかく歌いたい。そういう切迫感というのでしょうか、生き急いでいるようなパンク的な感覚は重要ではないでしょうか。

デジタル写真の誕生で、誰でも写真が撮れるようになりました。技術の習得も必要なくなりました。言いたいことがあれば、すぐできるようになりました。それは写真だけではなく、コンピューターで演奏することが主流になった音楽もそうです。わたしが写真を始めた理由の一つには、写真はそれほど技術の習得に時間がかからないだろうと思っていたからです。技術を

極めるなんていうことを目指していたら、たちまち老人になってしまう。技術が高度に発達した今だからこそ反技術的でパンク的なアチチュードが必要なのだと思います。

　　写真集『Ectoplasm Profiling』の文章のなかで、「コミュニスト」という語が使われています。この言葉は、この本全体において、もっともパワフルで議論を喚起する記号であると感じました。あなたにとってこの言葉は何を意味しますか?作品をつくるとき、とりわけ美学的選択や好みにおいて、イデオロギーはどのような役割を持ちますか?あなたにとって「コミュニズム」とは何を意味しますか?

全ての革命家は死刑を宣告された存在だとネチャーエフは言い、革命家は休暇中の死者だとレーニンは言いました。共産主義社会が目指す目標は、国家や民族、階級の消滅です。そして共産党とは、レーニンが言うにはそれらが消滅した世界を先取りした存在であり、予て実現される社会を体現している存在です。革命家はあらかじめ死刑を宣告された者であるというネチャーエフの発言は、自分達はすでに死者であって、死を先取りした存在だということです。ネチャーエフやレーニンの発言の主旨は、革命家や前衛党としての共産党は死や消滅を先取りした存在であり、消滅や死を現実の中で体現しているのが革命家や共産党なのではないかということだと思います。

　写真は、今存在している対象を"かつてあったもの"に変容させる芸術だと思うのです。写真は、対象を写した瞬間に、それをすぐに過去のものにしてしまう。写っている対象は"それはかつてあったもの"になる。それが写真の原理だと思うのですが、それならば写真に写っているものは、今はそれが存在しないということの証明です。写真は"写っているものは、今はない"という、写っているものの消滅を表すものではないでしょうか。写真は対象の消滅を具体化するのです。写真はそれがかつて存在したということ

を表しますが、"それはもう今はない"という消滅も表します。コミュニストが自己の死や国家の消滅を体現している存在なら、写真もまた対象の消滅を具体化するのです。死や消滅の具体化というところがコミュニストと写真家の共通するところだと思います。

写真は死や消滅と非常に馴染み深い芸術だと思います。"それがかってあった、けれど今はないもの"を写す写真は、幽霊のようではないですか。写真は此岸の存在を彼岸の彼方に連れていく芸術なのだと思います。

革命家が休暇中の死者なら、革命とは死者の世界から此岸の世界への呼びかけです。此岸の存在を彼岸化する写真もまた死者の世界からの呼びかけではないかと思います。革命と写真は死と消滅と近似的な関係にあり、そこに写っているものお、すでにないものにしてしまう写真は、死者、特に屍体とよく似ている。屍体もまたそこにありながら、すでにその屍体の持ち主は、ここにはいないことを体現している存在です。

ロシア社会民主党が分裂したときレーニンが率いた左派グループは少数派でしたが、彼は自らのグループをボリシェヴィキ＝多数派と名付けました。少数派ではあるけれど、我々こそがプロレタリア階級の真実を代表しているという矜持がそれを名乗らせたのでしょうが、多数派という言葉を字義通り解釈すれば、人類の多数派とは生者ではなく死者です。革命家とは休暇中の死者であると語るレーニンには、無意識下に死者のことが浮かんだのではないでしょうか。レーニンにとってプロレタリア階級とは、生者の階級ではなく、死者の階級のことだったのではないでしょうか。革命家が死者を先取りした存在であるなら、ボリシェヴィキの言う権力奪取は、生者の代わりに死者や霊的存在が権力を掌握するということだったのではと思います。コミュニストとは死者を先取りして今現在に現れている存在であり、それは写した全てのものを屍体化して表してしまう写真の原理とそっくりなのではと思います。

美学とは、つねになんらかのイデオロギーの存在によって決定されるものだと思います。純粋に美しいものは存在しない。わたし達が何かを見て

美しいと思うのは、たいていの場合イデオロギー操作によって作られた結果です。

写真家はスタイルを持っています。スタイルというのは、わたしは世界をこのように見ているという写真家の立ち位置の表明だと思うのです。スタイルをどのように確立するかというのが、写真家になる人の最初の課題でしょう。どのような立ち位置で世界と接するのかというアチチュードを明らかにすることが写真家ですから、それは一度確立されたらそう容易には変えられないと思います。色々とスタイルを変え続ける写真家もいますが、わたしはそのような人はいかがなものかと思っています。

自前のスタイルを持つということは、マスメディアが美しいといい続けるものに対して疑問を持つことだと思います。マスメディアの喧伝する美しさ、例えば日本なら桜や富士山が美しいといわれていますが、それは風景を美学化することで、風景を消費物として商業主義的に再構成することです。そのような美学は資本主義社会のイデオロギーに立った者の発言ですから、自身のスタイルを持つということは、そのようなイデオロギーに対して疑いを持たなければいけない。

パリの風景を見て、パリを写した観光写真と同じように見えると感動しながら言う人がいますが、それは実際の風景を見る前に、観光写真のイメージを頭の中に刷り込んでから見るので、それは観光写真に洗脳された見方です。そして観光写真の立ち位置というのは、経済的、民族的、宗教的な矛盾で渦巻いているパリを、美というヴェールで覆うことでそれらの諸矛盾を覆い隠そうというブルジョワ側のイデオロギーに立った写真なのです。スタイルを持つということは、無反省に美を肯定するのではなく、イデオロギーによって操作された美に抗うことではないでしょうか。

コミュニズムの芸術とは、ベンヤミンのいう美学の政治化だと思うのです。コミュニストはあらゆる美学に対して、その背後に存在するイデオロギーを検証しなければいけません。全ての美学にはイデオロギーが隠蔽されている。イデオロギーの存在なしで、美学は成立しません。

　例えばイタリアの未来派は、戦争は美しいと宣言しました。その宣言が意味するものは、近代テクノロジーの肯定です。テクノロジーの発展によって作られた飛行機、大砲の存在が戦争を美しくする。原子爆弾がその究極でしょう。それらの大量殺戮兵器は遠距離で操作されるので、直接敵対する人間を見ないですみます。それにそれら近代テクノロジーによって作られた兵器は、とても写真写りがいいのです。写真写りや映像の写りがいいことが、20世紀以降の戦争の条件です。それは写真写りの美しさによって戦争の背後に存在するブルジョワのイデオロギーを隠蔽するために要求されたものなのです。

　写真は美を表現するのではなく、美を成立させる地平を写してしまうものだと思います。それは美がどのような環境で成り立っているのかという、美が立脚している構造を露わにするのではないかと思っています。わたしがクローズアップの技法をあまり使わないのは、それがどのような環境で存在しているのか見えなくなるからです。美しい花があってそれに近寄って撮れば確かにきれいに撮れるのですが、その花の美しさは、それがどのような場所で咲いているのかという、環境を見せないことで成り立つ美しさです。例えばその花の咲いている場所がアウシュビッツの跡地だったら、単純にその花が美しいとは言えないでしょう。物事を美しく撮るのにクローズアップが有効なのは、それがどんな場所にいるのかという地平を覆い隠してしまうからです。

　マルクスが共産主義とは達成されるべき目標ではなく、その過程のことだといいましたが、わたしの写真や映像もまた達成されるべき目標がそこには存在しないと思います。全ては過程の段階です。わたしの作品は全て過程の段階であり、完成することはないでしょう。もし完成というものが存在するのなら、わたしが死んだときだと思います。

　足立正生の映画『略称・連続射殺魔』では、都市の風景がもっとも大きなテーマになりました。足立さんの作品は、あなたのヴィデオ作品にインスピレーションを与えましたか?風景をイデオロギーとして用いることは、今なお可能なのでしょうか?　風景写真は政治写真の新境地を切りひらくことができるのでしょうか?また、現代の都市風景が人びとの行動に及ぼす影響について、どのようにお考えですか?写真、風景、それから犯罪——これらのあいだに関連性はありますか?写真とテロリズムに何らかの共通点はあるでしょうか?

　『略称・連続射殺魔』は、わたしが二十歳のときに見ました。ストーリーも俳優もなくて、風景だけでも映像が成り立つのだという驚きがありました。永山則夫が見た風景だろうという想像だけで作られた映像があんなにもリアリティーを表出することができたのは、映像の力だと思います。ストーリーや言葉がなくても映像は、映像だけで成立する。青森の路地裏の風景やヒマワリ畑にタクシーのフロントガラスから撮影されたリンゴ畑の風景の細部に目を凝らしていると眩暈がする思いです。映像は細部が写っていればそれだけでいいのだとそのとき納得しました。

　『略称・連続射殺魔』が松田政男の風景論をベースにして作られたというのは、後から知りました。あの映画は、それまでの政治的ドキュメンタリー映像と違って、情感とヒューマニズムが欠けています。冨樫雅彦と高木元輝の作った音楽はかなりセンチメンタルな匂いがするのですが、基本的には情感とヒューマニズムを画面から追放しようとした映像なのだと思います。

　『略称・連続射殺魔』の制作者の一人の松田政男が、この映像を評して「風景こそが、まずもって私たちに敵対してくる＜権力＞そのものとして意識されたからなのである。おそらく、永山則夫は、風景を切り裂くために、弾丸を発射したに違いないのである。国家権力ならば、風景を大胆に切断して、たとえば東名高速道路をぶち抜いてしまう。私たちが、快適なドライブを楽しんだとき、まさにその瞬間に、風景は私たちを呪縛し、

＜権力＞は私たちをからめとってしまうのだ」と書いていましたが、資本主義社会は永山則夫の犯罪でしか表現できなかった憤りでさえも風景化してしまうのです。そんな資本主義のイデオロギーに対して、情念で闘ってもそれはすぐに風景化されてしまう。60年代の日本はどちらかというと情念的なものが主流でした。機動隊の盾に対して、材木や鉄パイプで襲撃する武装デモを、自己の実存を機動隊の盾に投企するという言い方で理論化していました。政治的な課題に対して自己の実存を問題の中心に置く情念的な政治思考が60年代では普通だったようです。情念は社会環境やシステムによって作られたものでしかない。そのような作られたものを政治的な課題の中心に置くことで権力と対峙するというのは、対峙する権力に飲み込まれるだけではないでしょうか。資本主義社会の中で情念を中心に置くことは、システムの中で消費されるだけでしかないのです。

　『略称・連続射殺魔』が写した風景は、人間の領域からかけ離れた彼岸のような遠さを感じます。『略称・連続射殺魔』の風景には、ヒューマニズムが入る余地がない。細部の集積によって成り立つ『略称・連続射殺魔』は、人間が画面から追放された後の世界を思わせます。情況から情が切り離され、情況は風景に取って代わられると松田政男が書いていましたが、それは資本主義社会の非人間性を訴える言葉でありながらもまた、映像の本質を表した言葉でもあるのです。資本主義が人間を労働力という商品に変質させるなら、映像は人間を風景の細部に変質させる。

　『略称・連続射殺魔』は人間の情念や心情には回収できない風景を表しました。風景映画としての『略称・連続射殺魔』は、今でも十分刺激的です。風景映画や風景写真には、まだ可能性があると思います。

　東京では駅の改札口を出た瞬間に、あちらこちらに設置されているモニターから商品広告の映像が流れてきます。電車に乗れば車内放送で、体の不自由な人に席を譲って下さいとか、ホームで困っている人がいたら助けてあげて下さいとか、電車に乗ることとは関係のない道徳的な説教が

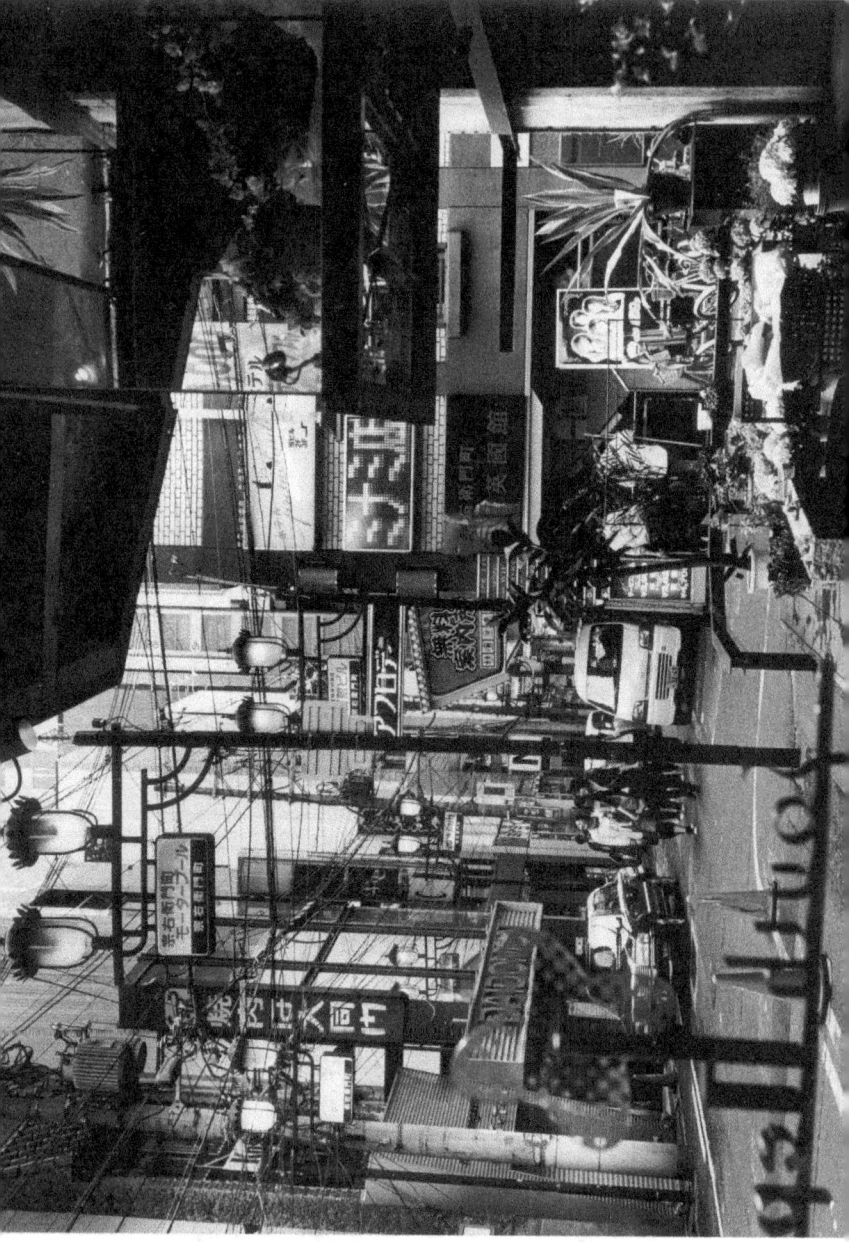

一日中流れています。そのような社会に住んでいれば、精神的に色々な影響を受けるでしょう。

　駅の構内放送では、お客様の安全を最優先しておりますと朝から晩まで放送し続けています。お客様の安全が最優先されますという放送のべつ幕無しに放送されているので、安全という言葉を聞くと妙に腹が立ってくる。車内放送では車内暴力をお客様トラブルと、鉄道自殺を人身事故と言葉を言い換える。言葉を言い換えることで、暴力や自殺という殺伐とした事件を覆い隠すのです。電車はつねに快適で楽しい乗り物でなければならないという日本独特のレジャー・ファシズムの結果です。日本の電車は、車両のあちこちに小さいモニターが設置されていて、そこからいつも人生を楽しく過ごすように強要する映像が朝から晩まで流れています。そのような欺瞞の言葉を聞かされ続けると人間はどこかおかしくなるのではと思います。テレビを見れば人よりもワンランク上の生活を目指せというコマーシャルばかりで、ひたすら商品の洪水です。駅では安全と助け合いという道徳的説教を強要され、街を歩けば、商品を買い続けることが資本主義社会で暮らす人間の幸せだと喧伝される。当然犯罪も多発するでしょうし、わたしの写真に見られる商品広告の看板の多さを見れば、こんな所に住みたくないと思います。

　テロリズムと写真や映像は、原理的な部分でとても関係が深いと思います。小さな行動で大きな恐怖心を煽るのがテロリズムの原理です。フィルムに強い光を当てて、レンズで幕やスクリーンなどに拡大映像を投映して見せるファンタスマゴリーという初期の映像とテロリズムの原理は似ているように思います。むしろテロリズムとはファンタスマゴリーのことではないでしょうか。ベンヤミンがパサージュのショーウィンドウをファンタスマゴリーの原理で説明していましたが、テロリズムもまたファンタスマゴリーの魔法を利用しています。テロリズムに恐怖することは、テロリストが作り出す幻影に恐怖するのと似ている。最近の日本では、北朝鮮からミサイルが発射されるたびに、すぐに大きな建物に隠れろとテレビで警報が流されたり、電車

を緊急停止させたりしていますが、それは日本のマスメディアが、北朝鮮のミサイルをファンタスマゴリー的な恐怖に見せようとしているのです。アメリカの北朝鮮政策に賛意を示す日本政府のイデオロギー操作です。

写真は実体的な反映ではありません。対象を切り取ることで違うものを生み出すのです。現実を切り取り、再構成するという操作は、ある種の幻影を作り出すことだと思うのですが、例えばわたしの撮る東京はこんなにゴミゴミした場所だけではない。もっとさっぱりした場所もあります。けれどそのような混沌とした場所を集中的に撮り続けることで、現実の東京とは違うリアリティーが生まれる。それはテロリストが作り出す幻影と似ているのですが、幻影だからこそ妙にリアリティーを持つ。増幅されたイメージの方が、リアリティーがあるのです。テロリズムも写真も映像もファンタスマゴリー的な要素を共有しています。

そしてテロリズムとは暴力と情報の操作だと思うのです。小さな行動を周知に効果的に知らしめるためには、自爆テロやハイジャック、そのような行動を効果的な場所で何度も執拗に反復する。それは資本主義の宣伝パターンとそっくりです。わたし達は日々、商品テロリズムの攻撃を受けているのです。

テロリストは世界を恐怖させるという目的がありますが、彼らにとってファンタスマゴリー的なイメージは手段でしかない。それに対して写真家や映像作家は、ファンタスマゴリー的に増幅されたイメージに取り憑かれた者です。それは手段ではなく目的であって、そのようなイメージに取り憑かれた人間は、現実ではなく、イメージの中を生きるようになる。テロリストもまたイメージを手段として使っているのかもしれませんが、いつか自分達の作り出したイメージに飲み込まれるでしょう。写真家もテロリストもイメージに取り憑かれた人間なのです。

日本で作品を展示する機会はあまりなく、ヨーロッパでの展覧会が多かったとおっしゃいました。私はヨーロッパ人ですが、あなたの作品を、コンセプチュアルなベッヒャー派以降につくられた、もっとも厳密で重要な研究の一つだと考えています。作品（写真やヴィデオだけでなく文章も含めて）の潜在的影響を考えると、金村さんの写真に対する貢献は、ベッヒャー派よりもはるかに重要なものであるように思います。

　1）あなたのモノクロ写真は、視覚的なノイズと情報の集積を写真に持ち込み、完全に新しい構図、場所との関係性を実現しました。写真家にとって、あなたの白黒の東京のイメージをみたあとでは、以前と同じように空間とフレーミングを関連づけることができません。

　2）あなたはヴィデオに対するまったく新しいアプローチを切りひらきました。あなたのヴィデオ作品は、まったく新しい方法と視座をもって、物語ること（ナレーション）の本質について問いかけています。

　3）「Z-Trash diary」では、イメージ製作においてさらに踏み込んだ境地に達しています。このように、異なるメディアをもちいて、あなたは少なくとも3度、写真の新しくてパワフルな可能性を切りひらいたのです。

　あなたの写真史に対する貢献が今以上に認められるようになったら、これから撮影される写真、あるいは写真をめぐる人びとの意識にどのような変化が起こると思いますか？一体、何がイメージを現代的なものにするのでしょう？あなたにとって現代的なイメージとは何ですか？現代的なイメージという概念は納得できるものでしょうか？

ロラン・バルトが言うように写真はプンクトゥム的なものだと思います。一つのコードに収まり切れない過剰な細部を集積することで写真が成立するのです。原発事故や東北大震災以降の日本の写真はドキュメンタリー的な要素を求められ、映像の持つ過剰な細部を表現するのではなく、社会的なメッセージを伝えるための道具のように扱われています。わたしの作品が今

以上に認められるようになったら、社会的なコードに収まることだけが写真ではないということにみんなが気づくでしょう。写真はメッセージではないし、メッセージを説明するための便利な挿絵ではないのです。

イメージとは、わたしは幻影だと思います。それは実体のないものなのですが、実体がないゆえに、奇妙な魅力を発揮する。イメージが現代的なものと結びつくのは、イメージが社会的なコードに回収され、それが現実と結びついた実体だと思われた結果だと思うのです。社会的なコードに回収されたことで、イメージが説明可能な挿絵のようなものに変質する。イメージを実体の反映だと思うことは、イメージの持つファンタスマゴリー的な魅惑やフェティシズムを廃棄させることだと思います。イメージとは理解可能なものではない。それはいつまでも分からないものでありながらも、人々を魅了するものです。

写真はイメージだと思いますが、言語や貨幣もまたイメージだと思います。人間はリアルなものに直接触れることができない存在だと思うのです。つねにイメージを介在することで対象と向き合う。イメージを通して現れてくるものが人間にとっての現実です。わたし達はイメージの海に囲まれて、そこから出ることができない。

現代を理解するには、イメージの介入が必要とされますが、けれどイメージはファンタスマゴリー的な幻影を持って介在してくるので、つねにバイアスがかかり、ストレートに現代が理解できるわけではないのです。共有可能なイメージは存在しません。わたし達はそれぞれ、ばらばらなイメージを持つことしかできない。みんなが納得できるような共通するイメージを持って現代を理解することはできないと思います。各自によって現代の現れ方は違います。現代的なイメージという一言で現代を理解することは不可能なのです。それにイメージはイデオロギーの操作によって生み出すこともできる。ファシストやコミュニストが現代の日本を見たら、正反対のイメージを持つでしょう。もしそのような共有可能なイメージがあるとしたら、それは資本主義社会によって操作されたイメージです。

中平卓馬にはどのようにして出会ったのですか?彼を大阪で撮影する
のはどのような感じでしたか?若い写真家たちが中平卓馬から学ぶこと
のできる、もっとも重要な教訓とは何ですか?中平卓馬が若い世代の
写真家たちに遺したものとは何ですか?

中平卓馬の写真は学生時代から知っていました。写真もよかったのです
が、彼の書いた文章がとてもよかった。写真にとって重要なのは、わたし
ではなく、世界の方だとカフカのようなことを書いていて、とても感心しま
した。

　大阪で中平さんを撮影したとき思ったのですが、彼が撮影している姿は
とても彫刻的でした。ジャコメッティの彫刻を思い出させる立ち姿だった
です。

　日本の写真は私写真がとても多いです。けれど自分のアイデンティ
ティーというのは、社会によって構成されているわけで、そこが分からない
で、私写真を撮る写真家が多い。先天的にわたしのアイデンティティーが
存在するわけではないのです。わたしのアイデンティティーを決定するの
は、わたしだと思っている人が多いのですが、中平卓馬の写真には、その
ような先天的で不動なわたしのアイデンティティーを揺り動かす力があると
思います。わたしの存在は世界によって構成されたものであり、わたしは
世界の一部でしかない。そう思わせる力が中平卓馬の写真や文章にはあ
るのではないでしょうか。

　日本の若い写真家に、中平卓馬的な影響はまだあまり浸透していない
気がします。どちらかといえば森山大道のような情念的な写真の影響の方
が強いようです。写真は、写真家の美学によってコントロールする芸術だと
思っている人がたくさんいます。

同世代の人たちの政治的背景についてはいかがですか?同世代の人
たちは何らかの政治的背景を共有していると思いますか?生活、ある
いは創造的側面において、金村さんの政治的な意識はどのようにし
て、どれくらいの年月をかけて育まれていったのでしょう?芸術家でな
かったとしたら、異なる政治的見解を持っていたと思いますか?

同時代の人達の政治意識というのは、ブルジョア的なヒューマニズム意
識が強いのではと思います。3月11日に東北の大震災で原発が破損しま
した。東北という場所は日本国内における植民地であり、工業社会で働
くプロレタリアを恒常的に供給するために、農民を流動化させ、労働力と
してプールされ続けた場所でした。ブルジョアジーは格差を利用すること
で利潤を追求するのですが、そのために国内格差を意識的に作り上げま
す。商業の中心地があちこちに点在している日本の西側と違い、東北にと
って商業交換できる相手は東京だけです。東京以外の交渉相手を持たな
い東北は、最初から力関係で東京の植民地になることを運命付けられてい
ました。二毛作と一毛作という農産物の収穫システムの問題もあるのでは
と思いますが、東京と東北では、商業取引の関係としては明らかに非対
称的でした。

　東北は農村地帯だったのですが、明治維新以降、日本は農業社会か
ら工業社会に社会システムを転換させるために、土地に住み着く農民の労
働力を流動化させます。工業社会が必要とする労働力を確保するために、
農村の共同体を破壊して、流動化させ、土地と深い関係を結んでいた農
民を、何も持たないプロレタリアートという労働力に変質させました。東北
は労働力をプールし続ける場所でしかない。工業社会を成立させるために
流動化された東北に対して、さらに安い労働力を求める資本家がその視
線を東南アジアに向けたとき、東北は見捨てられ、残ったのは貧困だけ
です。70年代の自民党の政治家達は、東北を中心に富の再分配を行おう
と、開発という名目でインフラ整備に税金を投入しました。原発が東京で

はなく、東北に持ち込まれたのも、富の再分配と東北地域の活性化という名目です。原発が持ち込まれることで政府や電力会社から助成金が大量にばら撒かれるので、貧困化された東北としてそれは絶好のアイテムだったのです。

東北の犠牲によって、東京の人間は快適な生活を送れたのです。地域活性化と富の再分配という名目で自民党政府は危険な原発を東北に持ち込んだのですが、一度震災が起きれば、そのような格差を生み出す資本主義の構造的な矛盾にみんな目をつぶり、がんばろう東北とか、みんなで繋がろうとか、ブルジョア・ヒューマニズム的な偽善を語るだけで、資本主義社会の構造には目をつぶっているだけでした。わたしは震災による原発の破壊とその結果としての放射能の日本国内への拡散は、長年植民地化された東北の復讐ではと思っています。福島原発が破損したとき、家族のことを思って、国内から外国へ移住することを考えていると公言する人がたくさんいましたが、東北の犠牲の上に成り立った生活を享楽しておいて、今更なんだという気もしました。日本の繁栄は、国内植民地や第三世界の収奪の上に成り立っているのです。さんざん収奪をしておいて今さら自分だけ放射能から逃げようというのは、どうなのでしょうか。搾取し続けた人間の運命だと思って放射能を浴びる以外に日本人に何があるのかと思うときもありました。

同世代の人で政治的な背景を共有していると思える人は何人かいますが、その人達はやはりわたしと同じように反ヒューマニズムです。ブルジョアのヒューマニズムは全ての政治的な問題を覆い隠します。けれど写真家はマグナムに代表されるように、基本的にヒューマニズムで動いている人が多いので、わたしのような政治意識を共有する人は少ないと思います。

わたしは日本ではマイノリティーのクラスの出身なので、政治と私生活を切り離して考えたことがない。芸術と私生活と政治を分けて考えている人が日本には多いですが、わたしにはそれがよく分からない。

　日本では言葉の言い換えが多いのです。かつて新聞では、サラリーマンのことを賃金奴隷と表現していました。まさに的を得た表現だとわたしは思うのですが、今ではそのような言い方は、PC的に禁止です。労働者階級という言葉が使用されなくなり、わたし達はみんな市民という存在になりました。わたしは市民という言葉には子供の頃から違和感を感じていて、市民という言い方にはすごくフラットな感じがするのです。労働者階級という言い方には具体的な働く人間の姿を想起できますが、けれど市民と言われると抽象的な感じを受けて、そこには何もない感じがするのです。わたしの世代はまだ言葉の言い換えが進んでいなくて、物事の本質を指し示すようなリアルな言葉が使われている環境で育ちました。そのような長い言語環境がわたしの政治意識を育てたのだと思います。

　わたしが芸術家でなくて、市井の人であったとしても政治意識は変わらないと思います。いきなりお金持ちにでもなったならば、政治意識も変わるかもしれませんが、多分変わらないと思います。子供の頃から身についたものは、環境が変わってもなかなか変わらないのではと思います。

　スライドショーについて。「Elvis the Positive Thinking Pelvis」はスライドショーをじつに興味深いやり方で進化させたものとみなすことができます。複雑なスライドショーです。

　　過去に、スライドショーをつかって展覧会をなさったことがありますね。あなたにとってスライドショーはどのような重要性を持ちますか？スライドショーを使った展覧会という着想はどのように閃めいたのですか？スライドショーとヴィデオを使用することの違いとは何ですか？

何年か前に銀座のギャラリーでスライドショーの展覧会をやりました。スライド映写機を20台ぐらい用意して、アットランダムにそれらを床に置いて、天井に投影したり、壁に投影したりする展覧会でした。五千円払う

と、その会場の中でわたしがポラロイドでお金を払ったお客さんを撮影するというパフォーマンスもやりました。

わたしの展示は、60cm×50cmサイズの写真をギャラリーの壁面に四段掛けでかける展示がほとんどだったので、そのときの様子はずいぶんスペクトラムな感じを受けました。

最初にスライド上映の話を持ちかけられたとき、デジタルの映写機は使いたくないと直感的に思いました。スライド映写機のあのガタガタと音を立ててフィルムがチェンジしていくアナログな感じでやりたいと思いました。その考えはフィルム写真に対する郷愁からきたわけではなく、スライド映写機が鳴らすあの音が気持ちいいだろうと思ったのです。映写機の光が点滅しながら消えていく会場で、ガタガタと音が鳴っている空間は美しいだろうと思いました。

ヴィデオでもそんな風にやってみたいですね。会場に何台もヴィデオ映写機を持ち込んで、映写したいと思っています。

わたしは60年代から70年代に実験映画の世界で流行っていたエクスパンデッド・シネマが好きです。複数の映写機を使ってひとつのスクリーンに映写したりとか、ループ映写というのもありました。ループで映写されているフィルムにミシンを操作して穴を開けるアナベル・ニコルソンの『Reel Time』や、二台の映写機を使って黒みのフィルムを映し続ける映写機に、何も写っていない白みのフィルムを投影する飯村隆彦の『デッド・ムービー』。そういう感じの映像インスタレーションに興味があります。スライドショーがわたしにとって重要性を持つとしたら、映像インスタレーションをやってみたいと思わせたことでしょうね。

そのときのスライドショーは今思うと少しノスタルジックな気がしますが、デジタル・ヴィデオの場合はそういう情感がないような気がします。ケネス・アンガーは彼の映像ボックスセットのタイトルを『マジック・ランタン・サイクル』と名付けましたが、わたしのヴィデオもまたマジックであり、スライドが醸し出すランタン的な雰囲気を出せないかと思っています。

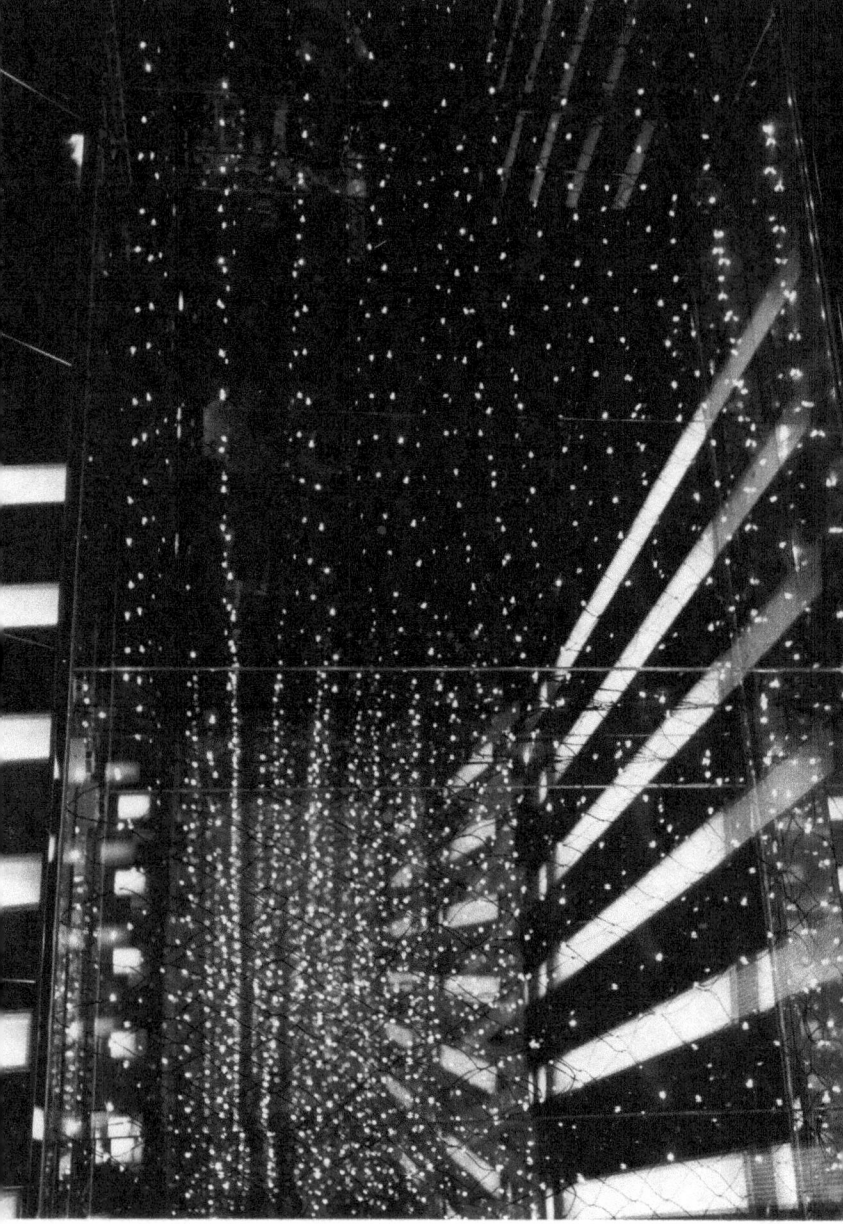

　デジタル・ヴィデオはスライドと違って先端のテクノロジーであり、それは
もっと非人間的です。無機質な感じがします。けれど先端のテクノロジーこ
そがマジックを生み出すものだとわたしは思っています。例えば50年代当
時の最先端だったエレキギターでブルースを演奏すると、黒人ブルースが
内包していたヴードゥー的なマジックが露わにされたように、先端のテクノ
ロジーはマジックを呼び出します。70年代の最先端のテクノロジーだったメ
ロトロンやアナログシンセ等々、それらは必ずマジック的なものを内包して
いました。ビートルズの『ストロベリー・フィールズ・フォーエバー』のメロトロ
ンの使い方は、とてもマジカルだった記憶があります。ヴィデオはスライド
のノスタルジアとは違う、新しいマジック性を持っているのではないかと思
っています。

　小松浩子さんは、わたしのヴィデオを見て、霊的なものを感じると言って
くれましたが、先端のテクノロジーにこそマジック・ランタン的な霊性が現れ
るのではないかと思っています。

　　ファインダーの代わりに、液晶ディスプレイ画面を使うときの感覚はど
　　のようなものですか？どのような種類のデジタル・カメラを使っていま
　　すか？どのようにしてデジタル・カメラを選びますか？デジタル・カメラの最
　　大の限界とは何だと思いますか？

液晶ディスプレイは慣れないですね。いまだに慣れません。フィルムカメ
ラのファインダーと違って、覗き込めないから、カメラと一体化できないの
です。液晶ディスプレイのカメラにはいつも軽い違和感を感じますが、け
れどそれがいいのかもしれませんね。液晶ディスプレイで撮影していると写
真を撮っているというよりも、カメラを操作しているような気にさせられます。
自分が写真家というよりも、カメラのオペレーターという感じがするのです。

　デジタル・カメラはリコーのGRを使っています。宣伝のために使ってく
れとGRの人に頼まれたのです。あと最近はiPhoneのカメラも使ってい

ます。ズームができて便利です。来年ぐらいにはiPhoneの動画映像を取り入れたものを作りたいと思っています。

この間久しぶりにフィルムで上映されたマイケル・スノウとジェームス・ベニングと松本俊夫と伊藤高志と奥山順一という豪華なメンツを続けて見ました。今見てもやはり感動します。フィルムは画面に厚みが出るというのか、すごく物質感を感じさせます。あの物質感がデジタルにはないような気がするのです。要するに軽いのですよね。それに画面もフィルムと比べると、フラットな感じがします。

ただデジタルは編集に便利ですし、コスト的にもフィルムとはまるで違います。2時間ぐらいのフッテージで、わたしは20分ぐらいの映像を一本作るのですが、それをフィルムでやるとコストが大変かかります。

デジタルはフィルムに比べると確かに軽くてフラットな感じを受けるのですが、その軽さがフィルムにはないデジタル特有の長所になるのではないでしょうか。コストの問題かもしれませんが、実際フレデリック・ワイズマンやジェームス・ベニングもデジタルに移行しています。

デジタルの限界は画面がきれいすぎて、なんだかフラットな感触しか持てない。フィルムのイメージには物質性を感じるのですが、デジタルはそのような物質性に欠けている。そこがデジタルの限界だと思うのですが、物質性を感じさせないデジタルの限界が、繰り返しになりますが、もしかしたらそれがデジタルの長所になるのではと思います。

リュミエール兄弟がスクリーンに初めて投影した『列車の到着』に映っている列車は、フィルムに光を当てて、スクリーンに拡大したイメージとしての列車ですから、それは現実の列車ではないし、物質でもない。けれど人々が『列車の到着』を見てパニックになったのは、投影されたイメージの列車でしかないと知りつつも、そこに現実の列車とは別の物質的な何かを感じたから逃げ出したのではないでしょうか。例えば進行する列車と共に表れるフィルムの粒子。彼らは初めてそこでスクリーンに拡大された粒子を見たわけです。それは列車と共に粒子が襲いかかってくるような、列車では

なく、フィルムそのものが襲いかかってくるような感覚があったのかもしれません。

　それに比べるとデジタルは、ひたすらきれいな映像でしかない。現実よりもきれいに感じるのは、フィルムと違ってメディアの持つ物質性を完全に切り捨てているからでしょうか。デジタル映像は、物質性を持たない。そのような物質性が欠落したデジタルで、『列車の到着』のような物質性を表現することができるのでしょうか。

　物質性がないメディアを使って物質性を表現する。わたしはカメラやフィルムというメディアの持つ物質性に興味がありました。けれどデジタルには、そのようなメディアの物質性が完全に排除されています。フィルムカメラがメディアの物質性を露わにしたのに対して、デジタルはメディアの物質性が初めから存在していない。より純粋な現実の再現を求めるデジタルカメラは、そこにフィルムカメラが持っていたメディア特有の夾雑物の存在を許さないでしょう。4Kカメラや8Kカメラの出現でみられるように、その異常なぐらいの現実の再現性の追求は、映像からノイズや物質性を追放します。4Kカメラや8Kカメラで撮られた映像は、それはもう現実の再現ではない。現実がこんなにクリアで、平べったくて、美しいわけがない。

　デジタルカメラの物質性の欠けた美しさは、わたしが子供の頃に思っていた天国のイメージに近いです。美しいイメージがフラットな空間を漂っている。物質の裏付けを欠いたイメージとしてのデジタル映像は、幽霊のようではないでしょうか。幽霊が怖いのは、それが物質の裏付けを欠落させたまま現実の世界に表れるから怖いのであって、デジタル映像に可能性があるとしたら、物質的な裏付けを欠いたイメージが持つ幽霊性ではないかと思います。

　そしてそのようなデジタル映像がもし物質性を持つとしたら、それは幽霊の物質性です。幽霊は物質性が欠けていると分かっていながら、わたし達はそこに物質性を見ようとしてしまう。いくら見て、探してもそこには物質性が完全に欠落している。そして欠落していればしている程、更にそこに物

質の存在を探してしまう。物質性の完全な欠落が、新たな物質性を希求させるのです。そして物質性がデジタル映像の中に表れることは絶対にないという絶望感が、デジタルの新たな物質性だと思います。

それにモノクロ写真はプリントの操作で、写真を見る人に感情を喚起させる画面を作ることができますが、デジタル写真の場合、エフェクト処理でそれをやると、まるで冗談みたいな映像になります。デジタルで情感を出そうとすると、それは情感の廃墟のようなものになってしまう。人間的な要素からデジタルは縁遠いメディアだと思うのです。けれどそのようなデジタルの非人間性はわたしにとってとても魅力的です。

『Ectoplasm Profiling』を読んで、あなたの文章は絵画に少し似ていると感じました。例えば、東島毅の絵画を想起したのです。これまでに絵画の表現を用いたことはありますか？絵画に興味はまったくないのでしょうか？

東島毅の絵は、線と面という対照的な二つの要素が、画面の中でぶつかりあったり、統合したりしている絵画だと思います。確かにわたしの文章は分裂的で体系化しづらい文章です。東島毅は絵の中の対立を重要視する画家のように思いますが、わたしの文章や、特に写真や映像もまた対立が複数存在しているのではないでしょうか。対立が対立されたまま止揚されないところがわたしの文章や写真、映像の特徴なのかもしれません。その意味ではわたしの文章を読んでもらって、東島毅を想起するのは正しいことだと思います。

絵画の表現を意識的に持ち込んだことはモノクロ写真に関してはないですね。無意識的にならあるのかもしれませんが。例えばわたしの撮る電線でごちゃごちゃになった街並みが、ジャクソン・ポロックに似ていると外国のプレスに書かれたことがあります。絵画には興味がありますが、わたし

が写真に意識的に持ち込んだ方法というのは映画です。引っかき傷のような電線は、実験映画のスタン・ブラッケージの無意識的な影響だと思いますし、レンズの手前にいくつものものが後ろの風景を遮るように撮るのは、小津安二郎の影響です。

ピントがぶれて対象が何だかよく分からないアブストラクトな感じの『Ectoplasm Profiling』は、絵画の方法を取り入れています。わたしのモノクロ写真は全てピントが合っていてクリアな写真ですが、『Ectoplasm Profiling』は、わたしのモノクロの方法論とはまるで違う方法を取り入れました。簡単に言ってしまうと、絵画の筆線のような曖昧さを導入しようと思いました。『Ectoplasm Profiling』はコラージュや絵画の影響下で撮られています。

モノクロの写真集は一点、一点きっちりと見せる方法論ですが、『Ectoplasm Profiling』は複数のイメージと言葉の組み合わせで見せようとしたかったのです。バラバラで色々な素材の紙を使っているのは、手触り感を変化させたかったからです。

GRのカメラで撮影したデジタルの写真を見るとき、わたしはすごく早いスピードで見ます。多分0,5秒ぐらいのスピードで見ています。何が写っているかにはあまり興味がなくて、たくさん撮った写真をコマ落としの映像のように、ただ早くして見るのが好きなのです。そのような網膜に残響のように表れるイメージを再現したくて、『Ectoplasm Profiling』お作りました。

『Ectoplasm Profiling』を作る直前にフランシス・ベーコンの展覧会を東京で見ましたが、ベーコンの描く、輪郭が崩れて、人間の姿が何か別のものに変容していくようなイメージにインスパイアされました。クリアなものではなく、ものが網膜に明確に表れる直前のなにかが蠢くような雰囲気を表現してみたいと思いました。それには写真だけではなく、文章をパラフレーズ的に写真のあちこちに挟み込んで、コラージュ的にやろうと思いました。

　ちなみに『Ectoplasm Profiling』は、日本では不評でした。日本ではわたしはモノクロしか撮らない写真家だと思われていることと、コラージュ的な本の作りが、よく分からなかったのでしょう。ほとんど黙殺された感じです。

　　どのようにして文章をつくりますか？　まずアイデアがあってそこから始めるのですか？あるいは、書きながら生まれてくるのでしょうか？『Ectoplasm Profiling』の文章はどのようにして書かれたのですか？吉増剛造の文章に興味をもったことはありますか？

文章は書きながら思いつくのです。書く前に何か考えてということはしません。パソコンの前に座ると自動的に指が動くのです。なんだかシャーマンみたいだなと自分でも思いますが、考えをまとめて、それを文章で再現しようとすると突然書けなくなるのです。喋るのもそうですね。最初の頃は何を喋るかメモ用紙を持って喋ったりしたのですが、それだと上手く喋れないのです。何も考えないで舞台に立ってみたらよく喋れた。生まれながらのシャーマン体質なのでしょうか。

　『Ectoplasm Profiling』の文章もそんなシャーマン的な感じで書いた本です。

　72年に連合赤軍という極左グループが日本にありまして、イタリアでいえば「赤い旅団」のようなグループなのですが、『Ectoplasm Profiling』の文章を書いているとき、わたしは連合赤軍についての本をよく読んでいました。その影響であの文章になったのです。連合赤軍は結局内輪の粛清と警察との銃撃戦で崩壊するのですが、連合赤軍の最高幹部の森恒夫が、スパイ行為お疑われたメンバーの査問中に、本当の共産主義者なら死ぬはずがないと、そのメンバーの心臓にアイスピックを打ち込みました。当然その人は死ぬのですが、森恒夫は本当の共産主義者なら死なないはずだから、彼はスパイだったと結論付けたのです。それを読んで、

共産主義者は死を超えなければいけない存在なのかとわたしは大変に驚いた思いがあります。

アンドレ・バザンが書いたように写真は、防腐処理を施された永遠の生命を持つものなら、生まれて死ぬという、始まりと終わりのプロセスを持つ有機的生命の持続的時間から対象を、切り離すことで写真は成立します。現実の時間から切り離されたことで、写真化された対象は永遠の生命を持つ。時間の持続から対象を切り取る写真は、対象を始まりと終わりの時間から超越させます。それは有機的生命が持つ死を超えることではないでしょうか。

森恒夫は共産主義者とは不滅の肉体を持つ存在だと思ったのかもしれません。彼からみれば共産主義者とは有機的生命を持った存在ではなく、物質的な存在なのでしょう。人間が物質に転化されるのが、森恒夫の考える共産主義者です。ドストエフスキーの『悪霊』で、ネチャーエフをモデルにしたキリーロフの、死を越えろ、それが新しい人類だというセリフがありました。革命家は死刑を宣告された存在であると書いたネチャーエフにとって、革命家は既に死んでいる存在なのだから、死は恐怖ではないのです。そして死ぬことに恐怖感を抱かない人間というのは、それは人間ではなく物質です。不滅の肉体を持つということは、死を超えることであり、共産主義者とは、だから物質の別名ではないでしょうか

共産主義者は有機的な肉体を持つ人間を物質に転化させる者達です。スターリンというペンネームが鉄の男という意味を表すように、共産主義者は自ら物質になろうとする存在です。それは現実の対象を印画紙という物質に定着させる写真家と似ているのではないでしょうか。森恒夫がメンバーの心臓をアイスピックで貫くことで、死を克服させようとしたように、写真もまた永遠の生命を与えるために対象を有機的な時間から切り離します。それは有機的な生命に対して死を宣告することです。

対象を有機的な時間のサイクルから切り離して防腐処理を施し、永遠の生命を与える写真家と、本当の共産主義者なら死なないという、死を超

越した無機的な物質を志向する共産主義者は似ているのではないかと思い、その影響下で書きました。

　吉増剛造は文章もいいと思いますが、わたしは吉増剛造の写真の方が好きなのです。彼の二重露光の方法は画期的だと思いました。一度撮ったフィルムを何年も寝かせて、適当なときに取り出してまた撮る。最初に自分が何を撮ったか忘れてから撮るという方法にとても驚きました。自分が撮ったものをそんな風に突き放せるというのが驚きの理由です。

　吉増剛造の写真は何かの対象を撮るというよりも、対象と自分の関係の痕跡を撮っているような気がします。彼の写真はだから吉増剛造という以外ほかに何もいいようがない。ジョナス・メカスの映像が、メカスという以外にジャンル分けできないように、吉増剛造の写真や映像もそんな気がします。

　　物語る行為（ナレーション）のルールを破ること、物語る行為を壊すこと、物語る行為をひっくり返すことは、政治的芸術をつくるための方法でもありえます。テレビ・コマーシャルの多くでは、比較的スタンダードな語りと象徴の構造が使われています。反-物語る行為というアプローチをとることも一つの政治的選択です。『Ectoplasm Profiling』についてお聞きしますが、この作品は物語る行為を覆すものだと思いますか？ヴィデオ「Everyday XXX」と写真集『Ectoplasm Profiling』には、物語る行為という点に関して共通する点があると思いますか？

わたしは昔から映像の物語には興味がありませんでした。『Ectoplasm Profiling』は反物語的な写真集です。写真や映像は物語の奴隷ではない。物語という体系の中に収まりきれない過剰な細部が写真や映像には存在します。細部の集積こそが写真であって、物語に回収される写真は所詮挿絵と変わりがありません。写真を始めた頃、エルスケンのパリの写真集を見ましたが、全編に漂う物語性をうっとうしく感じました。あれでは

写真の物質的な細部が見えてこない。サンジェルマンにたむろしている実存主義かぶれの青年男女の説明でしかない。なぜ写真や映像には物語が必要なのでしょうか。ものが写る。それだけで写真はいいではないかと思います。

民族や宗教、階級や国家というのは、物語だとわたしは思うのです。そしてそれらはとてもよくできた物語だと思うのですが、民族や宗教、階級や国家の消滅を目指すコミュニストなら、反物語の立ち位置でなければいけません。なぜならそれらは物語によって作られたものだからです。

わたしは自分の写真や映像をとてもミニマルなものだと思っています。なぜミニマルな方法を選んだかというと、その方法だと物語が発生する余地が写真の中に生まれないと思ったからです。何年か後に自分の回顧展が開催されたとき、会場はすべて同じような写真しか並ばないでしょう。同じような写真が入り口から出口まで続いている。その様子に物語の入ってくる余地があるでしょうか。

今日わたし達は物語に囲まれて生きています。民族や宗教という昔からの物語に、20世紀に入ってプラスして作られたヒューマニズムや階級や国家という物語に囲まれて生きています。物語の存在は、わたし達の意識よりも先行して存在する。物語とは、わたし達の存在を決定付ける上位概念です。わたし達が物語を語るのではなく、物語というのは、わたし達にそれを語らせてしまうものです。自分が主体的に語っているつもりでも、実は物語によって語らされている。そしてそのように誰もが語ってしまう物語は、誰もが了解できる凡庸な物語ばかりです。誰もが知っている物語を、わたし達は独自の物語を見つけたかのように、嬉々として語ってしまう。わたし達は主体的に物語を選ぶことができないのです。物語を語るということは、物語の奴隷になることです。語りたくて、語るのではなく、語らされているのに、まるでそれが自分独自の物語のように語る。物語は、そのように語らせさせることで、共同体にアイデンティティーを見

出す人間を増産ます。同じ陳腐な物語を語らせることで、物語は人々に同一意識を持たせるのです。

"これはAだ"と誰かが言ったら、わたしを含めて誰もがそのAを理解できるのだと想像、了解することで共同体が成り立ちます。誰もが理解できるというところが重要です。写真や映像は誰もが理解することを拒否しますが、共同体は誰もがそれを理解しているはずだという想像で成り立っているのです。だから共同体に属する人間はみんな同じ考えになるし、自分もまた誰もが考えていることと同じ考えを持っていることに納得して、そこに仲間を求め、自己のアイデンティティーを見出します。

物語は、人々にとっての理解装置です。物語という理解装置を共有することで、みんなが同じ考えを共有できると信じているのです。物語を覆すことは、理解装置なしで現実を見ることです。物語という装置を外して現実を見れば、理解できない細部によって現実が成り立っているということが分かるでしょう。

愛国心という物語を語るとき、人はみんな、生まれた国を愛するのが当たり前だという前提でしか語らない。生まれた国を愛するのは、人間として当たり前のことだというそれは虚構の物語でしかないのですが、人々は、愛国心は物語ではなく、人間の条件として先天的に存在すると思っている。根拠もないのにそれが当たり前のことだと思われ、流通しているのが物語です。国家や階級の消滅を目指すコミュニストの立場に立つ芸術家なら、物語に対して、つねに否と言い続けなければならないでしょう。

ある組み合わせを見ると、そこになんらかの意味を見出そうとする人間の習性を利用したモンタージュ技法に対して、『Everyday XXX』と『Ectoplasm Profiling』は、互いのショットがつながらないということを目指しています。それはショットをつなげることで意味を産出させない反モンタージュ技法です。隣り合うショット同士が意味を生み出さず、ただ隣接されるだけです。つながらないものをつながったように見せるモンタージュ技法に対して、つながらないものを、つながらないままつなげたのが、この二つの映

像の共通するところです。『Everyday XXX』もまた反物語の意識で作られています。

　「Z-Trash Diary」を本のかたちで印刷しようと計画したことはありますか?あるいは、つねにオンラインの素材なのでしょうか?なぜ写真をインターネット上でみせようと考えたのですか?

「Z-Trash Diary」は本で出したいと思っていますが、日本ではどこの出版社も興味を持たないでしょう。イタリアで興味を持つ出版社はありますか?

　「Z-Trash Diary」を本で作るとしたら、多分『Ectoplasm Profiling』のような形になるとは思いますが、もっとコラージュ的な要素が強くなると思います。わたしはコラージュに興味があります。写真というのは本質的にコラージュなのではないかとも思っています。わたしの撮る、つぎはぎだらけの建築に行き当たりばったりの都市計画で作られた東京の風景は、コラージュのように見えるのです。

　わたしのモノクロ写真の展示は、壁面に直接写真をたくさん貼る方法なのですが、それはコラージュの方法を意識しています。

　"つねにオンラインの素材なのでしょうか?"というわけでもないのです。「Z-Trash Diary」に関しては、インターネット上で見せる以外に発表する場所がないと思ったからです。あとデジタルカメラで撮った写真は、モニターで見るのが一番しっくりくるのではないかと思いました。今はデジタルの印刷もずいぶんよくなったから、いいプリントで見せられるかもしれません。インターネット上で見ていると、一点一点でしか見せられないもどかしさを、わたしいつもは感じます。動画もプラスして、『Ectoplasm Profiling』を拡大した展示をやってみたいと思います。

　あと「Z-Trash Diary」は、フィルム写真でいえばコンタクト・プリントを見せている感じですね。セレクトする前の写真を見せているのです。だから

失敗もあるし、なんだかよく分からない写真もある。モノクロ写真は慎重に
セレクトして発表していますが、「Z-Trash Diary」は別です。もっとルーズで
す。けれど失敗した写真も、成功した写真もインターネット上で発表し続け
ていると、良い悪いの区別が曖昧になる。何が成功で何が失敗なのか分
からなくなります。セレクトの基準というのは何だろうと思うときもあります。

　フィルム写真のことですが、ちょっと昔の写真を見ると、撮影してすぐ見
たときは失敗だと思って発表しなかった写真が、今見るととてもよく見えるこ
とがあります。不思議です。時間が経てば経つほど、すべての写真が面
白く見えるのです。それが写真の特性なのでしょうか。それならば、はたし
て写真に失敗や成功があるのでしょうか。

　撮影して現像した写真をファイルボックスの中で数年間寝かすことで、
また違うものが生まれるのかもしれません。写真は瞬間を切り取る芸術だと
言われていますが、瞬間を切り取るだけではなく、そのような熟成に近い
時間感覚を写真は持つのかもしれません。

　　ヴォルフガング・ティルマンスは、自分は「新しい」車のイメージをつく
　　ることで頭がいっぱいだと述べました。ある人はホンマタカシが「新し
　　いヴィジョン」をつくったと言いました。もっとも個人的には同意しませ
　　んが……。多くの写真批評家は、あたかも終わりなき「変化と変容の
　　プロセス」が起こりうるかのごとく、「次に何がくるか」にとらわれていま
　　す。あなたの場合、写真は「新しさの獲得」や、批評言語を理想的未
　　来にむかって絶えず刷新しつづけることとは無関係だと言います。イタ
　　リアでは、いまだにモノクロ写真は「古く」て、カラー写真は「新しい」と
　　考える、とてもナイーヴな批評家や写真家たちがいます。どうして人び
　　とや社会は今なおイメージ、それから詩人を必要としているのでしょう?

新しいものが見たい、体験したいという感覚ほど古いものはないと思います。つねに新しいものを求める心情というのは最も保守的な心情です。例えばアジェ以降の写真の歴史を見て、写真は何か進歩したでしょうか。芸術は進歩しなければいけないという進歩史観こそ近代社会の罠だと思います。

芸術に新しいものをつねに求め続ける人々の心情というのは、要するに芸術を消費物だと思っているのでしょう。消費はつねに新しいものを必要とします。新しくフレッシュなものを求めるように資本主義社会は、わたし達に要求します。消費者もまた新しい商品を買うと、自分も少し新しくなったような気がするのでしょう。消費することが自分のアイデンティティーをつねにリセットする行為だと思い込む、買い物依存症のような人々を資本主義社会は日々生み出し続けています。

ニューモードの芸術を求める人というのは、買い物依存に陥った人間が、つねに新しいものを買い続ける様とよく似ています。芸術品ときちんと対峙していないのです。資本主義社会では芸術は所詮アクセサリー扱いなのです。自分のイメージアップのために芸術について見たり、語ったりしている人がほとんどです。みんな芸術が好きなのではなく、芸術を見たり、語ったりする自分が好きなだけです。だから新しいものを追い求めるのでしょう。

わたしは同じような写真をもう20年以上撮り続けているので、すごく保守的な写真家だといわれることが多々あります。『Ectoplasm Profiling』を発表したら、新しいことに挑戦していると言われましたが、都市の細部を撮るという意味では、前のモノクロ写真の方法論と何も変わらないと思っています。わたしは繰り返しが好きです。繰り返し続けることに快楽を感じるタイプの人間なのでしょう。

"韻の踏み方も知らない奴が、詩を書きたがる"と歌ったのはLou Reedでした。『Sweet Jane』という曲です。日本の商品広告のコピーを見ていると、その言葉に納得がいきます。去年発表したわたしの動画のタイトルは、伊勢丹のクリスマス商戦のときに使われた"Life is a Gift"というキャ

ッチコピーをそのまま使いました。クリスマスプレゼントは伊勢丹で買って、あちらこちらにそのプレゼントを配ろうという、消費を訴える以外に何も言っていないコピーです。今や日本では、広告代理店が詩人です。ヘルマン・ヘッセの『さようなら世界夫人』を日本のロックバンド頭脳警察が対訳してこう歌っていました。「世界はがらくた中に横たわりかつてはとても愛していたのに今僕等にとって死神はもはやそれほど恐ろしくないさ世界は僕等に愛と涙を絶えまなく与え続けてくれたでも僕等は君の魔法にはもう夢など持っちゃいない」と、みんなが世界夫人に対して、「君の泣き声と君の笑い声にはもう飽きた」と別れを告げる詩があります。詩人が必要とされるのは、世界ががらくたのような屑の集積場になってしまったからです。けれど資本主義社会の詩人に、かつては美しかった世界夫人のような詠嘆を再現することはできません。マルコさんの書いたように、「自分は「新しい」車のイメージをつくることで頭がいっぱい」になるぐらいです。資本主義社会の魔法は既に時代遅れになってしまったのです。世界に対して、新しいイメージを寄与してみたり、美しい詩を捧げてみたりすることに何の意味があるのでしょうか。屑を黄金に見せる手品は破綻してしまったのです。

　写真は詩よりも散文に近いのではと思っています。カメラの機能は即物的で、ただ対象を写すだけです。写真には意味がありません。写した対象を指示しているだけで、そこには指示以上の意味が出てこない。そのような無意味性が、見る人間に色々なイメージを抱かせる。その意味では、写真はアレゴリー的な見方を喚起させます。

　写真を見るとき画面に写っているものに合わせて視線が動きます。今見ているものの隣にとつねに視線が動き続ける。写真を見ることは隣接性であり、写っているものの横や上下に視線を移動させる。写真を見るということは、視線の隣接運動です。

　人間が生きていく上でイメージが必要だと先ほど書きましたが、わたしはいつかイメージを超えて、現実そのものに触れてみたいという願望があります。けれど人間にとってイメージが物質なのであり、イメージの向こうに行

くことはできないのです。多くの人々はイメージという媒介なしに直接現実と触れ合っていると思っている人が多い。例えば天気のいい日に森に行って葉っぱの緑を見れば、とても美しいと思いますが、それがなぜ美しいと思うのかといえば、それは直接葉っぱを見ているのではなく、イメージをそこに介在させて見ることで、葉っぱが美しく見えるのです。葉っぱそのものに美しいも汚いもありません。

　けれどそのような美しいという形容詞が排除された世界を写すことが写真にはできるのではないでしょうか。写真にとって形容詞は敵といってもいい存在だと思います。形容詞がイメージと結びつくとそれは、最悪の美学を生み出します。形容詞というのは生成変化し続ける現実の運動を、言葉の中に回収し、停止させてしまう回収装置です。イメージとは形容詞ではありません。イメージが人間にとって現実なら、それは物質的な存在でなければならない。写真は風景からあらゆる形容詞を剥ぎ取ることで、物質としてのイメージを顕します。イメージの物質化。イメージを美しいや汚いといった形容詞に回収させるのではなく、物質の側に奪還するのです。

　　　　　　　　　　　　　　質問＝マルコ・マッツィ2017年7月30日
　　　　　　　　　　　　　　答＝金村修2017年9月1日